D1423244

Palgrave Studies in European Union Politics

Series Editors
Michelle Egan
American University
Washington, USA

Neill Nugent
Manchester Metropolitan University
Manchester, UK

William E. Paterson
Aston University
Birmingham, UK

Following on the sustained success of the acclaimed European Union Series, which essentially publishes research-based textbooks, Palgrave Studies in European Union Politics publishes cutting edge research-driven monographs. The remit of the series is broadly defined, both in terms of subject and academic discipline. All topics of significance concerning the nature and operation of the European Union potentially fall within the scope of the series. The series is multidisciplinary to reflect the growing importance of the EU as a political, economic and social phenomenon.

Editorial Board:
Laurie Buonanno (SUNY Buffalo State, USA)
Kenneth Dyson (Cardiff University, UK)
Claudio Radaelli (University College London, UK)
Mark Rhinard (Stockholm University, Sweden)
Ariadna Ripoll Servent (University of Bamberg, Germany)
Frank Schimmelfennig (ETH Zurich, Switzerland)
Claudia Sternberg (University College London, UK)
Nathalie Tocci (Istituto Affari Internazionali, Italy)

More information about this series at
http://www.palgrave.com/gp/series/14629

Helena Carrapico · Antonia Niehuss
Chloé Berthélémy

Brexit and Internal Security

Political and Legal Concerns on the Future
UK-EU Relationship

With contributions by Arantza Gomez Arana, Raphael Bossong, Sophie Carr,
Elaine Fahey, Benjamin Farrand, Massimo Fichera, Daniela Irrera,
Anita Lavorgna, Alex MacKenzie, Camino Mortera-Martinez,
Giacomo Orsini, Maria Grazia Porcedda, Steffen Rieger,
Ariadna Ripoll Servent, Christof Roos,
Anna Sergi, Florian Trauner, Gijs de Vries,
Tim J Wilson, and Sarah Wolff

Helena Carrapico
Department of Politics and
International Relations
Aston University
Birmingham, UK

Chloé Berthélémy
Sciences Po Lille
Lille, France

Antonia Niehuss
School of International Relations
University of St Andrews
St Andrews, UK

Palgrave Studies in European Union Politics
ISBN 978-3-030-04193-9   ISBN 978-3-030-04194-6   (eBook)
https://doi.org/10.1007/978-3-030-04194-6

Library of Congress Control Number: 2018962045

© The Editor(s) (if applicable) and The Author(s), under exclusive license to Springer
Nature Switzerland AG, part of Springer Nature 2019
This work is subject to copyright. All rights are solely and exclusively licensed by the
Publisher, whether the whole or part of the material is concerned, specifically the rights
of translation, reprinting, reuse of illustrations, recitation, broadcasting, reproduction
on microfilms or in any other physical way, and transmission or information storage and
retrieval, electronic adaptation, computer software, or by similar or dissimilar methodology
now known or hereafter developed.
The use of general descriptive names, registered names, trademarks, service marks, etc. in this
publication does not imply, even in the absence of a specific statement, that such names are
exempt from the relevant protective laws and regulations and therefore free for general use.
The publisher, the authors, and the editors are safe to assume that the advice and
information in this book are believed to be true and accurate at the date of publication.
Neither the publisher nor the authors or the editors give a warranty, express or implied,
with respect to the material contained herein or for any errors or omissions that may have
been made. The publisher remains neutral with regard to jurisdictional claims in published
maps and institutional affiliations.

Cover illustration: Magic Lens/Shutterstock

This Palgrave Pivot imprint is published by the registered company Springer Nature
Switzerland AG
The registered company address is: Gewerbestrasse 11, 6330 Cham, Switzerland

ACKNOWLEDGEMENTS

The following book is the result of two projects, whose funders we would like to thank. The first project, which was financed by the 'UK in a Changing Europe' initiative of the Economic and Social Research Council and which began shortly before the UK's referendum on exiting the European Union, addressed the potential consequences of Brexit for the UK and EU's internal security. The authors were particularly concerned by the fact that internal security had scarcely been discussed in the debate running up to the referendum in June 2016 and wanted to draw academics and policy-makers' attention to this area. This first project allowed for the development of a second project, funded by the British Academy, which focused on the development of a future UK-EU security relationship, its negotiation and the transition/implementation phase from membership to third country status. We are therefore sincerely grateful to both the 'UK in a Changing Europe' initiative and to the British Academy for their invaluable support of the present publication.

Furthermore, the authors would like to thank the academic community working on EU and UK justice and home affairs; this book was very much a collective journey. As part of the projects mentioned above, the authors were able to organise a number of workshops that aimed to reach out to the academic and policy communities, and the general public. The present book is the result of academic discussions among UK- and non-UK-based experts in internal security, feedback on the fears and concerns of the younger UK-based population, and questions and insights from policy-makers. In this context, we would like to express our most sincere thanks to the academics and practitioners who took part in the workshops: Ana Aliverti, Arantza Gomez Arana, Alex Balch, Ian Bond, Raphael Bossong, Caroline Chatwin, Justin Clements, Jon Coaffee, Anne-Lynn Dudenhoefer, Martin Elvins, Lord Jay of Ewelme, Elaine Fahey, Ben Farrand, Maria Fletcher, Jamie Gaskarth, Cristina Greco, Marion Greziller, Line Haidar, Ester Herlin Karnell, Christian Kaunert, Anita Lavorgna, Alex MacKenzie, Camino Mortera-Martinez, Giacomo Orsini, Stefania Paladini, Maria Grazia Porcedda, Mohammed Rahman, Christof Roos, Patrycja Rozbicka, Stephen Rozee, Anna Sergi, Balazs Szent-Ivanyi, Ed Turner, Matilde Ventrella, Ben Wagner, David Wall, Auke Willems, Aaron Winter, Uwe Wunderlich and Lucia Zedner.

The authors would also like to acknowledge the Aston Centre for Europe for providing the necessary structure and support for the development of both projects. Last but not least, we would also like to say a special thanks to Alex MacKenzie for his dedication to this project and insightful comments, and to Fraser Logan for the excellent linguistic revision of the book.

We hope that this book can contribute to the academic discussions on the future UK-EU relationship, as well as inform the development of future policy positions.

Contents

Notes on Contributors

Arantza Gomez Arana is a Lecturer in Security and Criminology at Birmingham City University. Dr. Gomez Arana has published extensively on European Union External Relations. In particular, her research has discussed Latin America and Mediterranean relations with the European Union. She is also a member of the Centre for Brexit Studies at BCU and is currently writing a book on Brexit and Gibraltar.

Chloé Berthélémy holds a Master's Degree from Aston University and Sciences Po Lille in European affairs with a particular focus on European internal security, notably cybersecurity policies. She has been working as a research assistant for projects funded by the ESRC and the British Academy on Brexit and internal security since 2016.

Raphael Bossong is a researcher at the German Institute for International and Security Affairs, where he focuses on EU Justice and Home Affairs. His recent publications include *Theorising EU Internal Security* (OUP) and *EU Borders and Shifting Internal Security* (Springer). He holds a Ph.D. from the London School of Economics.

Sophie Carr is the Associate Head of Department for Applied Sciences at Northumbria University and a member of the Northumbria Centre for Evidence and Criminal Justice Studies (NCECJS). Her research focuses on the application and understanding of expert evidence within the criminal justice system. Prior to joining Northumbria University, Sophie was a Senior Forensic Scientist with the Wetherby Laboratory of the Forensic Science Service. Her role was that of a scene attending scientist with expertise in the analysis and interpretation of body fluids and DNA, including blood pattern analysis.

Helena Carrapico is a Senior Lecturer in Politics and International Relations at Aston University and a co-director of the Aston Centre for Europe. Her research focuses on European Union Justice and Home Affairs governance, namely organised crime and cybercrime policies. She has published extensively on European internal security topics in journals such as the *Journal of Common Market Studies, European Foreign Affairs Review, Crime, Law and Social Change, European Security* and *Global Crime.*

Elaine Fahey is Professor of Law and Associate Dean (International) at the Institute for the Study of European Law (ISEL), the City Law School, City, University of London. Her research interests span the relationship between EU law and global governance, transatlantic relations, the EU's Area of Freedom, Security and Justice, and the study of law beyond the State and are the subject of over 60 publications including books, articles, edited volumes and special issues, including a monograph, *The Global Reach of EU Law* (Routledge, 2016).

Benjamin Farrand is Associate Professor in Law at the University of Warwick. His research focuses on the dynamics of law-making in areas of political uncertainty and technological change, with a particular emphasis on online intellectual property enforcement, cybersecurity and network governance. He has recently published an article in *European Politics and Society* on the EU's approach to combating the sale of counterfeit goods online, as well as an article on intellectual property law post-Brexit in the *Journal of Common Market Studies.*

Massimo Fichera is Adjunct Professor in EU Law at the Faculty of Law of the University of Helsinki and Academy of Finland Research Fellow. His research and teaching interests lie in the area of constitutional theory and EU Law, in particular the interplay between EU and international law. He is also interested in the discipline of comparative constitutional law and the notion of transnational law. He holds a Ph.D. in Law (University of Edinburgh, UK) and a Master's in International Affairs (ISPI, Milan, Italy). He has published extensively in the above mentioned areas of research, including a monograph, *The Foundations of the EU as a Polity* (Edward Elgar, 2018).

Daniela Irrera is an Associate Professor of International Relations at the University of Catania. She currently serves as President of the European Peace Research Association (EuPRA) and is a member of the Steering Committees of the ECPR Standing Group on International Relations and ECPR Standing Group on Organized Crime. She is also on the editorial committee of EuropeNow and is a Book Review Co-Editor at the *Journal of Contemporary European Studies*, and one of the editors of the *Palgrave Handbook on Global Counterterrorism Policies*. She has published extensively in the field of International Relations and EU politics, dealing with global terrorism, transnational organised crime, civil society and humanitarian affairs.

Anita Lavorgna is a Lecturer in Criminology within the Department of Sociology, Social Policy & Criminology at the University of Southampton (UK). She is currently leading research projects on Internet-facilitated wildlife trafficking and health frauds. Her research focuses on cybercrimes (especially Internet-facilitated trafficking activities), organised crime and the propagation of fake/fraudulent health information online.

Alex MacKenzie is a Lecturer in International Politics in the Department of Politics at the University of Liverpool, UK. His research interests revolve around the EU's global role in counterterrorism. He has published widely on the EU as a counterterrorism actor, the EU-US security relationship and the role of EU institutions in counterterrorism.

Camino Mortera-Martinez is a Research fellow and Brussels representative at the Centre for European Reform, a think tank based in London. She is responsible for the CER's work on EU justice and home affairs. She holds a Master's degree in law from the University of Oviedo (Spain), an Exchange diploma in legal studies from Cardiff University (UK) and a Master of Arts in European political studies from the College of Europe in Bruges (Belgium). She is a regular contributor to newspapers and media in Europe and the US and has given evidence to the British Parliament on matters of Brexit and EU security and migration policies.

Antonia Niehuss is a Ph.D. candidate in International Relations at the University of St Andrews and specialises in Critical Security Studies, more specifically gender and terrorism. She has, throughout her studies at the University of Konstanz, Aston University and the University of Bamberg, continuously worked on European security and has been working as a research assistant for projects funded by the ESRC and the British Academy on Brexit and internal security since 2016.

Giacomo Orsini is a Postdoctoral Researcher in the LIMA Project at the Institute for the Analysis of Change in Contemporary and Historical Societies (IACS), Louvain School of Political and Social Sciences, Université Catholique de Louvain, Belgium. Focusing on border management, migration and contemporary governance systems, he has conducted fieldwork research in several European borderlands. He also teaches international migrations at the Université Libre de Bruxelles and collaborates with the Vrije Universiteit Brussel.

Maria Grazia Porcedda is a postdoctoral Research Fellow at the School of Law, University of Leeds, where she is a member of the EPSRC-funded CRITiCaL project. Maria Grazia's research and publications focus on EU law and technology, particularly data protection and cyber security matters. She is a member of EDEN (Europol Data Experts Network) and, until Spring 2018, of the EUISS Task force on Cyber Capacity Building. She holds a Ph.D. in Law from the European University Institute. Her early work was awarded grants and prizes by the Accademia Nazionale dei Lincei and the Italian Association of Information Security (CLUSIT).

Steffen Rieger holds two M.A. degrees in Political Science from Aston University Birmingham and the University of Bamberg, with a focus on internal security in the European Union. After an internship at the German Institute for International and Security Affairs, he now is a Probationary Commissioner at the Federal Police in Germany.

Ariadna Ripoll Servent Ariadna Ripoll Servent has been Assistant Professor of Political Science and European Integration since 2013. She is also visiting professor at the College of Europe in Bruges, where she teaches a course on the European Parliament. Her research focuses on European integration, EU institutions and EU internal security policies (particularly asylum, immigration and data protection). Among her recent publications are the 'Routledge Handbook of Justice and Home Affairs Research' (co-edited with Florian Trauner) and 'The European Parliament' (published by Macmillan International Higher Education).

Christof Roos is Junior Professor of European and Global Governance at Europa-Universität Flensburg and associate researcher at the Institute for European Studies at the Vrije Universiteit Brussel. His work focuses on EU integration in Justice and Home Affairs, EU immigration and asylum policy, and freedom of movement.

Anna Sergi is Lecturer in Criminology and Deputy Director of the Centre for Criminology at the University of Essex, UK. She is an International Visiting Fellow at the University of Melbourne, Australia and Chair of the Early Career Researchers Network of the British Society of Criminology.

Florian Trauner is Research Professor at the Institute for European Studies of the Vrije Universiteit Brussel and Visiting Professor at the College of Europe. His research interests concern the field of European integration, notably migration and asylum policies, the role of EU institutions and European foreign policy. He recently co-edited *The Routledge Handbook of Justice and Home Affairs Research.*

Gijs de Vries is a Visiting Senior Fellow at the European Institute of the London School of Economics and Political Science (LSE). He was State Secretary of the Interior in the government of The Netherlands. He was the Dutch government's representative in the Convention on the Future of the European Union. From 2004 to 2007, he served as the European Union's first Counter-Terrorism Coordinator.

Tim J Wilson is Professor of Criminal Justice Policy at Northumbria University Law School and a member of the Northumbria Centre for Evidence and Criminal Justice Studies (NCECJS). His academic interests and internationally funded research cover how criminal justice systems respond to rapid scientific and technological development; international criminal justice cooperation in response to increasingly globalised threats to society; and epistemic and ethical issues at the interface of science, law and politics. More recently, he has been called to give oral evidence on the implications of Brexit for criminal justice to the Commons Justice Committee in 2017 and the House of Lords EU Home Affairs Sub-Committee in 2018.

Sarah Wolff is Director of the Centre for European Research and Senior Lecturer in Public Policy at Queen Mary, University of London. She is also Senior Research Associate Fellow at the Netherlands Institute for International Relations (Clingendael). Her research interests concern Justice and Home Affairs, EU migration and border management policies, particularly in relation to the Middle East and North Africa as well as the role of religion and secularism in EU foreign policy. Her most recent research project deals with the situation in Calais.

Abbreviations

ACIST	Anti-Counterfeiting Intelligence Support Tool
ACRIS	Anti-Counterfeiting Rapid Intelligence System
AFSJ	Area of Freedom, Security and Justice
API	Application Programming Interface
CCTV	Closed-Circuit Television
CEAS	Common European Asylum System
CEPOL	European Union Agency for Law Enforcement Training
CETA	EU-Canada Comprehensive Economic and Trade Agreement
CFD	Common Framework Decision
CJEU	Court of Justice of the European Union
CSDP	Common Security and Defence Policy
CTA	Common Travel Area
CTG	Counterterrorism Group
DNA	Deoxyribonucleic acid
DRD	Data Retention Directive
EAW	European Arrest Warrant
EC3	European Cybercrime Centre
ECHR	European Court of Human Rights
ECR	European Conservatives and Reformists
ECRIS	European Criminal Records Information System
EEA	European Economic Area
EFTA	European Free Trade Association
ENISA	European Union Agency for Network and Information Security

ENSFI	European Network of Forensic Science Institutes
EP	European Parliament
EPPO	European Public Prosecutor Office
ESCN	European Strategic Communications Network
EU	European Union
EUIPO	European Union Intellectual Property Office
Eurodac	European Dactyloscopy
Eurojust	European Union's Judicial Cooperation Unit
Europol	European Union Agency for Law Enforcement Cooperation
FADO	False and Authentic Documents Online
FIUs	Financial Intelligence Units
Frontex	European Border and Coast Guard Agency
G8	Group of Eight
GDPR	General Data Protection Directive
GNS	European Global Navigation Satellite Systems Agency
HM Government	Her Majesty's Government
IntCen	European Union Intelligence and Situation Centre
Interpol	International Criminal Police Organization
J-CAT	Joint Cybercrime Action Task Force
JHA	Justice and Home Affairs
JITs	Joint Investigation Teams
LIBE	European Parliament Committee on Civil Liberties, Justice and Home Affairs
MENA	Middle East and North Africa
MEP	Member of European Parliament
MP	Member of Parliament
NATO	North Atlantic Treaty Organisation
NGOs	Non-Governmental Organisations
NIS	Network and Information System
OCTA	Organised Crime Threat Assessment
OLAF	European Anti-Fraud Office
PNR	Passenger Name Record
RAN	Radicalisation Awareness Network
SIENA	Secure Information Exchange Network Application
SIGINT	Signals Intelligence
SIS	Schengen Information System
TFEU	Treaty on the Functioning of the European Union
TFTP	Terrorism Financing and Tracking Programme
TFTP	Trivial File Transfer Protocol
UK	United Kingdom
UN	United Nations

USA/US	United States of America
VCRS	Victim Crisis Response Team
VIS	Visa Information System
WA	Withdrawal Agreement

CHAPTER 1

Introduction

Abstract This book explores the viability of future UK-EU internal security arrangements, including their impact on the UK's security and international standing, by departing from the current relationship between the two parties, discussing on-going negotiations, and addressing the main political and legal concerns arising from different possible arrangements. As the UK prepares to leave the EU, it is faced with having to develop new forms of cooperation with its neighbours to fight ever more transnational security threats, as well as new strategies to maintain its leading role as an international security actor. As outlined in this introductory chapter, the book has three main objectives: to contribute to the general knowledge on the risks and opportunities associated with the disentanglement of the UK from European internal security cooperation; to clarify some of the debates currently taking place within the context of the negotiations; and to inform the policy discussions which form the basis of proposed cooperation models, and which are likely to shape the future UK-EU security relationship significantly.

Keywords European union · Brexit · Area of Freedom, Security and Justice · Political and legal consequences

Internal security—including the fight against terrorism, organised crime and cybercrime—has traditionally been one of the main concerns of the British public. In April 2017, YouGov conducted a survey which revealed

© The Author(s) 2019   1
H. Carrapico et al., *Brexit and Internal Security*,
Palgrave Studies in European Union Politics,
https://doi.org/10.1007/978-3-030-04194-6_1

that 90% of the population believes that terrorist attacks are very likely to take place in the United Kingdom (UK), while 73% believes that the threat of terrorism is rapidly increasing (Smith 2017). Compared to other European countries, the UK also has one of the highest proportions of respondents indicating that they do not consider their country to be a safe place to live, expressing concerns related to terrorism, organised crime, border insecurity and cybercrime (European Commission 2017). From a historical perspective, there has been a clear increase in anxiety, in relation to security issues, over the past 10 years; though the UK population has always had one of the highest levels of concern for insecurity among European Union (EU) countries (European Commission 2011, 2009).

Surprisingly, however, such concerns were seldom reflected in the debate running up to the EU exit referendum in June 2016. While the Remain Campaign focused on the negative consequences of Brexit for the UK's economy, the Leave Campaign argued that the UK's membership of the EU had led to a deterioration of the country's sovereignty and to an inability to control UK borders, which was in turn presented as resulting in a reduced pool of available jobs and an overburdening of public services (in particular the National Health Service). With the exception of brief references by Nigel Farage and Ian Duncan Smith to the link between free movement and the possibility of further terrorist attacks, internal security was rarely mentioned (*The Guardian* 2016). It was, in any case, far from being the object of serious or in-depth discussion.

This situation began to change, however, in January 2017 with Theresa May's Lancaster House Speech, followed by the UK government's White Paper in February and the issuing of the letter triggering Article 50 in March. Although the objective of these three documents was to present the UK general negotiation stances and to project a vision of future UK-EU relations, they also served to highlight that security would potentially be a contentious topic in Brexit negotiations. Whereas the Lancaster House Speech referred to Britain's willingness to continue to assist EU counterterrorism efforts through its intelligence capabilities (Prime Minister's Office 2017a), the underlying tone of the letter triggering Article 50 was far less diplomatic. In fact, the letter warned the EU that a potential failure to reach an agreement would have serious consequences for security cooperation, and in particular for the EU's fight against cross-border crime and terrorism (Prime Minister's Office 2017b). This growing debate enabled the emergence of more detailed arguments, namely those of current and former security professionals.

These included the views of, for instance, former Europol Director Rob Wainwright, according to whom Brexit will potentially leave the UK in a less secure position as a result of more restricted access to EU intelligence databases (Wright 2018); and Sir Richard Dearlove, former head of MI6, who argues that the EU intelligence community has more to lose from Brexit than the UK does as, in his view, most EU security arrangements have little operational impact (Reuters 2016).

If the security debate had, until then, been characterised by limited visibility in terms of the wider public, the terrorist attacks that took place between March and June 2017[1] brought about a repositioning of the topic (Warrell 2017). By further politicising it, these events triggered a multiplication of Brexit and security references among pre-2017 General Election discourses. Suddenly, police cuts, counterterrorism strategies, cyber threats, intelligence sharing with the EU, nuclear weapons, and the causes of terrorism were some of the main concerns being raised in the context of future Brexit negotiations. Despite an increase in the visibility of these issues, namely in the context of political party leaders' debates and interviews,[2] security proposals for Brexit negotiations remained essentially vague. In fact, despite attempts on the UK side to concretise a negotiation position in this area, namely through the production of position papers, a great deal of ambiguity remains with regards to what the future UK-EU security relationship will look like, what kind and degree of cooperation can be achieved, and how long this new relationship would take to emerge. For the moment, the only certainty is that at the end of December 2020 (on the basis of an expected transition/implementation phase), the cooperation mechanisms and instruments of the Area of Freedom, Security and Justice (AFSJ) will no longer be available to the UK, following its exit from the EU in March 2019.[3] This end point will mark the conclusion of several decades of European internal security integration for the UK—a process that, although not straightforward, has come to benefit both Britain and the EU.

---

[1] We are referring specifically to the Westminster attack on 22 March 2017, the Manchester Arena bombing on 22 May, and the London Bridge attack on 3 June.

[2] The interviews of Theresa May and of Jeremy Corbyn by Jeremy Paxman, on the 29th of May 2017, on SkyNews, and the BBC leaders' debate on the 31st of May illustrate how security became more prominent among political concerns in the later stages of the General election campaigns.

[3] The date of December 2020 is based on the draft Withdrawal Agreement, as stated in Art. 121, and on the fact that so far (August 2018) no extension to the transition has been requested by the negotiating parties.

Even though the present book originated in a willingness to address a gap in public debates, the increased awareness of the importance of security issues in the context of Brexit negotiations enabled it to also become an instrument for exploring and responding to rapidly emerging technical policy concerns and questions. As such, this volume has a very large target audience, ranging from policy-makers and academics to members of the public interested in Brexit and security matters. It is, above all, a view of the progress achieved and the challenges remaining in current negotiations, as seen through the eyes of some of the leading academics in this field. The objectives of the book are: firstly, to contribute to the general knowledge on the risks and opportunities associated with the disentanglement of the UK from European internal security cooperation; secondly, to clarify some of the debates currently taking place within the context of the negotiations; thirdly, to inform the policy discussions which form the basis of proposed cooperation models, and which are likely to shape the future UK-EU security relationship significantly; and fourthly, to contribute to the growing academic literature on the future of the AFSJ, specifically the consequences of differentiated disintegration.

The book is composed of two main sections. The first gives a comprehensive overview of the current internal security relationship between the UK and the EU, the possible consequences of Brexit in this area, the negotiation positions of both parties, and the most important current debates. More specifically, the book begins by contextualising, in Chapter 2, the UK-EU relationship in the area of internal security, based on the analysis of the UK's negotiated arrangements in this area and its historical evolution. The potential impact of Brexit on the UK's internal security, as well as the EU's AFSJ, is outlined in Chapter 3, focussing specifically on police and judicial cooperation, and migration, asylum and border issues. Chapter 4 discusses the emerging EU and UK negotiation positions and explores their strengths and limitations, as well as the responses they have triggered. Finally, Chapter 5 highlights the main political and legal considerations that play into the current negotiations, by focusing on transitional arrangements, alternative models to UK-EU membership, enforcement and dispute resolution, and the maintenance of the UK's influential position within European security.

Section two is composed of specialised sectoral views from a large number of experts on internal security, which further expand the points developed in the first section. As the relationship between the UK and the other EU Member States in the area of internal security has developed for years, leaving the EU does not simply mean leaving a few pieces of legislation behind: a complex network of cooperation will have to be transformed, which will hopefully have the best outcome for EU and UK citizens in mind. Based on various disciplinary perspectives—including International Relations, Law and Criminology—the sectoral views of the second section of the book firstly offer detailed assessments of the different parts of this cooperation, and secondly reflect not only the possible direct consequences, but also the possible indirect consequences of Brexit in these areas, while highlighting issues that will play into the negotiations and offering guidance to both sides of the negotiation table. Chapter 6 opens the second section of the book by focusing on different aspects of the future UK-EU security relationship, as developed by Massimo Fichera, Ariadna Ripoll Servent, Camino Mortera-Martinez and Elaine Fahey. Chapter 7 explores the future cooperation between the UK and the EU in the area of police and judicial cooperation, as seen through the eyes of Gijs de Vries, Raphael Bossong, Steffen Rieger, Alex MacKenzie, Anna Sergi, Florian Trauner, Ben Farrand, Anita Lavorgna, Maria Grazia Porcedda, Tim J Wilson and Sophie Carr. Finally, Chapter 8 provides detailed accounts of the challenges related to migration and border control with contributions from Arantza Gomez Arana, Daniela Irrera, Giacomo Orsini, Christof Roos and Sarah Wolff.

In the conclusion, the authors draw on the expertise of all of the contributors to propose priorities and considerations for the UK and the EU to take into account when shaping their future security relationship.

References

European Commission. 2009. *Awareness of Key Policies in the Area of Freedom, Security and Justice-Analytical Report*. Eurobarometer Survey, January.

European Commission. 2011. *Internal Security—Report*, Special Eurobarometer 371, November.

European Commission. 2017. *European Attitudes Towards Security—Special Eurobarometer 464b Report*. Directorate-General for Migration and Home Affairs and Directorate-General for Communication, December.

Prime Minister's Office. 2017a. *The Government's Negotiating Objectives for Exiting the EU: PM Speech*. Available from: https://www.gov.uk/government/speeches/the-governments-negotiating-objectives-for-exiting-the-eu-pm-speech. Last accessed 31 May 2018.

Prime Minister's Office. 2017b. *Prime Minister's Letter to Donal Tusk Triggering Article 50*. Available from: https://www.gov.uk/government/publications/

prime-ministers-letter-to-donald-tusk-triggering-article-50. Last accessed 31 May 2018.

Reuters. 2016. EU *Exit Could Make Britain Safer—Former MI6 Spy Chief*, 24 March. Available from: https://uk.reuters.com/article/uk-britain-eu-security/eu-exit-could-make-britain-safer-former-mi6-spy-chief-idUKKCN-0WQ0NE. Last accessed 31 May 2018.

Smith, M. 2017. *Nine in Ten Brits Think Further Terror Attacks Are Likely*, YouGov Survey, 24 March. Available from: https://yougov.co.uk/news/2017/03/24/nine-ten-brits-think-further-terror-attacks-are-li/. Last accessed 31 May 2018.

The Guardian. 2016. *Nigel Farage Defends Linking Brussels Attacks and EU Migration Rules*. Available from: http://www.bbc.com/news/uk-politics-35879670. Last accessed 31 May 2018.

Warrell, H. 2017. Terror Attacks Shaped UK Election But Failed to Lift May. *Financial Times*, 8 June. Available from: https://www.voanews.com/a/terror-attacks-may-drive-security-issues-upcoming-brexit-talks/3889359.html. Last accessed 15 May 2018.

Wright, R. 2018. Europol Head Warns of Security Impediments After Brexit. *Financial Times*, 7 March. Available from: https://www.ft.com/content/b74ec3d0-2213-11e8-9a70-08f715791301. Last accessed 31 May 2018.

CHAPTER 2

The Current UK-EU Internal Security Arrangements

Abstract This chapter shows that internal security has evolved into one of the most dynamic and prioritised policy fields of the EU. The UK's unique opt-in and opt-out arrangements with the EU in this field have enabled it to selectively participate in measures which it perceives to be in its national interest, contributing to the field's complex differentiated integration. However, the UK has deeply shaped the AFSJ, with the UK's involvement having benefitted both the UK and the EU, leading to Brexit potentially having a deep impact on the internal security of both parties.

Keywords Brexit · UK-EU relationship · Selective participation · Differentiated integration · Opt-ins and Opt-outs · Sovereignty

Justice and Home Affairs (JHA) has become, over the past 15 years, one of the most dynamic policy areas of European integration, having grown exponentially in terms of policy content and institutional structures (Monar 1999). It has also developed into one of the most important political priorities of the European Union (Treaty of Lisbon 2007). This policy area covers matters that are traditionally associated to national Home Affairs and Justice ministries, such as border controls, asylum, immigration, judicial cooperation in civil and criminal matters, and police cooperation.

© The Author(s) 2019   7
H. Carrapico et al., *Brexit and Internal Security*,
Palgrave Studies in European Union Politics,
https://doi.org/10.1007/978-3-030-04194-6_2

THE DEVELOPMENT OF THE AREA OF FREEDOM, SECURITY AND JUSTICE

The institutionalization of JHA began to accelerate when early inter-governmental developments were subsumed into the European structure, with the Treaty of Maastricht's introduction of the Third Pillar and the identification of areas of common interest in the field of JHA. These areas of common interest emerged in particular out of the perceived need to protect the developing Internal Market against criminal abuse, and from the understanding that national law enforcement bodies were in a position of disadvantage in relation to organised crime groups, which were free to profit from the disappearance of internal borders (Uçarer 2016). Thus, the development of EU Justice and Home Affairs rests on a neo-functionalist logic, which assumed that the best way to achieve the completion of the Internal market was through the creation of European synergies in the area of police and judicial cooperation (Monar 2006). JHA then evolved in the direction of further integration, with the coming into force of the Treaty of Amsterdam and the creation of the AFSJ: parts of the Third Pillar were communitarized, and the Schengen *acquis* was incorporated into the EU's legal order. More recently, the Lisbon Treaty eliminated the Pillar structure and attempted to streamline the decision-making process in JHA by expanding qualified majority voting. The evolution of JHA has allowed for the emergence of a 'space of protection' (Boin et al. 2006), characterised by a shared willingness to provide individuals living in the EU with effective access to justice, improved safeguards against crime and terrorism, and the right to circulate freely within Schengen. Examples of measures which have contributed to the development of the Area of Freedom, Security and Justice include, among others: Europol—the EU's law enforcement agency—, Eurojust—the EU's judicial cooperation agency—, the European Arrest Warrant—a legal instrument that aims at harmonising and expediting extradition—, and the Schengen Information System—a database that enables the exchange of information on individuals and property for the purpose of border management and law enforcement.

THE RATIONALE BEHIND SELECTIVE PARTICIPATION IN JUSTICE AND HOME AFFAIRS

Despite the impressive development of this area, however, not all Member States take full part in its activities. The United Kingdom, Ireland and Denmark have chosen not to engage fully in the integration process of JHA, by opting-out from specific parts of the *acquis communautaire*. The argument presented by these countries is that they wish to maintain control over matters of key importance to their national sovereignty, in particular immigration, asylum, and security policies (Adler-Nissen 2009). In the case of the United Kingdom, the government feels that the current European arrangements in this area do not favour its national interests, which have been constructed around the protection of its common law system and unique geographical characteristics (Home Office 2013a). As argued by Geddes, the United Kingdom has focused its attention on external border controls, rather than internal security measures (2013), unlike other Member States which request, for example, that all national and non- national residents be registered with the local police.

Decisions like those of the United Kingdom, Ireland and Denmark have led to a 'differentiated integration' (Adler-Nissen 2009), or 'variable geometry' (Usher 1997) in the area of JHA, which goes back to the partial communitarisation of the Third Pillar introduced by the Treaty of Amsterdam. The period ranging between the entry into force of the Treaty of Maastricht and that of the Treaty of Amsterdam was characterised by an intergovernmental approach to JHA, which allowed for Third Pillar matters to be decided unanimously and for Member States to safeguard their national interests. With the introduction of the Treaty of Amsterdam, however, immigration and asylum matters were transferred from the Third to the First Pillar, leading to a change in the decision-making process for these areas. The prospect of replacing the unanimity rule with qualified majority voting quickly led specific Member States to raise concerns about loss of sovereignty in the area of internal security, and to submit requests for derogations and opt-outs.

The UK's Opt-In and Opt-Out Arrangements

The UK has negotiated three opt-outs in the field of JHA: the first two (Protocols 19 and 21) were introduced with the Treaty of Amsterdam and the third one (Protocol 36) came about with the Treaty of Lisbon. The Amsterdam derogations allow the UK to opt in to measures relating to migration and asylum and to opt out from the Schengen legislation. The more recent derogation constitutes a mass opt-out from all pre-Lisbon measures relating to police and judicial cooperation in criminal matters. This sub-section of this chapter analyses these opt-outs in further detail.

Protocol 21, the *Protocol on the position of the United Kingdom and Ireland in Respect of the Area of Freedom, Security and Justice* exempts the UK from the application of measures comprised in Title V of Part Three of the Treaty on the Functioning of the European Union, which covers visas, asylum, immigration and other policies related to the free movement of persons. Although the United Kingdom is under no obligation to adopt the measures in Title V of the Treaty, the protocol enables it to opt in to any individual measures which it might consider capable of enhancing its security. This legal arrangement allows the UK to feel that it is protecting its border security interests, while at the same time being free to join the remaining EU members in more advanced integration measures of its choice in the area of immigration and asylum. In practice, the Protocol allows the UK to opt into a given measure within three months of it being presented to the Council. If the opt-in takes place within this time frame, the UK is given the possibility to participate in its negotiation. If the opt-in is agreed at a subsequent stage, the UK is still free to adopt and implement the measure, but it is no longer allowed to influence its negotiation. Until now, the United Kingdom has made use of this opt-in right to participate in measures mainly related to asylum and illegal migration, having chosen not to opt into measures on legal migration and border control (Home Office 2013b).

Protocol 19, the *Protocol on the Schengen Acquis Integrated into the Framework of the European Union* clarifies the conditions of the application of the Schengen Agreement, which aims to abolish checks at the internal borders of the EU. By setting the provisions for all Member States taking part in Schengen, the Protocol also refers to the conditions applicable to the United Kingdom. Namely, it clarifies that, although

Britain does not generally participate in Schengen, it is able to request an opt in to specific provisions in this acquis (Article 4 of Protocol 19). After opting in to a given measure, Britain is considered to be included in subsequent related measures, unless it asks the Council for an opt out from those new measures (Article 5 of Protocol 19). On this basis, the UK has chosen not to take part in border control provisions but has opted in to police and judicial cooperation measures. According to the Home Office and the Ministry of Justice, these opt-ins have been key in helping the country fight organised crime and terrorism by facilitating information exchange with other Member States (2015). As will be further detailed in Chapter 3, these police and judicial cooperation measures include instruments such as the Schengen Information System, Europol, Eurodac and Eurojust. Whereas Protocol 21 allows the UK to opt in to legislation solely based on its own decision, Protocol 19 requires all Member States to unanimously decide on whether the UK can take part in the measure it has asked to opt into. Such a system has generally worked to the UK's advantage, though at times it was not allowed to take part in instruments which it considered as beneficial (as was the case with Frontex) (Kaunert et al. 2014).

This form of selective participation was further expanded by the Treaty of Lisbon, when the UK was faced with the prospect of numerous JHA measures becoming subject to the jurisdiction of the Court of Justice, following a five-year transitional period starting from the entry into force of the treaty. During treaty negotiations, the UK requested for the *Protocol On Transitional Provisions* (Protocol 36) to include the possibility of obtaining a block opt-out from pre-Lisbon measures regarding police and judicial cooperation in criminal matters (around 130 measures) (see Fichera, this volume, Chapter 6). The proposal to activate this opt-out was presented in October 2012, opening the door to a period of national debate. Numerous actors, including practitioners and the House of Lords EU Select Committee, responded to this political decision by discussing a vast array of evidence on the consequences of a mass opt-out,[1] eventually pushing the Government to partly backtrack by opting back into 35 of those measures (including, for instance, Europol and the European Arrest Warrant). What is particularly interesting about the

---

[1] For the complete set of evidence and for the video recording of the discussions, please visit http://www.parliament.uk/2014opt-out.

block opt-out is that, in a way, it can be understood as a Brexit trial run, given the level of complexity in opting out from a large number of measures, as well as the decision to opt back into some of them, based on concerns for UK security.

To conclude this chapter, it is important to underline that, although this form of selective participation is often presented as evidence of the UK's nature as an 'awkward partner' (George 1998) and of the AFSJ's growing complexity (Peers 2018), it has also served as an important mechanism for the development of this policy area, benefitting not only the UK itself but also the EU and its other Member States. On this basis, Chapter 3 will explore the possible consequences of Brexit for the UK and the future of the AFSJ.

References

Adler-Nissen, R. 2009. Behind the Scenes of Differentiated Integration: Circumventing National Opt-Outs in Justice and Home Affairs. *Journal of European Public Policy* 16 (1): 62–80.

Boin, A., M. Ekengren, and M. Rhinard. 2006. Protecting the Union: Analysing an Emerging Policy Space. *Journal of European Security* 28 (5): 405–421.

Geddes, A. 2013. *Britain and the European Union*. Basingstoke, Hampshire: Palgrave Macmillan.

George, S. 1998. *An Awkward Partner. Britain in the European Community*. Oxford: Oxford University Press.

Home Office. 2013a. *Information About the JHA Opt-In and Schengen Opt-Out Protocols*. Ministry of Justice, February 2013. Available from: https://www.gov.uk/government/publications/jha-opt-in-and-schengen-opt-out-protocols. Last accessed 26 April 2017.

Home Office. 2013b. *List of JHA (Title V) Opt-In and Schengen Opt-Out Decisions Taken Between 1 December 2009 to Date*. Home Office and Minister of Justice, February 2013. Available from: https://www.gov.uk/government/publications/jha-opt-in-and-schengen-opt-out-protocols. Last accessed 26 April 2017.

Home Office and Ministry of Justice. 2015. *Background Information: JHA Opt-In Protocol and Schengen Opt-Out Protocol*. Available from: https://www.gov.uk/government/publications/jha-opt-in-and-schengen-opt-out-protocols-3. Last accessed 7 July 2017.

Kaunert, C., S. Léonard, H. Carrapico, and S. Rozée. 2014. The Governance of Justice and Internal Security in Scotland: Between the Scottish Independence Referendum and British Decisions on the EU. *European Security* 23 (3): 344–363.

Monar, J. 1999. Justice and Home Affairs in a Wider Europe: The Dynamics of Inclusion and Exclusion. *ESRC One Europe or Several?* Working Paper 07/00, ESCRC, Swindon.

Monar, J. 2006. Cooperation in the Justice and Home Affairs Domain: Characteristics, Constraints and Progress. *Journal of European Integration* 28 (5): 495–509.

Peers, S. 2018. Differentiated Integration and the Brexit Process in EU Justice and Home Affairs. In *The Routledge Handbook of Justice and Home Affairs Research*, ed. A. Ripoll Servent and F. Trauner, 253–263. London: Routledge.

Uçarer, E. 2016. The Area of Freedom, Security and Justice. In *European Union Politics*, ed. M. Cini and N. Perez-Solorzano Borragan, 5th ed, 281–294. Oxford: Oxford University Press.

Usher, J. 1997. Variable Geometry or Concentric Circles: Patterns for the European Union. *International and Comparative Law Quarterly* 46 (2): 243–273.

CHAPTER 3

The Consequences of Brexit for the UK and for the Area of Freedom, Security and Justice

Abstract This chapter outlines the potential impact of Brexit on the UK's internal security, as well as the EU's Area of Freedom, Security and Justice, focusing specifically on police and judicial cooperation, and migration, asylum and border issues. Despite the UK's limited participation in judicial cooperation and migration and asylum policies, there are manifold potential consequences of Brexit in these areas, with the chapter concluding that Brexit holds both positive and negative consequences for the EU in these fields while damaging the UK's internal security and involving a number of challenges for future cooperation.

Keywords Brexit · Police cooperation · Judicial cooperation in criminal matters · Asylum and migration · Border management

THE POSSIBLE IMPACT OF BREXIT ON UK INTERNAL SECURITY

This chapter, which is based on the selective participation of the UK in the Area of Freedom, Security and Justice, explores possible consequences for the UK's internal security. The measures in which the UK participates in the field of EU Justice and Home Affairs broadly concern the fields of police cooperation, judicial cooperation, asylum and migration, according to which this section is structured.

© The Author(s) 2019   15
H. Carrapico et al., *Brexit and Internal Security*,
Palgrave Studies in European Union Politics,
https://doi.org/10.1007/978-3-030-04194-6_3

Police Cooperation

The UK is heavily involved in and has shaped EU police cooperation. This includes operational cooperation, information exchange and supporting action, which means the training and funding of police cooperation and security-related research (European Commission 2017a). This sub-section starts by exploring the information exchange mechanisms which the UK has mainly benefited from and the roadblocks that could emerge in future cooperation agreements. It then shifts its focus to operational cooperation instruments and their development and finally discusses the UK's current and possible future participation in supporting action.

The most relevant information exchange instrument for UK internal security is most likely to be Europol, which constitutes a forum for Member States to share information and intelligence, while also facilitating operational cooperation (for a detailed discussion on Brexit and Europol, see Bossong and Rieger, this volume, Chapter 7. For Europol's EC3, see Porcedda, this volume, Chapter 7). Its significance has increased in recent years (Carrapico and Trauner 2013), after being strengthened by the new Europol regulation of 2016, which clarifies the obligation of Member States to share data (European Parliament and the Council 2016a). According to the UK Government, Britain uses this agency 'more than almost any other country' (HM Government 2016: 4). Both the British Government and the EU have signalled their interest in cooperating, with regards to Europol in the future (May 2017). However, any deal is likely to lessen cooperation, given that third countries with Europol agreements do not have direct access to its databases, nor are they able to influence its strategic development, as they do not sit on the management board (see de Vries; Lavorgna, this volume, Chapter 7). Although the UK's policing and intelligence expertise (House of Lords 2016) and its membership of the Five Eyes (Mortera-Martinez 2017) are expected to strengthen its position in the Brexit negotiations (based on intelligence collection capacity), future cooperation may be hindered by the fact that the UK would have to keep up with EU data protection standards in relation to all information sharing measures (Peers 2016). Equally problematic would be Europol's accountability to the European Court of Justice (European Scrutiny Committee 2017a), given that the jurisdiction of this institution was one of the prominently discussed reasons for leaving the EU.

The exchange of information for police cooperation purposes is not limited to Europol databases (see Trauner; Wilson and Carr, this volume, Chapter 7). The UK also shares information through other instruments, namely: (1) the Schengen Information System (SIS II), used to disseminate and consult alerts on wanted or missing persons and objects (European Commission 2017b); (2) the Prüm Decisions, which allow states to search each other's databases for DNA profiles (within 15 minutes), Vehicle Registration Data (within 10 seconds) and fingerprints (within 24 hours) (Council of the European Union 2008a, b); and (3) the new European Passenger Name Record (PNR) directive, which obligates air carriers to provide PNR data for flights entering or departing from the EU, and which enables Member States to collect PNR data for intra-EU flights on a voluntary basis (European Parliament and the Council 2016b).

These measures add considerable value to the UK's internal security. Where SIS II is concerned, the National Crime Agency and the National Police Chiefs Council pointed to its relevance for mainstream policing, providing police officers on the street with the possibility of checking alerts on persons or objects from other EU countries (House of Lords 2018). Within the first year of the UK connecting to SIS II, over 6400 alerts from other Member States received hits in the UK and over 6600 alerts issued by the UK were responded to by other countries (HM Government 2016). Regarding Prüm, its value is difficult to measure as it is not yet fully implemented.[1] Nevertheless, its potential for the UK was made clear during a 2015 pilot project, which led to 118 DNA profile matches (HM Government 2016).[2] Then Home Secretary Theresa May pointed to the fact that Prüm allows national authorities to check a EU citizen's DNA records in 15 minutes, rather than the 143 days it would take pre-Prüm (May 2016). The National Crime Agency called the Interpol arrangement on sharing DNA and fingerprints on which

[1] By mid-2017, 24 Member States were expected to be operational for automated data exchange regarding DNA, 22 regarding Fingerprints, and 23 regarding vehicle registration data (Council of the European Union 2017). The UK, which has struggled with technical and data protection problems in the past (Santos 2016), was scheduled to be operational for all three types of exchange in the course of 2017, although in March 2018 that was still not the case (MOPAC 2018).

[2] The 2015 Prüm pilot project involved the UK, the Netherlands, France, Spain and Germany.

the UK could fall back on 'time consuming, bureaucratic and nowhere near as effective for protecting the public' (House of Lords 2016: 30). According to UK law enforcement agencies, the European PNR directive is also a very valuable tool, in particular for counterterrorism and border management (House of Lords 2016).

Post-Brexit cooperation in relation to these instruments is also not without its challenges. The UK's participation in SIS II would be unprecedented insofar as all countries using this system are members of the EU or the Schengen area. Where Prüm is concerned, the only third countries taking part are Norway and Iceland, which are also Schengen members. Still, as Prüm Decisions are not part of the Schengen *acquis*, it is unlikely that the UK's opt out from Schengen will constitute an obstacle to a future deal (House of Lords 2016). Regarding the European PNR, while the EU already has PNR agreements with the United States, Australia and Canada (which do not, however, include the exchange of intra-EU PNR data) (House of Lords 2016), the European Parliament has referred the new draft agreement with Canada to the European Court of Justice due to privacy concerns (European Parliament 2017). The Court's decision could call all PNR agreements into question and impact any future agreement with the UK (for more details regarding the jurisdiction of the Court, see Chapter 5).

Where operational cooperation is concerned, the Joint Investigation Teams (JITs) are one of the instruments most frequently used by the UK (Eurojust 2017; House of Lords 2016). JITs are fixed-term arrangements set up to deal with cases involving at least two Member States (Council of the European Union 2002a). The Crown Prosecution Service and the National Crime Agency emphasised the tool's importance for efficiently dealing with cases involving multiple Member States (House of Lords 2016). Given that third countries can participate in JITs with the agreement of all other participants (Eurojust 2017), it is quite likely that the UK will be allowed to participate in this instrument in a post-Brexit context. Such involvement, however, will be dependent on two Member States wishing to initiate a JIT with the UK and taking the initiative of involving it as a third country. Given that most UK-related JITs are bilateral, future cooperation along the same lines might have to rely on Council of Europe instruments, such as the Second Protocol of the European Convention on Mutual Legal Assistance in Criminal Matters (for more details on this option, please see Chapter 5) (Niehuss et al. 2018).

Europol is also increasingly involved in operational cooperation: while it does not have autonomous investigative or coercive capabilities, it can ask Member States to initiate or coordinate investigations. It offers technical, financial and operational support to cross border investigations and can suggest setting up JITs, in which it can also participate (European Parliament and the Council 2016a: Articles 5 and 6). The criminal analysis Europol provides is becoming less and less dependent on information from Member States thanks to the increase in the number of experts directly employed by Europol (Occhipinti 2015). This trend implies that, by leaving Europol, the UK may lose access not only to a forum for information exchange with other Member States but also to additional networks of experts who contribute to operational cooperation.

Brexit's influence on current arrangements in the field of supporting action, which includes the training and funding of police cooperation and security-related research, is limited: the UK is not considered a Member State in relation to CEPOL, the European Union Agency for law enforcement training, but a partner country, since it did not opt into the new CEPOL regulation of 2015 due to concerns about costs and its autonomy on training police (House of Lords 2014a). Furthermore, Brexit will have no direct impact on the funding of police cooperation as the UK chose not to participate in the police-cooperation part of the Internal Security Fund[3] due to budgetary concerns (Home Office 2013). In contrast, with regard to research and innovation funding, the UK has received the highest and the second highest amount of funding in 2014 and 2015, from the security-related section "Secure Societies" (European Commission 2016a) of the EU Research and Innovation Programme Horizon 2020, worth 1.7 billion Euros in total for 2014–2020 (European Commission 2014). As with all EU research funding, it is uncertain if it will be possible for the UK to fully participate in this funding post-Brexit.

As the above measures show, the current police cooperation arrangements contribute to the UK's internal security in fields such as serious crime and terrorism, but also mainstream policing. Future cooperation is essential for successful and prompt investigations, but will most likely require a degree of legal creativity with regard to specific measures.

---

[3]The UK does not participate in the external borders and visa part of the Internal Security Fund either, as this development is based on the provisions of the Schengen acquis, in which the UK does not take part.

Judicial Cooperation

Judicial cooperation in criminal matters is built on the principle of mutual recognition and involves substantive criminal law, legislation on the rights of victims, suspects and accused, laws on mutual recognition, and agencies to foster judicial cooperation (European Commission 2017d). The UK does not participate in most substantive criminal law legislation—with the exception of measures on the rights of victims, suspects and accused—but has been engaged in the field of mutual recognition, especially regarding the European Arrest Warrant (EAW) (Peers 2016). The British law enforcement community identified Eurojust, the EAW and the European Criminal Records Information System (ECRIS) as particularly useful to the UK (House of Lords 2016), with the EAW being one of the few security-related policies discussed in the run-up to the referendum.

Eurojust's casework has, since its establishment in 2002, steadily increased to 2306 new cases in 2016, of which 373 (about 16%) involved the UK (Eurojust 2017). Eurojust supports coordination and cooperation between Member States' investigative and prosecuting authorities in cases where serious crime affects two or more countries. It constitutes a forum in which national authorities discuss and agree on specific approaches to cases, and provides legal, technical and financial support to JITs (Eurojust 2017). Precedents for future cooperation with the UK can be found in the agreements with the US, Norway, and Switzerland, which have Liaison Prosecutors based in the agency, but which do not sit in its management board and cannot access its case management system (House of Lords 2016). British law enforcement agencies identified Eurojust as highly valuable for working multilaterally, as it provides a neutral space to talk to several other Member States in real time with translation services provided, increasing the speed of communication (House of Lords 2016) (see Porcedda, this volume, Chapter 7).

One of Eurojust's duties is to support Member States' use of the European Arrest Warrant (EAW), an instrument that speeds up and facilitates the extradition of criminals within the EU (Council of the European Union 2002b). In 2015, 1149 people were surrendered to other countries by the UK through this mechanism and 123 people were returned to the UK by other participating states (National Crime Agency 2016). The Government and law enforcement agencies have highlighted that the EAW has significantly decreased the time and resources needed for extradition, from an average of 10 months for a non-EU extradition to 3 months under the EAW mechanism, for which strict time limits are imposed. They have also underlined that its relevance will increase further as crime becomes increasingly transnational (Dawson et al. 2017). Norway and Iceland have extradition agreements with the EU (which have yet to enter into force) that are similar to the European Arrest Warrant, although they do not involve the surrendering of their own nationals (House of Lords 2016). The more bureaucratic 1957 Council of Europe Convention on Extradition would be the instrument which the UK could potentially fall back on[4] (European Scrutiny Committee 2013) in the case of no future agreement over the EAW. Under the Convention, 22 EU Member States could still refuse to surrender their nationals to the UK (House of Commons 2014) and applications for extradition are made through diplomatic channels, which requires political approval, while the EAW simply operates between judicial authorities (Dawson et al. 2017).

ECRIS, the European Criminal Records Information System, gives prosecutors complete information on a person's criminal records upon request (The Council of the European Union 2009). The UK opted into a draft proposal from 2016 aimed at upgrading the system to facilitate the exchange of criminal record information on third country nationals (European Commission 2016b), and a supplementary proposal is expected mid-2017 that aims to enable authorities to locate criminal record information on third country nationals without having to consult all Member States (European Commission 2017d). No third countries currently have access to ECRIS, which, according to UK law enforcement agencies, is critical in assessing the risk a person poses and in properly prosecuting individuals (House of Lords 2016: 27). Home Secretary Amber Rudd called for more proactive sharing of criminal records in a meeting of EU Interior and Justice Ministers in January 2017 (Rudd 2017), pointing to the UK's interest in this exchange of information.

As a final comment regarding judicial cooperation, it is also be important to mention that Brexit could lead to divergence in criminal laws between the UK and the EU, which would put the UK's internal security at risk (see Lavorgna, this volume, Chapter 7). Criminals

---

[4]Problems could emerge as some Member States repealed the domestic legislation that underpinned the Convention (Dawson et al. 2017).

use asymmetries in law to their advantage, which could lead to the UK becoming a more attractive place for conducting illegal activities (Sergi 2016; see Farrand; Sergi, this volume, Chapter 7). Furthermore, Brexit could negatively influence the rights of victims, suspects and accused in the UK as future legislation in this area may diverge from Britain's current opt-ins in this area (The Law Society of Scotland 2016).

Asylum and Migration

The EU's influence on the UK in matters of asylum and migration is considerably more limited (Peers 2016). As mentioned above, the UK does not participate in the Schengen legislation regarding EU visas and border controls,[5] despite having opted in to a few Schengen measures with regard to criminal law and policing (Peers 2016), such as the SIS II. Regarding the Common European Asylum System, the UK participates in the Dublin regulation (Home Office 2013) and the first wave of directives setting out minimum standards for an asylum system[6]—standards which could become lower in the UK after Brexit. It participates in the Asylum and Migration Fund (European Parliament and the Council 2014), which it mostly uses to develop projects that aim to return third country nationals (DCLG and Home Office 2018).

Regarding the consequences of Brexit for asylum and migration, while the UK's future relation with the Dublin system will impact immigration and asylum from non-EU countries (Peers 2016), Eurodac adds a security dimension to this field (see Goodwill in: European Scrutiny Committee 2016). The Dublin regulation enables the UK to return individuals who have already claimed asylum in another Member State, with the UK being a net beneficiary and transferring more asylum seekers to other Member States than it receives through the system (European Scrutiny Committee 2017b). Eurodac, a biometric database

---

[5] As the CJEU ruled that it would then have to opt in to the entirety of Schengen (Peers 2016).

[6] This first phase of the Common European Asylum System included the Reception Conditions Directive 2003/9/EC, the Qualification Directive 2004/83/EC and the Asylum Procedures Directive 2005/85/EC. Although the UK takes part in this first stage, it has decided not to opt into the second phase of the Asylum System (including a Qualification Regulation, an Asylum Procedures Regulation, and a Recast Reception Directive (Peers 2016)).

for fingerprints of asylum seekers and irregular migrants entering the EU, enables border authorities to verify whether a person has already claimed asylum in another Member State. It can also be accessed by law enforcement authorities for the purpose of fighting terrorism and other serious criminal activities (European Parliament and the Council 2013).[7] In 2016, the UK opted into the new Eurodac proposal, which sets out to store larger amounts of information for longer periods of time (European Commission 2016c), a development that former Immigration Minister Robert Goodwill called 'of significant value in terms of law enforcement access' (European Scrutiny Committee 2016). Exiting the Dublin system and Eurodac could thus result in the UK having less available information about asylum seekers and irregular border crossers entering the UK via the EU (see Wolff; Roos, this volume, Chapter 8). While there are association agreements with third countries that include Dublin and Eurodac, those countries are all part of the Schengen area, making any possible future participation of the UK in Dublin unprecedented (Peers 2016).

Borders

One of the most prominent issues likely to affect the UK's internal security is the changes to UK border arrangements. Since the Referendum campaign, there have been numerous attempts to claim that Brexit would allow the UK to 'take back control of its borders' (Boris Johnson in Reuters 2017). This idea equates closing borders with a reduction in migration and in criminality, a highly problematic association for three main reasons: (1) Not only does it portray migrants in a negative light, but it also erroneously assumes that most illegal migrants crossed the border in an irregular way, when it is actually the case that most arrived on a visa and overstayed (see Roos, this volume, Chapter 8); (2) this idea also conveys the impression that borders are water tight instruments capable of efficiently performing security functions as closed independent systems (see MacKenzie, this volume, Chapter 7); and (3) it implies that the majority of organised crime and terrorism originates from outside the EU, thus ignoring the importance of home-grown activities (see Sergi,

---

[7]Eurodac can currently only be used for criminal investigations if other available databases, including Prüm, have been searched first (European Scrutiny Committee 2017b), which means that future access to Eurodac for law enforcement bodies is also dependent on arrangements regarding these databases.

this volume, Chapter 7). This is, in fact, a gross simplification of how borders work and what they are able to achieve. Not only is it impossible to patrol kilometres of land and sea border, but a border is only as efficient as the information contained in its database. Given the possible loss of access to shared databases, there is the risk that UK borders might become more insecure (see Farrand; Sergi, this volume, Chapter 7). Following Brexit, border points with the Republic of Ireland, France and Spain (see Wolff; Orsini; Gomez Arana; Irrera, this volume, Chapter 8) have the potential to become external borders of the EU, with the possible reinstatement of hard borders characterised not only by physical changes, such as large security apparatuses and customs and immigration controls, but also by psychological changes, including re-definitions of individual and collective identities.

Where the Irish crossing is concerned, the border between Northern Ireland and the Republic of Ireland has mainly functioned as an open border since 1923, when a Common Travel Area (CTA) was established between the UK and the Republic of Ireland. The free movement of people agreement implies minimum border controls and a degree of policy coordination, with nationals of the CTA not being subject to passport checks. The CTA not only facilitates the flow of 30,000 frontier workers and supports both sides' economies, but also represents a crucial element of the relationship between Northern Ireland and the Republic of Ireland by creating a frictionless crossing point. Furthermore, the CTA is recognised and accepted by EU law (Protocol 20 of the Treaty of Lisbon), even though it predates the creation of the European Union (Tonge 2017). It is also important to mention that the CTA does not include provisions regarding customs, trade, and free movement of goods, capital and services (Hayward and Phinnemore 2018).

A hard border could entail the reinstatement of strict border controls and, consequently, a redesign, if not disappearance, of the CTA, which could negatively influence the peace process (Tannam 2017). More specifically, Brexit poses short-term and medium-term challenges to this specific crossing point. Regarding the short-term challenge, opportunities for criminal actors could emerge from the confusion surrounding potential new rules and procedures being imposed on individual and commercial users. Given that there already is substantial abuse of the CTA reported by border authorities, namely regarding drug-related organised crime (An Garda Siochana and Police Service of Northern Ireland 2016), Brexit has the potential to further exacerbate the situation. In order to counter this possible consequence, the UK and the EU would likely have to dedicate more resources to the prevention of criminality. Regarding the medium-term challenges, the potential creation of a border crossing regime that corresponds to an EU external border would be a serious trial for future security cooperation. Questions that will need to be answered include what kind of border can and should be created, given the historical context of this border crossing; and whether such a border is feasible in practice. It is important to bear in mind that border creation implies the coordination of a large number of services, not only customs and immigration, but also health and environment. An additional medium-term challenge—losing EU funding—should also not be overlooked. Currently, Northern Ireland is a recipient of funding, such as the PEACE IV Programme, which supports reconciliation for local communities. Although this type of funding is not directly related to border crossing, its loss has the potential to exacerbate existing security tensions, and perhaps even to lead to a regression of the stability of the area, which could result in the need for further border cooperation in the future (see Irrera, this volume, Chapter 8).

As the border between Northern Ireland and the Republic of Ireland has been historically contentious, it has been the focus of most political discussions over post-Brexit border issues. It is, however, not the only border the UK and the EU will have to reflect on: the crossing points in Calais/Dover and in Gibraltar will also constitute important challenges. Currently, the port of Dover is responsible for 17% of the UK's overall trade in goods, which makes it the main entry point for hauliers travelling from other European countries (Port of Dover 2018). This large trade volume involves the entry of 2.7 million lorries per year, most of which travel from Calais, in France. Therefore, the consequences of Brexit for this border point are not only economic (associated with potential long delays following the re-introduction of border controls for goods and people) but also security related.

The UK and France are mainly concerned with the smuggling of illegal goods and people (Home Office 2018; see Farrand, this volume, Chapter 7). Such concerns led these countries to sign the Le Touquet Treaty in 2003, which allowed for juxtaposed border controls, with UK authorities checking passengers and freight in Calais, and France carrying out Schengen entry controls in Dover (see Orsini; Wolff, this volume, Chapter 8). This joint border management is credited with reducing unauthorised entries, with 56,000 crossing attempts prevented in 2016 (Home Office 2018). As part of this agreement, the UK has invested considerably in securing the Calais side, namely by funding high-security fencing, additional border staff, CCTV, and infrared detection technology. In January 2018, a new agreement complementing the Le Touquet Treaty was signed by both countries with an aim to providing France with additional support in addressing the border pressures stemming from the refugee crisis. It also demonstrated the UK's commitment to welcoming larger refugee numbers, namely children (HM Government 2018a). Both the 2003 and 2018 treaties are bilateral agreements, which in principle should not be directly affected by Brexit. And yet, the most recent agreement already indicates that bilateral relations are also impacted by EU-level changes. When campaigning for election, Emmanuel Macron was clear that he wanted to re-negotiate the Le Touquet Treaty, claiming that Brexit was likely to lead to the need to reinforce security in Calais (due, for instance, to longer lorry queues facilitating illegal migration). Arguing that the UK would have the most to lose from the French border becoming more porous, he declared that he wanted to ensure the UK was paying a fair share of this future investment (Henley 2016). In this sense, the 2018 agreement can actually be seen as the result of a shifting balance of power, with France seizing Brexit as an opportunity to be more demanding of the UK.

Often forgotten in Brexit-related discussions, the crossing point between Gibraltar and Spain is the UK's second land border with the EU (See Orsini; Gomez Arana, this volume, Chapter 8). Although it does not share the history of violence of the Irish border, this border is not without its problems, given Spain's claim over the control of this territory. Gibraltar has been under British rule since the eighteenth century, when it was seized by Dutch-British forces during the War of Spanish Succession, and formally ceded by the Spanish Crown through the Treaty of Utrecht (House of Lords 2017a). Its historical importance derives from its strategic location, which gave it control of the entries and exits to the Mediterranean Sea (see Gomez Arana, this volume, Chapter 8). Currently, Gibraltar has its own government and legal system, with UK responsibilities limited to external relations and defence. Furthermore, and unlike other British Overseas Territories, Gibraltar is part of the EU, sharing the UK's opt-outs from the Area of Freedom, Security and Justice. As a result of being outside of Schengen, every individual crossing this border is subject to document controls, including a criminal record check. As Gibraltar is highly dependent on Spanish labour force (with 12,000 Spanish citizens entering Gibraltar on a daily basis), border crossings are particularly time consuming (Couzens 2017). In fact, the Spanish Government is often accused by Gibraltar of purposely tightening border controls as part of a retaliation and bullying strategy. Relations between Spain and Gibraltar have been particularly tense since 2011, with a number of agreements and dialogue channels falling through (Valle Galvez 2017).

In this diplomatically difficult context, Brexit poses a number of risks to this border crossing. Similarly to the Calais/Dover border, the first impact that Brexit could have on Gibraltar is economic. Although the main trade partner of Gibraltar is the UK, a hard Brexit may exclude this territory from the Single Market (House of Lords 2017a). Given that the economy of Gibraltar is mainly service-based (financial services, online gambling and tourism), it comes as no surprise that the Government of Gibraltar is greatly concerned about Brexit (Benwell and Pinkerton 2016). Beyond economic survival, Brexit is also understood as constituting an existential threat to Gibraltar's sovereignty (Picardo 2015). Spain has seen Brexit as a window of opportunity for renegotiating the status of Gibraltar and for proposing co-sovereignty by claiming that the territory would be entirely isolated outside of the EU. The possibility of co-sovereignty has gained further credibility with Spain's request to include in the negotiation guidelines what is in practice a right to veto any decision about the future of the Gibraltar-EU relationship (European Council 2017: Article 24). Finally, Brexit may also have a security impact in the sense that the current cooperation between law enforcement agencies on both sides of the border may be at risk of disappearing. One of the most important drug trafficking centres in Spain, La Linea de la Concepcion, is located just outside of Gibraltar (Jones 2018). Given the rapidly increasing trafficking flows and the scale of related violence, any disruption to the cooperation (in particular the possible disappearance of the EAW in Gibraltar) would be harmful to both sides (see Orsini, this volume, Chapter 8).

THE POTENTIAL IMPACT OF BREXIT ON THE FUTURE OF THE AREA OF FREEDOM, SECURITY AND JUSTICE

Brexit, however, will not only impact the UK but also the entire Area of Freedom, Security and Justice. The UK's departure will decrease its influence within the different EU political fora addressing internal security matters, which will in turn impact EU integration in Justice and Home Affairs (see Ripoll Servent, this volume, Chapter 6). Indeed, even if the UK relationship with the EU in this area has been based on an intricate set of opt-ins and opt-outs, it has been a leading and influential Member State, which has deeply shaped security priorities, approaches and instruments (see Trauner; Lavorgna, this volume, Chapter 7). As a result, Brexit currently poses two main challenges for the Area of Freedom, Security and Justice: (1) how to compensate for the loss of UK capacities and knowledge that have so far been used to advance this area and (2) who will replace the UK as one of the main EU security entrepreneurs? This section will analyse the potential consequences for the AFSJ by following a similar structure as the previous one.

Police Cooperation

The UK demonstrated genuine interest over the years in taking part in, and even fostering, European action in the fields of police cooperation, counter-terrorism and the fight against organized crime. Starting with a UK proposal to establish a working group to coordinate the fight against terrorism[8] (Monar 2014), the UK consistently tried to push for greater cooperation, while advocating for intergovernmental and informal structures, rather than supranational and legalised approaches. Despite its 2014 block opt-out and its cherry-picking practice in the area of Justice and Home Affairs, the UK's influence at the EU level is relatively significant insofar as it managed to upload a number of its own security norms and use its expertise to shape policy developments (for examples of UK influence see Chapter 5). Considering the complexity of this relationship, there is a genuine risk that Brexit will negatively impact EU police cooperation (see Fichera, this volume, Chapter 6).

---

[8]At the December 1975 Council of Ministers' meeting, the UK Prime Minister proposed that a platform be created to enable Member States to discuss internal security matters. This idea led to the establishment in 1976 of a working group to combat terrorism, exchange best practices and facilitate police cooperation, which would become known as the TREVI group.

The primary example of Brexit's potential impact on European internal security measures is embodied by Europol: the agency is highly dependent on the UK's contributions and expertise (Wainwright 2016), and has been significantly shaped by Britain. In addition, the UK has been and continues to contribute a great deal of intelligence to the agency, which is particularly valuable considering that a large portion of the cases dealt by Europol is linked to the UK. In March 2017, Rob Wainwright, Director of Europol, reiterated that "Europol would be weaker without active British engagement" (Peck 2017) as the UK is involved in 40% of its cases (Wainwright 2016). The field of counterterrorism is also heavily influenced by the UK, with the 2005 EU Strategy on Counterterrorism being modelled after the UK's CONTEST strategy (House of Lords 2017b).

Other policy areas where the UK has been an important agenda-setter at the EU level are data retention, data collection and data sharing, and cybersecurity. Although the UK managed to upload parts of its policies on telecommunications data retention (Friedrichs 2008; Council of the European Union 2006), its European partners may be more reluctant, after Brexit, to pursue the mass collection of user data that the UK has so far advocated. In addition, the European Court of Justice recently ruled against this British approach of a blanket collection and retention of data (BBC 2016). Also related to data collection, the European PNR was actively promoted by the UK, the first country in the EU to adopt a national PNR, with a view to making its own database more efficient (House of Lords 2016). Regarding cybersecurity policy, the UK is already considered a leading Member State, whose practices other Member States are encouraged to follow (Christou 2016) (see Porcedda; Lavorgna, this volume, Chapter 7). This essential role is illustrated, for instance, by its leadership of the Joint Cybercrime Action Task Force (J-CAT), which is aimed at fighting bank theft malware, and whose operations are hosted at Europol's European Cybercrime Centre (EC3). J-CAT was led by Andy Archibald, who served as the deputy director of the UK National Cybercrime Unit. Ultimately, the UK's influence in shaping the nature and direction of European cooperation in the field of policing, as well as its power of initiative and leadership in the operational aspects of the sector might well imply that the EU's internal security will be negatively impacted by the UK's departure. In particular, a less influential UK in security matters could also mean a weaker EU, not only at the internal level, but also in terms of the external dimension of the Area of Freedom, Security and Justice. The EU may have less capacity to project its norms and principles, which would reduce its influence over its neighbours, and their possible conflicts (de Vries, this volume, Chapter 7).

Judicial Cooperation

The UK has traditionally favoured mutual recognition in the area of judicial cooperation, whereby one decision taken by legitimate authorities in one Member State takes effect and is recognised as such by the corresponding authorities in another Member State (Peers 2004). Mutual recognition is also a better fit with the Common Law tradition, whereas harmonization can be incompatible with certain British legal principles (Friedrichs 2008). As such, Brexit could mean stepping away from mutual recognition and moving in the direction of greater legal harmonization for remaining Member States. Often being a beneficial contributor to the European judicial instruments, the UK's departure could imply both positive and negative consequences for the EU's efficiency in the field.

When it comes to analysing the use of the European Arrest Warrant, other European partners benefit considerably from the UK's participation in this instrument. As mentioned above, whereas 1149 individuals were surrendered to other countries by the UK through this mechanism in 2015, only 123 suspected criminals were returned to the UK by other participating states (National Crime Agency 2016). If future EU-UK relations do not include an agreement regarding swift extradition, EU nationals who currently reside in the UK and who are sought by other Member States' judicial authorities may find it easier to avoid being sent back for prosecution (Carrera et al. 2016), which is not to mention the fact that the UK may also start refusing to extradite its own nationals.

On the other hand, Brexit could have a positive impact on the creation and development of the European Public Prosecutor Office (EPPO) as the UK has been one of the strongest barriers to its progress. The EPPO is a body created to investigate and prosecute crimes affecting the financial interests of the EU (Giuffrida 2017). The reason for the UK's opposition resides in the fact that the EPPO model, whereby the prosecutor is in charge of conducting the investigations, is contradictory to the UK model, in which law enforcement bodies are the sole decision-makers (House of Lords 2014b). Despite the fact that the EPPO was initially set up on the basis of an "enhanced cooperation" with 16 participating Member States (Council of the EU 2017), the body would progressively develop into a real supranational judicial agency (Bond et al. 2016) by being open to the gradual accession of other EU countries and by extending its competences, as hinted by Giovanni Kessler, head of the EU anti-fraud office Olaf (Nielsen 2013).

Borders, Asylum and Migration

As the UK is in full control of its borders, its withdrawal from the EU is expected to have limited impact on the Schengen zone. Although the UK decided to adopt certain aspects of the Schengen acquis relating to police and judicial cooperation in criminal matters, its influence on EU Schengen policies has been rather limited to all appearances. Indeed, the UK's opt-in arrangements have relied on the Council of Ministers' unanimity; and where such approval is given, the UK is then also bound to subsequent measures issued in the same field (Ryan 2016). Requests for opt-ins have been refused with regard to access to the Visa Information System (VIS) and full participation in Frontex (Trauner 2014). Britain's involvement in SIS is also limited as the UK does not have access to alerts for third country nationals who have been refused entry into Schengen (Ryan 2016). In addition, the UK Government has opted out from all substantive EU legislation on immigration of third-country nationals (Carrera et al. 2016), and thus has never had the opportunity to influence visa policies.

Brexit may also have little effect on the EU asylum policy, in particular on the Dublin system and on the Common European Asylum System. Due to its geographical position, the UK is traditionally not a first-entry country and has, therefore, welcomed and accommodated small numbers of asylum seekers. Compared to other large Member States, the UK receives very few asylum applications: while Germany and Italy recorded 77,235 and 37,765 first time asylum applications respectively in the last quarter of 2016, the UK only received 9255 (Eurostat 2017). It is always possible, however, for UK figures to increase post-Brexit as a result of being outside of the Dublin System. As the UK will no longer have the possibility of returning asylum seekers to the first-entry country, its attractiveness may increase (see Fichera, this volume, Chapter 6). Furthermore, with the UK's departure, the European Commission will lose a relevant opponent to its European quota system, which aims to achieve solidarity with first-entry countries by distributing asylum claims among Member States. Indeed, the UK has persistently advocated a resettlement approach rather than relocation, meaning that it favours asylum claims being submitted and processed in the regions of origin or in dedicated centres in countries of transit (Léonard and Kaunert 2016), thus "sourcing" its own refugees from non-EU refugee camps. Notably, the UK has chosen not to participate in any of the EU's relocation schemes, which transfer asylum seekers from entry points to other Member States. Instead, the British government created the Gateway Protection Programme, a resettlement scheme transferring refugees from camps in Lebanon, Turkey and other non-EU countries, as part of the global resettlement programme of the United Nations High Commissioner for Refugees (Guild 2016).

Although current legal arrangements imply the exclusion of the UK from migration policies, it has in many instances managed to be involved in the decision-making process, thanks to informal consensus-seeking in the Justice and Home Affairs Council, a pragmatic norm which permits taking 'everybody on board' despite national opt-outs (Adler-Nissen 2009). For example, the British Government had an interest in promoting the introduction of biometric identifiers in identification documents at EU level. Although the UK was ultimately not allowed to adopt the Regulation on biometrics in passports given its classification as part of Schengen border measures, it nonetheless managed to "participate in the discussions about what to include in the regulation arguing as a 'normal' Member State" (Adler-Nissen 2009). Moreover, it was possible for the British representatives to attend Frontex Management Board meetings, holding an observer status, and participate in several joint operations set up by the border management agency, providing staff and equipment (Taylor 2017).

For the EU, a hard Brexit could also represent an opportunity for greater coherence in terms of its migration and asylum policies, as it could move towards greater harmonization of norms and deeper integration without having to cope with the operation of two or more parallel systems. This is notably the case for the CEAS (Common European Asylum System), whose first generation the UK opted into, although it subsequently made a different decision over the Recast Reception Directive. If the UK manages to strike a deal regarding the CEAS, it may also achieve a similar result with the future Dublin IV Regulation, given the UK

Immigration Minister's reference to the country continuing to take part in the Dublin system on the basis of the Dublin III provisions without opting into the new regulation (European Scrutiny Committee 2017c). Finally, and on a less optimistic note, it is important to mention that a soft Brexit (where a future agreement would include these policy areas) could also see the AFSJ becoming even more differentiated by adding an additional level of complexity (see Ripoll Servent, this volume, Chapter 6).

By way of concluding this chapter, through its special legal status in the Area of Freedom, Security and Justice, the UK was able to cherry-pick instruments valuable to its national security, which means that the current arrangements with regard to police and judicial cooperation and asylum, migration and borders strongly reflect the UK's preferences. As shown in this section, Brexit could impact the work of investigative and prosecutorial authorities in the UK in various ways and may negatively shape the UK's internal security, although this depends on the agreement which the UK and the EU potentially reach. The extent to which this deal will accommodate the UK's preferences cannot be foreseen, though future access to many instruments will require legal creativity and political will from both sides. Of course, besides the UK's current arrangements, its participation in future developments of the Area of Freedom, Security and Justice is also at stake: be it with the European Investigation Order which will soon be implemented in the UK (European Commission 2017f), or the new developments that will strengthen and connect information systems (see European Commission 2017e), Brexit will reduce the UK's influence and involvement in these developments.

REFERENCES

Adler-Nissen, R. 2009. Behind the Scenes of Differentiated Integration: Circumventing National Opt-Outs in Justice and Home Affairs. *Journal of European Public Policy* 16 (1): 62–80.

An Garda Siochana and Police Service of Northern Ireland. 2016. *Cross Border Organised Crime—Threat Assessment.*

BBC. 2016. *EU Data Retention Ruling Goes Against UK Government,* 21 December. Available from: http://www.bbc.com/news/uk-politics-38390150. Last accessed 16 June 2017.

Benwell, M., and A. Pinkerton. 2016. Brexit and the British Overseas Territories. *The RUSI Journal* 161 (4): 8–14.

Bond, I., S. Besch, A. Gostyńska-Jakubowska, R. Korteweg, C. Mortera-Martinez, and S. Tilford. 2016. *Europe After Brexit: Unleashed or Undone?* Centre for European Reform, April 2016. Available from: https://www.cer.org.uk/sites/default/files/pb_euafterBrexit_15april16.pdf. Last accessed 24 June 2017.

Carrapico, H., and F. Trauner. 2013. Europol and Its Impact on EU Policy-Making on Organised Crime. *Perspectives on European Politics and Society* 14 (3): 357–371.

Carrera, S., E. Guild, and N. Chun Luk. 2016. What Does Brexit Mean for the EU's Area of Freedom, Security and Justice? *CEPS Commentary.* Available from: https://www.ceps.eu/system/files/What%20does%20BREXIT%20mean%20for%20the%20EU.pdf. Last accessed 28 March 2018.

Christou, G. 2016. *Cybersecurity in the European Union: Resilience and Adaptability in Governance Policy.* Basingstoke: Palgrave Macmillan.

Council of the European Union. 2002a. Council Framework Decision of 13 June 2002 on Joint Investigation Teams. *Official Journal* L162: 1–3.

Council of the European Union. 2002b. Council Framework Decision of 13 June 2002 on the European Arrest Warrant and the Surrender Procedures Between Member States. *Official Journal* L190: 1–18.

Council of the European Union. 2006. *Press Release 21st February.* Available from: http://www.eu2006.at/en/News/Council_Conclusions/JAISchluss folgerungen.pdf. Last accessed 14 June 2017.

Council of the European Union. 2008a. Council Decision 2008/615/JHA of 23 June 2008 on the Stepping Up of Cross-Border Cooperation, Particularly in Combating Terrorism and Cross-Border Crime. *Official Journal* L210: 1–11.

Council of the European Union. 2008b. Council Decision 2008/616/JHA of 23 June 2008 on the Implementation of Decision 2008/615/JHA on the Stepping Up of Cross-Border Cooperation, Particularly in Combating Terrorism and Cross-Border Crime. *Official Journal* L210: 12–72.

Council of the European Union. 2009. Council Decision 2009/316/JHA of 6 April 2009 on the Establishment of the European Criminal Records Information System (ECRIS) in Application of Article 11 of Framework Decision 2009/315/JHA. *Official Journal* L93: 33–48.

Council of the European Union. 2017. *European Public Prosecutor's Office: 16 Member States Together to Fight Fraud Against the EU Budget*, Press Release, 3 April. Available from: http://www.consilium.europa.eu/en/press/press-releases/2017/04/03-eppo/. Last accessed 15 June 2017.

Couzens, G. 2017. Gibraltar Border Delays: Spanish MP Demands Answers Over Long Queues. *Express*, 6 April. Available from: https://www.express.co.uk/news/world/788585/gibraltar-border-delays-spanish-mp-answers-long-queues. Last accessed 4 April 2018.

Dawson, J., S. Lipscombe, and S. Godec. (2017). The European Arrest Warrant. *House of Commons Briefing Paper* 1: 14.

DCLG and Home office. (2018). *Controlling Migration Fund: Prospectus.* Available from: https://assets.publishing.service.gov.uk/government/uploads/system/uploads/attachment_data/file/733160/CMF_ Prospectus_2018_-_2020.pdf. Last acessed 20 March 2018.

Eurojust. 2017. *Annual Report 2016,* 1–69. Available from: http://eurojust. europa.eu/doclibrary/corporate/Pages/annual-reports.aspx. Last accessed 25 May 2017.

European Commission. 2014. *Security in 2020: Meeting the Challenge,* 1–32. Available from: https://ec.europa.eu/home-affairs/sites/homeaffairs/ files/financing/fundings/research-forsecurity/docs/security_research_bro- chure_2014_en.pdf. Last accessed 20 June 2017.

European Commission. 2016a. *Commission Staff Working Document. Horizon 2020 Annual Monitoring Report 2015,* SWD (2016) 376 final: 1–260.

European Commission. 2016b. *Proposal for a Directive of the European Parliament and of the Council Amending Council Framework Decision 2009/315/JHA, as Regards the Exchange of Information on Third Country Nationals and as Regards the European Criminal Records Information System (ECRIS), and Replacing Council Decision 2009/316/JHA,* COM (2016) 7 final, 2016/0002 (COD): 1–38.

European Commission. 2016c. *Proposal for a regulation of the European parliament and of the Council on the establishment of 'Eurodac' for the comparison of fingerprints for the effective application of [Regulation (EU) No. 604/2013 establishing the criteria and mechanisms for determining the Member State responsible for examining an application for international protection lodged in one of the Member States by a third-country national or a stateless person], for identifying an illegally staying third-country national or stateless person and on requests for the comparison with Eurodac data by Member States' law enforce- ment authorities and Europol for law enforcement purposes (recast),* 2016/0132 (COD): 1–107.

European Commission. 2017a. *Joint Statement by President Jean-Claude Juncker and Prime Minister Theresa May,* 16 October, Brussels. Available from: http://europa.eu/rapid/press-release_STATEMENT-17–3969_en.htm. Last accessed 26 March 2018.

European Commission. 2017b. *Position Paper Transmitted to EU27 on the Use of Data and Protection of Information Obtained or Processed Before the Withdrawal Date,* TF50 (2017) 14. Available from: https://ec.europa.eu/ commission/sites/beta-political/files/use-data-protection-information_en.pdf. Last accessed 18 December 2017.

European Commission. 2017c. *Joint Report from the Negotiators of the European Union and the United Kingdom Government on Progress During Phase 1 of Negotiations Under Article 50 TFEU on the United Kingdom's Orderly Withdrawal from the European Union*, 8 December, Brussels.

European Commission. 2017d. *Proposal for a Regulation of the European Parliament and of the Council Concerning the Respect for Private Life and the Protection of Personal Data in Electronic Communications and Repealing Directive 2002/58/EC (Regulation on Privacy and Electronic Communications)*, (Communication) COM (2017) 10 Final, 2017/0003 (COD).

European Commission. 2017e. *Communication from the Commission to the European Parliament, the European Council and the Council. Seventh Progress Report Towards an Effective and Genuine Security Union*, COM (2017) 261 Final.

European Commission. 2017f. *Evidence*. Available from: http://ec.europa.eu/justice/criminal/recognition-decision/evidence/index_en.htm. Last accessed 4 July 2017.

European Council. 2017. *Special Meeting of the European Council (Art. 50)—Guidelines*, EUCO XT 20004/17, 29 April, Brussels.

European Parliament. 2017. *EU Passenger Name Record (European PNR)*, Legislative Train Schedule. Available from: http://www.europarl.europa.eu/legislative-train/theme-area-of-justice-andfundamental-rights/file-eu-passenger-name-record-(european-pnr). Last accessed 18 May 2017.

European Parliament and the Council. 2013. Regulation (EU) No. 603/2013 of the European Parliament and of the Council of 26 June 2013 on the Establishment of 'Eurodac'. *Official Journal* L180: 1–30.

European Parliament and the Council. 2014. Regulation (EU) No. 516/2014 of the European Parliament and of the Council of 16 April 2014 Establishing the Asylum, Migration and Integration Fund, amending Council Decision 2008/381/EC. *Official Journal* L150: 168–194.

European Parliament and the Council. 2016a. Regulation 2016/679/EU of the European Parliament and of the Council of 27 April 2016 on the Protection of Natural Persons with Regard to the Processing of Personal Data and on the Free Movement of Such Data. *Official Journal* L119: 1–88.

European Parliament and the Council. 2016b. Directive 2016/1148/EU of the European Parliament and of the Council of 6 July 2016 concerning measures for a high common level of security of network and information systems across the union. *Official Journal* L194: 1–30.

European Scrutiny Committee. 2013. The UK's Block-Opt Out of Pre-Lisbon Criminal Law and Policing Measures, House of Commons, Twenty-First Report of Session 2013–2014: 1–159.

European Scrutiny Committee. 2016. *European Union Agency for Asylum Debate*, 15 November 2015. Available from: https://hansard.parliament.uk/Commons/2016-11-15/debates/0bb691c4-3ce1-4d19-abcd-7bba69a853a9/EuropeanUnionAgencyForAsylum?highlight=eurodac#contribution-DD14A42BAFDF-4241-AD81-54D36F5AB275. Last accessed 24 June 2017.

European Scrutiny Committee. 2017a. *Documents Considered by the Committee on 19 April 2017. Europol: Agreement with Denmark.* Available from: https://www.publications.parliament.uk/pa/cm201617/cmselect/cmeuleg/71-xxxvi/7111.htm#_idTextAnchor016. Last accessed 02 June 2017.

European Scrutiny Committee. 2017b. *Fingerprinting of Asylum Applicants and Irregular Migrants: The Eurodac System.* Available from: https://www.publications.parliament.uk/pa/cm201617/cmselect/cmeuleg/71-xxxii/7109.htm. Last accessed 05 July 2017.

European Scrutiny Committee. 2017c. *EU Asylum Reform: Revision of the Dublin Rules and the Establishment of an EU Agency for Asylum.* Available from: https://www.publications.parliament.uk/pa/cm201617/cmselect/cmeuleg/71-xxiii/7110.htm. Last accessed 02 June 2017.

Friedrichs, J. (2008). *Fighting Terrorism and Drugs: Europe and International Police Cooperation.* London and New York: Routledge.

Eurostat. 2017. *First Time Asylum Applicants, Q4 2015–Q4 2016.* Available from: http://ec.europa.eu/eurostat/statisticsexplained/index.php/File:First_time_asylum_applicants_Q4_2015_%E2%80%93_Q4_2016.png. Last accessed 10 June 2017.

Giuffrida, F. 2017. *The European Public Prosecutor's Office: King Without Kingdom?* Centre for European Policies Studies, Research Report, No 2017/03, February 2017.

Guild, E. 2016. The UK Referendum on the EU and the Common European Asylum System, *freemovement.org*, 29 April. Available from: https://www.freemovement.org.uk/brexit-and-thecommon-european-asylum-system/. Last accessed 10 June 2017.

Hayward, K., and D. Phinnemore. 2018. *The Northern Ireland/ Ireland Border, Regulatory Alignment and Brexit: Principles and Options in Light of the UK-EU Joint Report of 8 December 2017*, Briefing Paper 3, February, Queen's University Belfast.

Henley, J. 2016. The Calais Border Treaty and Brexit: What Is France Saying? *The Guardian.* Available from: https://www.theguardian.com/uk-news/2016/mar/03/calais-border-treaty-brexit-what-is-france-saying. Last accessed 3 April 2018.

HM Government. 2016. *The UK's Cooperation with the EU on Justice and Home Affairs, and on Foreign Policy and Security Issues.* Background Note, 1–11. Available from: https://www.gov.uk/government/uploads/system/uploads/attachment_data/file/521926/The_UK_s_cooperation_with_the_EU_on_justice_and_home_affairs__and_on_foreign_policy_and_security_issues.pdf. Last accessed 1 June 2017.

HM Government. 2018. *Treaty Between the Government of the United Kingdom of Great Britain and Northern Ireland and the Government of the French Republic Concerning the Reinforcement of Cooperation for the Coordinated Management of Their Shared Border.* Available from: https://www.gov.uk/government/uploads/system/uploads/attachment_data/file/674885/Treaty_Concerning_the_Reinforcement_Of_Cooperation_For_The_Coordinated_Management_Of_Their_Shared_Border.pdf. Last accessed 03 April 2018.

Home Office. 2013. *List of JHA (Title V) Opt-In and Schengen Opt-Out Decisions Taken Between 1 December 2009 to Date.* Home Office and Minister of Justice, February 2013. Available from: https://www.gov.uk/government/publications/jha-opt-in-and-schengen-opt-out-protocols. Last accessed 26 April 2017.

Home Office. 2018. *Fact Sheet: The UK's Juxtaposed Border Controls.* Available from: https://homeofficemedia.blog.gov.uk/2017/07/11/fact-sheet-the-uks-juxtaposed-border-controls/. Last accessed 03 April 2018.

House of Commons. 2014. *10 November 2014 Daily Hansard—Debate.* Available from: https://www.publications.parliament.uk/pa/cm201415/cmhansrd/cm141110/debtext/141110-0002.htm. Last accessed 28 May 2017.

House of Lords. 2014a. *The United Kingdom Opt-in to the Draft CEPOL Regulation.* European Union Committee, 3rd Report of Session 2014–2015: 1–15.

House of Lords. 2014b. The European Public Prosecutor's Office (EPPO): The Impact on Non-participating Member States. *European Union Committee,* Oral and Written Evidence, 29 April. Available from: https://www.parliament.uk/documents/lords-committees/eu-sub-com-e/europeanpublic-prosecutor-office/EPPOVolofEvidence280414.pdf. Last accessed 15 June 2017.

House of Lords. 2016. Brexit: Future UK-EU Security and Police Cooperation. *European Union Committee,* 7th Report of Session 2016–2017.

House of Lords. 2017a. Brexit: Gibraltar. *European Union Committee,* 13th Report of Session 2016–2017, 1 March, HL Paper 116.

House of Lords. 2017b. Exiting the EU and Security, Law Enforcement and Criminal Justice. *European Union Committee,* Number CDP-2017-0015, 13 January.

House of Lords. 2018. Brexit: The Proposed UK-EU Security Treaty. *European Union Committee,* 18th Report of Session 2017–2019, HL Paper 164, July. Available from: https://publications.parliament.uk/pa/ld201719/ldselect/ldeucom/164/164.pdf. Last accessed on 25 August 2018.

Jones, S. 2018. Inside La Linea, the Spanish Town in the Frontline Against Drug Trafficking. *The Guardian,* 4 April. Available from: https://www.theguardian.com/world/2018/apr/04/spain-la-linea-drug-trafficking-gibraltar-hashish. Last accessed 04 April 2018.

Léonard, S., and C. Kaunert. 2016. *The Extra-Territorial Processing of Asylum Claims.* Available from: Fmreview.org/destination-europe. Last accessed 17 May 2018.

May, T. 2016. *Speech on Brexit.* Available from: http://www.conservativehome.com/parliament/2016/04/theresa-mays-speech-on-brexit-full-text.html. Last accessed 3 June 2017.

May, T. 2017. *Andrew Neil's Interview with Theresa May*, 29 March. Available from: https://blogs.spectator.co.uk/2017/03/transcript-andrew-neils-brexit-interview-theresa-may/. Last accessed 20 June 2017.

Monar, J. 2014. EU Internal Security Governance: The Case of Counter-Terrorism. *European Security* 23 (2): 195–209.

MOPAC. 2018. *Request for DMPC Decision—PCD 346*. Mayor of London, Office for Policing and Crime. Available from: https://www.london.gov.uk/sites/default/files/pcd_346_part_1_exchange_of_biometric_data_across_europe_-_the_prum_arrangements.pdf. Last accessed 23 May 2018.

Mortera-Martinez, C. 2017. *Good Cop, Bad Cop: How to Keep Britain Inside Europol. Center for European Reform Insight*. Available from: https://www.cer.org.uk/insights/good-cop-bad-cop-howkeep-britain-inside-europol. Last accessed 05 June 2017: 1–4.

National Crime Agency. 2016. *Wanted from the UK: European Arrest Warrant statistics 2009–May 2016 (Calendar Year)*. Available from: http://www.nationalcrimeagency.gov.uk/publications/european-arrest-warrant-statistics/wanted-fromthe-uk-european-arrest-warrant-statistics. Last accessed 1 June 201.

Niehuss, A., B. Farrand, H. Carrapico, and J. Obradovic-Wochnik. 2018. *European Union Member States' Judicial Cooperation Frameworks—A Focus on Extradition, Mutual Legal Assistance, and Joint Investigation Teams*. Report for the Home Office.

Nielsen, N. 2013. EU Prosecutor Likely to Expand Powers. *EUobserver*, 28 November. Available from: https://euobserver.com/justice/122285. Last accessed 25 June 2017.

Occhipinti, J.D. 2015. Still Moving Toward a European FBI? Re-examining the Politics of EU Police Cooperation. *Intelligence and National Security* 30 (2–3): 234–258.

Peck, T. 2017. Brexit Won't Stop the UK Won't Sharing Intelligence, Says (British) Europol Chief. *The Independent*, 7 March. Available from: http://www.independent.co.uk/news/uk/politics/brexitwont-stop-the-uk-wont-sharing-intelligence-says-british-europol-chief-a7616886.html. Last accessed 14 June 2017.

Peers, S. 2004. Mutual Recognition and Criminal Law in the European Union: Has the Council Got It Wrong? *Common Market Law Review* 41 (1): 5–36.

Peers, S. 2016. Migration, Internal Security and the UK's EU Membership. *The Political Quarterly* 87 (2): 247–253.

Picardo, F. 2015. Brexit Would Destroy Gibraltar. *Politico*, 5 March. Available from: https://www.politico.eu/article/brexit-would-destroy-gilbraltar/. Last accessed 4 April 2018.

Port of Dover. 2018. *Port of Dover Announces Fifth Consecutive Record Year for Freight*, Press Release, 9 January. Available from: https://www.doverport.co.uk/about/news/port-of-dover-announces-fifth-consecutive-record-y/13341/. Last accessed 03 April 2018.

Rudd. 2017. *Justice and Home Affairs Post-council Statement*, 2 February 2017, Vol. 620. Available from: https://hansard.parliament.uk/Commons/ 2017-02-02/debates/17020250000014/JusticeAndHomeAffairsPost CouncilStatementhighlight=Criminal%20Records#contribution-F8DE59D8- 34F0-4076-B773-5E201B4041D5. Last accessed 26 June 2017.

Ryan, B. 2016, Brexit and Borders: Schengen, Frontex and the UK. *Freemovement. org*, 19 May. Available from: https://www.freemovement.org.uk/brexit-and-borders-schengen-frontex-and-the-uk/. Last accessed 10 June 2017.

Santos, F. (2016). Overview of the Implementation of the Prum Decisions. Exchange-Forensic Geneticists and the Transnational Exchange of DNA Data in the European Union: Engaging Science with Social Control, Citizenship and Democracy. *European Commission*. Available from: https://estudogeral. sib.uc.pt/bitstream/10316/41091/1/Overview%20of%20the%20implementation%20of%20the%20Pr%C3%BCm%20Decisions.pdf. Last accessed on 25 April 2018.

Sergi, A. 2016. *Brexit Could Make Life Easier for Organized Crime Gangs*. Available from: https://theconversation.com/brexit-could-make-life-easier-for-organised-crime-gangs-60515. Last accessed 3 June 2017.

Tannam, E. 2017. *Brexit's Implications for Northern Ireland May Be Destabilising, But Not Fatal*, LSE Blog Post. Available from: http://blogs. lse.ac.uk/brexit/2017/04/06/brexit-and-peace-in-northernireland/. Last accessed 15 June 2017.

Taylor, B. 2017. *Leaving the European Union: Frontex and UK Border Security Cooperation Within Europe*, House of Lords, LIF 2017/0039.

The Law Society of Scotland. 2016. *Written Evidence—FSP0001*. Available from: http://data.parliament.uk/writtenevidence/committeeevidence.svc/ evidencedocument/eu-home-affairssubcommittee/brexit-future-ukeu-security-and-policing-cooperation/written/43327.html. Last accessed 2 June 2017.

Tonge, J. 2017. *The Impact and Consequences of Brexit for Northern Ireland*. European Parliament Policy Department C: Citizens' Rights and Constitutional Affairs PE 583, (116): 1–12.

Trauner, F. 2014. Migration Policy: An Ambiguous EU Role in Specifying and Spreading International Refugee Protection Norms. In *EU Policies in a Global Perspective: Shaping or Taking International Regimes?*, ed. Gerda Falkner and Patrick Müller, 149–166. London: Routledge.

Valle Galvez, A. 2017. Gibraltar, the Brexit, the Symbolic Sovereignty, and the Dispute: A Principality in the Straits? *Gibraltar Reports: Academic Journal About the Gibraltar Dispute* 2: 67–96.

Wainwright, R. 2016. *Foreword, in Maajid Nawaz and Julia Ebner the EU and Terrorism: Is Britain Safer in or Out?* Quilliam, May. Available from: http:// www.quilliaminternational.com/wpcontent/uploads/2016/05/The-EU-and-Terrorism_Maajid-Nawaz-and-Julia-Ebner.pdf. Last accessed 15 June 2017.

CHAPTER 4

Emerging EU and UK Negotiation Positions

Abstract This chapter explores how the emerging negotiation position of the UK regarding future cooperation in internal security with the EU is characterised by a largely unsubstantiated expectation that little will change in this area of cooperation for the sake of collective security. The EU, meanwhile, has signaled that it wants a partnership beneficial for both sides, but has also pointed out various challenges to future cooperation and voiced frustration with the UK's vague position and the experienced difficulties in the negotiations—feelings that, the authors warn, could reduce the political will necessary to reach a substantive future security agreement.

Keywords Brexit · Negotiations · Article 50 · Sovereignty · Political will · Trust

The EU-UK future security partnership will be subject to negotiations that are distinct from those on the future economic and trade relationship. Brexit negotiations are characterised by a phase-based approach which aims to avoid operational and legal gaps during the transition from the current relationship to new arrangements in all areas of cooperation. The first phase (June–December 2017) was dedicated to settling key priority issues in order to prevent the risk of legal uncertainty following Brexit. Following the UK's formal notification on March 29th 2017 to the European Council of its intention to leave the EU by triggering Article 50, six rounds of negotiation were required to tackle three

© The Author(s) 2019
H. Carrapico et al., *Brexit and Internal Security*,
Palgrave Studies in European Union Politics,
https://doi.org/10.1007/978-3-030-04194-6_4

pressing issues identified in this first phase: (1) EU and UK citizens' rights; (2) the financial settlement, including the UK's obligations undertaken while still being a member; and (3) the specific costs linked to the withdrawal process and the dilemma caused by the Northern Irish border.

In December 2017, the European Council estimated that there had been sufficient progress made in all three areas of concern and launched the second phase (which, at the time of writing, was still ongoing). This phase focused on the negotiation and ratification of a Withdrawal Agreement and on a preliminary discussion on the framework for the future EU-UK long-term relationship. On the basis of the European Council's suggestion and Theresa May's proposal in her Florence speech (May 2017), the EU-27 ministers agreed during the General Affairs Council of January 29th 2018 on a transition/implementation period starting immediately after the UK's EU membership ceases in March 2019 and concluding on December 31st 2020. During this expected transition/implementation period, all existing regulatory, budgetary, supervisory, judiciary and enforcement EU instruments and legislations will continue to apply to the UK. However, Britain will lose its voting rights, its participation in EU institutions and agencies' decision-making will be restricted, and it will not be able to join new Justice and Home Affairs measures. This transitional arrangement is understood as an extra buffer period aimed at avoiding an abrupt exit, whose possible gaps would be addressed only when the future EU-UK relationship enters into force. Given that such potential gaps would only be addressed once the UK has left the EU and after the new relationship agreement has been ratified by all Member States, the second phase also includes preliminary discussions on the future security agreement planned to come into effect once the transition/implementation period is over. The third and final phase, which is expected to start in March 2019, corresponds to the negotiation of the future UK-EU security agreement.

THE UK'S DEPARTING POSITION

Although negotiations in the area of security will not start until the Withdrawal Agreement is signed and ratified,[1] the UK has begun to articulate its position via a number of Prime Minister speeches and two

---

[1] As will be further explained in this section, agreement was reached on the withdrawal text in November 2018. At the time of proofs submission (May 2018), however, there was uncertainty on the UK side regarding the political acceptance of the agreement.

UK Government papers: 'Security, Law Enforcement and Criminal Justice: a future partnership' (HM Government 2017) and 'The Future Relationship between the United Kingdom and the European Union' (HM Government 2018). It is be important to mention from the onset that UK political debates have been largely characterised by an unsubstantiated, although dominant, idea that little will change in this area of cooperation. As Theresa May repeatedly mentioned, a similar level of security cooperation is expected to continue, despite the UK no longer being part of the AFSJ, in order to ensure that European security is not endangered (Lancaster House speech, January 2017; Florence speech, September 2017; Munich speech, February 2018). She argued at the Munich Security Conference in February 2018 that, while there is no security arrangement between the EU and a third country that reaches the UK's desired depth of cooperation, the extensive agreements between the EU and third countries in other fields, such as trade, could serve as a precedent for this area (House of Lords 2018). As she concluded, 'there is no legal or operational reason why such an agreement could not be reached in the area of internal security' (May 2018). In fact, the UK has called upon the EU to avoid 'rigid institutional restrictions or deep-seated ideology' (May 2018) and invites it not to 'be so inflexible that it confines cooperation to existing models' (House of Commons 2018b).

In line with the idea that much will remain unchanged for the sake of collective security, the UK is proposing a new relationship which is as strong and effective as the current one, and which would go far beyond the EU's existing cooperation models with third countries. More specifically, the UK wishes to develop a bespoke 'toolkit' designed to support coordination and cooperation between police and judicial authorities that will prioritise: (a) data-driven law-enforcement; (b) practical assistance to operations; and (c) multilateral cooperation through agencies (HM Government 2018). Although the 2017 Government paper does not go into further detail, it does state as a starting point that negotiations should cover all provisions the UK has opted into for Chapters 5 (judicial cooperation in criminal matters) and 6 (police cooperation) of Title V of the Treaty on the Functioning of the European Union, in addition to providing examples of instruments which it considers to be beneficial (including the Schengen Information System II, the European Arrest Warrant, the Europol Internet Referral Unit, and the Joint Cybercrime Taskforce) (HM Government 2017). The UK Government has also stated its intention to prioritise border-related issues, namely the maintenance of the Common Travel Area with the Republic of Ireland, the avoidance of a hard border between Northern Ireland and the Republic of Ireland, and the inclusion of Gibraltar's interests in the negotiations (HM Government 2017). The 2018 Government paper provides further detail regarding the elements it would like to see included in the future security agreement, but remains vague on how to achieve such result: the UK 'proposes a coherent and legally binding agreement on internal security that sets out respective commitments and reflects the integrated operational capabilities that the UK and the EU share' (HM Government 2018: point 18). Rather than propose legal or technical avenues for achieving the desired cooperation, the 2018 document simply reiterates the consequences of the UK not taking part in Justice and Home Affairs instruments. A particularly strong example is the proposal that legal barriers regarding extradition of EU nationals to the UK be surmounted on the simple basis of the 'mutual trust generated by the long history and experience of operating the EAW between the UK and the EU' (HM Government 2018: point 46).

When considering most of the measures that are included in this starting position, it is important to keep in mind that these are not the result of a rushed Brexit-related decision, but rather the product of a longer reflection dating back to the pre-mass opt-out discussion period of 2013–2014, as discussed in Chapter 2 of this volume. Faced with the prospect of increased European Court of Justice jurisdiction over police and judicial cooperation, Theresa May, who at the time was still Home Secretary, announced in 2012 the UK's intention of opting out entirely from this area, covering 133 EU pre-Lisbon measures. Following a long political and technical debate which focused on the transnational character of threats and the advantages and disadvantages of each of the measures (House of Lords 2013), the UK Government concluded that a mass opt-out would most likely endanger the UK's stability and the safety of its citizens, as it would be difficult to compensate for the loss of EU-level cooperation (May 2013). As a result, the UK still went ahead with the mass opt-out but asked to opt back into 35 of the most crucial instruments, including Europol and the European Arrest Warrant. It is these 35 measures together with post-Lisbon instruments that the UK is particularly keen to retain, given their potential impact on national law and order (HM Government 2017).

The UK also hopes it will manage, not only to strike an arrangement similar to the current relationship with access to the same valuable instruments, but also to secure the possibility of still taking part in the process of shaping current evolving EU mechanisms and future new proposals in the area of European security cooperation. This tells us that the UK is well aware that keeping access to the current toolbox of security instruments does not satisfy its ambitions, as these instruments will most certainly evolve in response to new emerging risks and opportunities (House of Commons 2018a).

There are a number of reasons why the UK believes that its proposed starting position is strong and realistic. Firstly, it notes that it shares the same fundamental values as the rest of Europe, including respect for human rights, rule of law, democracy and equality (May 2018). Consequently, it sees itself as having the same obligation to defend such values. Secondly, it feels that its security context and priorities are also very much aligned with those of the EU. Such context includes (a) the increasing threat posed by terrorism, extremism and instability, (b) the resurgence of State-based threats, (c) the erosion of the rules-based international order, (d) the ongoing growth in serious and organised crime, (e) the impact of technology, and (f) diseases, and natural hazards (HM Government 2018). Although there may be some degree of diversity in security priorities among the 28 Member States, there is a large consensus that current security problems transcend national jurisdictions, and that borders are limited in their capacity to tackle them (European Union 2010). From this perspective, the only way to effectively address terrorism and organised crime, among others, is to seriously invest in cooperation. As mentioned by the Prime Minister in her Munich speech, 'Europe's security is our security' (May 2018). The UK is acutely aware that its internal security directly depends on global security. Thirdly, and given that interdependence is not a one-way street, it also believes that the rest of Europe needs the UK's capacities in the area of security generally, and especially its intelligence, which is strengthened by the UK's membership of the Five Eyes, an intelligence alliance between the UK, the USA, Australia, Canada and New Zealand, for the purposes of maintaining stability. As an example, the UK explicitly mentioned when referring to the prospect of not taking part in ECRIS that it 'would deny EU Member States timely access to large volumes of vital information that currently protects the most vulnerable people and supports justice systems to be fair and effective across Europe' (HM Government 2018: point 34). Fourthly, the UK has been a key player in shaping the AFSJ, showing its expertise in security-related policy-making on many occasions and uploading several of its policies to the EU level (see Chapter 5). On top of its role as a norm-setter, it makes extensive use of existing instruments and is one of the main contributors facilitating and ensuring the quality of their operation (notably Europol's data systems). As a result, other Member States are also aware of the benefits of working with the UK in this policy field. Finally, from a technical perspective, the UK is also conscious that it may have a considerable advantage over third countries trying to strike security agreements, as it is departing, at least in theory, from a position of regulatory alignment, which should facilitate the expected transition/implementation phase and a future security agreement (see Porcedda, this volume, Chapter 7).

The view that the UK and the EU would be able to develop new forms of cooperation similar to the present ones, however, is not universally shared within the UK. The Home Affairs Committee of the UK Parliament, in a report from March 2018, warns of the complex legal and technical difficulties to be overcome before similar forms of cooperation can be reached, and urgently calls for both sides to show flexibility and commitment (House of Commons 2018b). The Committee expresses in particular its concerns for the UK government's 'apparent lack of investment and interest in contingency planning' to cope with a no security deal scenario.

The EU's Departing Position

From the EU's perspective, it is difficult to say at this stage whether the UK's initial security position is perceived as having any potential, or if it is convincing at all. While, on the one hand, Michel Barnier's response to the UK Government's security paper suggested the end of the UK's involvement in EU decision-making and of its capacity to shape new instruments (Barnier 2018), it admits, on the other hand, that EU and UK security priorities are fairly aligned (Barnier 2017b). In support of this view, Jean-Claude Juncker stated that 'we continue to need this security bridge, this security alliance between the UK and the European Union' (Juncker 2018). The EU wants a partnership that would benefit both sides and that would cover a broad spectrum of threats (see Mortera-Martinez, this volume, Chapter 6). The future UK-EU security partnership is essential, and the only way to tackle terrorism is to work together (European Commission 2017).

Nevertheless, the EU has also pinpointed a number of initial challenges to the future UK-EU security agreement, including the fact that it does not want to discriminate against other third countries by being seen to favour the UK and setting a precedent (see Trauner, this volume, Chapter 7), which would mean that the future agreement would need to have a delicate balance between rights and obligations (House of Lords 2018). According to Donald Tusk, 'the EU cannot agree to grant the UK the rights of Norway with the obligations of Canada' (Council of the EU 2018). In January 2018, the European Commission listed the 'factors determining the degree of the EU cooperation with third countries', including the security interest of the EU-27, potential shared threats and geographic proximity, the existence of a common framework of obligations with third countries (for example Schengen or the free movement area), the risk of upsetting relations with other countries, the respect for fundamental rights and equivalent data protection standards, and the strength of enforcement and dispute settlement mechanisms (European Commission 2018a). UK proposals would therefore have to meet the threshold for all these elements.

There have been indications that the EU perceives the UK's position as being too vague and opaque (see Mortera-Martinez, this volume, Chapter 6). In August 2017, Jean-Claude Juncker mentioned how disappointed he was at the insufficient depth of the UK Government Brexit sectoral papers (BBC 2017), which was followed by Michel Barnier's request for more clarity from the UK in relation to its proposals for Justice and Home Affairs, combined with the warning that 'any vision of the future must take into account the fact that the EU cannot and will not compromise on its founding principles' (Barnier 2018). Harsher criticisms have also portrayed the UK negotiation strategy as being at times incoherent. By example, the UK's decision to opt-in into new Justice and Home Affairs measures, only to abandon them at the end of the expected transition/implementation process, was labelled as surprising (European Commission 2018b).

Finally, the EU's discourse has also been characterised by a certain degree of frustration towards the UK's Brexit decision and the difficulty in reaching a Withdrawal Agreement. This frustration has at times been expressed in rather emotive language, as was the case with Michel

Barnier's Berlin Security Conference speech (Barnier 2017a), in which he portrayed the UK's decision to exit the EU, at a time when a series of terrorist attacks were occurring in European countries, as a form of betrayal of European principles and solidarity. More recently, the limited progress achieved between February and October 2018 has also heightened emotional reactions with the EU labelling the UK's negotiation strategy as fantasist, and the UK accusing the EU of insulting its negotiation team (Stone 2018). This frustration and potential subsequent lack of political will could seriously hamper the scope of the future agreement, as close coordination will require a great deal of flexibility, creativity, and persuasion to overcome the wide range of political, legal, and constitutional challenges to cooperation in the policy field of Justice and Home Affairs. The next chapter will examine some of these challenges.

References

Barnier, M. 2017a. *Speech by Michel Barnier at the Berlin Security Conference*, 29 November, Berlin. Available from: http://europa.eu/rapid/press-release_SPEECH-17-5021_en.htm. Last accessed 24 March 2018.

Barnier, M. 2017b. *Speech by Michel Barnier, Chief Negotiator for the Preparation and Conduct of the Negotiations with the United Kingdom, at the Plenary Session of the European Committee of the Regions*, SPEECH/17/723, 22 March, Brussels. Available from: https://www.ifa.ie/wp-content/uploads/2017/03/Speech-by-Michel-Barnier.pdf. Last accessed 30 March 2018.

Barnier, M. 2018. *Speech by Michel Barnier at BusinessEurope Day 2018*, 1 March, Brussels. Available from: http://europa.eu/rapid/press-release_SPEECH-18-1462_en.htm. Last accessed 29 March 2018.

BBC. 2017. *Brexit: Jean-Claude Juncker criticises UK's Position Papers*, 30 August. Available from: http://www.bbc.co.uk/news/uk-politics-41089257. Last accessed 26 March 2018.

Council of the European Union. 2018. *Statement by President Donald Tusk on the Draft Guidelines on the Framework for the Future Relationship with the UK*, 7 March, Statements and Remarks 109/18.

European Commission. 2017. *Joint Statement by President Jean-Claude Juncker and Prime Minister Theresa May*, 16 October, Brussels. Available from: http://europa.eu/rapid/press-release_STATEMENT-17-3969_en.htm. Last accessed 26 March 2018.

European Commission. 2018a. *Police and Judicial Cooperation in Criminal Matters*, 23 January. Available from: https://ec.europa.eu/commission/ sites/beta-political/files/police_judicial_cooperation_in_criminal_matters.pdf. Last accessed 4 April 2018.

European Commission. 2018b. *Press Statement by Michel Barnier Following This Week's Round of Article 50 Negotiations*, 9 February. Available from: http:// europa.eu/rapid/press-release_SPEECH-18-725_en.htm. Last accessed 25 May 2018.

European Union. 2010. *Internal Security Strategy for the European Union-Towards a European Security Model*, Brussels.

HM Government. 2017. *Security, Law Enforcement and Criminal Justice: A Future Partnership*. Available from: https://www.gov.uk/government/ uploads/system/uploads/attachment_data/file/645416/Security__law_ enforcement_and_criminal_justice_-_a_future_partnership_paper.PDF. Last accessed 22 March 2018.

HM Government. 2018. *The Future Relationship Between the United Kingdom and the European Union*. Available from: https://assets.publishing.service.gov.uk/government/uploads/system/uploads/attachment_data/ file/725288/The_future_relationship_between_the_United_Kingdom_and_ the_European_Union.pdf. Last accessed 21 July 2018.

House of Commons. 2018a. Oral Evidence: Home Office Delivery of Brexit: Policing and Security Cooperation. *Home Affairs Committee*, 635. Available from: http://data.parliament.uk/writtenevidence/committeeevidence.svc/evidencedocument/home-affairs-committee/home-office-delivery-of-brexit-policing-and-security-cooperation/oral/77427.pdf. Last accessed 29 March 2018.

House of Commons. 2018b. UK-EU Security Cooperation After Brexit. *Home Affairs Committee*. Available from: https://publications.parliament.uk/pa/ cm201719/cmselect/cmhaff/635/635.pdf. Last accessed 29 March 2018.

House of Lords. 2013. *Follow-Up Report on EU Police and Criminal Justice Measures: The UK's 2014 Opt-Out Decision*, 31 October. Available from: https:// publications.parliament.uk/pa/ld201314/ldselect/ldeucom/69/69.pdf. Last accessed 22 March 2018.

House of Lords. 2018. Brexit: The Proposed UK-EU Security Treaty. *European Union Committee*, 18th Report of Session 2017–2019, HL Paper 164. July. Available from: https://publications.parliament.uk/pa/ld201719/ldselect/ ldeucom/164/164.pdf. Last accessed 25 August 2018.

Juncker, J.-C. 2018. *Speech at the Munich Security Conference*, 17 February 2018, Munich. Available from https://www.securityconference.de/mediathek/ munich-security-conference-2018/video/statement-by-jean-claude-juncker/. Last accessed 29 March 2018.

May, T. 2013. Home Secretary Oral Statement to Parliament on 2014 Decision. 9 July, *Gov.uk*. Available from: https://www.gov.uk/government/speeches/home-secretary-oral-statement. Last accessed 22 March 2018.

May, T. 2017. *Andrew Neil's Interview with Theresa May*, 29 March. Available from: https://blogs.spectator.co.uk/2017/03/transcript-andrew-neils-brexit-interview-theresa-may/. Last accessed 20 June 2017.

May, T. 2018. *PM Speech at Munich Security Conference: 17 February 2018*. Available from: https://www.gov.uk/government/speeches/pm-speech-at-munich-security-conference-17-february-2018. Last accessed 24 March 2018.

Stone, J. 2018. EU Officials Tear into UK's Fantasy Brexit Negotiating Strategy as Talks Turn Bitter. *The Independent*, 24 May. Available from: https://www.independent.co.uk/news/uk/politics/brexit-latest-uk-eu-customs-plan-northern-ireland-theresa-may-a8368101.html. Last accessed 25 May 2018.

CHAPTER 5

Political and Legal Considerations Regarding the Negotiation of the Future UK-EU Security Relationship

Abstract In this chapter, the authors analyse potential transitional arrangements, discussing the possibilities of substantial delays in—or the no conclusion of—a security agreement, alternative models to the UK-EU relationship, dispute resolution and enforcement mechanisms in light of the UK Government's red line on CJEU jurisdiction, and the UK's potential reduced influence on future EU internal security.

Keywords Brexit · Transitional arrangements · Alternative relationship models · Dispute resolution · Loss of influence as an international actor

On the basis of the initial negotiation positions detailed above and the UK's current participation in EU Justice and Home Affairs, it is already possible to identify a number of issues that must be addressed over the course of the security negotiations. This section explores four of these issues, ranging from short-term to long-term concerns, including: (1) transitional arrangements; (2) alternative models to the current UK-EU relationship; (3) dispute resolution and enforcement mechanisms; and (4) the UK's continued role and influence in EU internal security.

Transitional Arrangements

The publishing of the draft Withdrawal Agreement in March 2018, followed by its agreed version in November 2018, has enabled us to have a first glimpse into the issues that need to be settled before the future UK-EU security agreement negotiations can begin (European Commission and HM Government 2018). The agreement covers a number of provisions relating to Justice and Home Affairs, including 'Access to network and information systems and databases' (Article 7, Common Provisions), 'Ongoing police and judicial cooperation in criminal matters' (Title V), and 'Data and Information processed or obtained before the end of the transition period' (Title VII). In other words, the agreement addresses the applicability of EU law to the UK during the expected transition/implementation phase, focusing in particular on what will happen to UK-EU operations and information exchange both during and after the transition/implementation period (see Fahey, this volume, Chapter 6). The text also includes a protocol on Northern Ireland, which underlines the need to avoid a hard border and to respect the Good Friday Agreement.

Whereas there was, during the Withdrawal Agreement negotiations, general consensus in areas relating to non-security issues, such as citizens' rights, this was less the case in the area of Justice and Home Affairs. Thanks to a colour-coded system created by the negotiating teams,[1] we were able to observe that, for most of the negotiation, security-related provisions were the object of either no agreement or only partial agreement. In fact, most of the provisions regarding what happens to ongoing cooperation, including the possibility of the UK benefitting from mutual legal assistance, European Arrest Warrants (EAW), and joint investigation teams, saw very limited agreement. Comparatively, quicker progress was achieved in defining what will happen to security information that has already been collected by both parties (namely in terms of whether it is possible to keep such data, how to protect it and

---

[1] The colour-coding system is explained as follows in the March 2018 version of the Draft Withdrawal Agreement: 'The colouring of the text corresponds to the following meanings: text in green is agreed at negotiators' level, and will only be subject to technical legal revisions in the coming weeks. For text in yellow, negotiators agreed on the policy objectives. Drafting changes or clarifications are still required. Text in white corresponds to text proposed by the Union on which discussions are ongoing' (p. 1).

dispose of it). Furthermore, by August 2018 the only element which seemed to be settled was that at the end of the transition/implementation phase, the UK would cease to have access to any network, information system, or database established on the basis of Union law unless a new agreement created for this purpose comes into force (Article 7, Common Provisions) (see de Vries, this volume, Chapter 7). It would also be important to point out that despite a general perception that the transition/implementation phase would mean business as usual with a continuation of the current legal regime, this would not apply to all internal security provisions. As an example, Article 185 clarifies that if the Withdrawal Agreement is ratified by both sides, the parties can issue reservations regarding the surrender of their nationals in the context of EAW already during the transition/implementation phase. As a result, Member States would already have the possibility of not extraditing their citizens to the UK from March 2019 onwards, even if the EU and the UK sign and ratify the Withdrawal Agreement (House of Lords 2018).

The difficulty experienced in reaching an agreement leads us to consider two possibilities: (1) that there could be substantial delays in signing and ratifying both the Withdrawal Agreement and the future UK-EU security agreement and (2) that there may be no agreement at the end of the process. Where the first possibility is concerned, although the Withdrawal Agreement negotiations are now concluded in principle, its still needs to be voted on and signed, with the ratification of this agreement ending on 29th March 2019. At this point, the official negotiations on the future of the UK-EU relationship would officially start (following an initial scoping period) (European Commission 2018). However, the current difficulties in reaching consensus on security related provisions could be a sign of things to come, particularly relating to data exchange and operational support. As demonstrated by the EU-US Safe Harbour Agreement (2000) and the EU-Canada PNR Agreement (2014), data protection and privacy provisions can be especially difficult to negotiate in view of the EU's very high protection standards (see Fahey, this volume, Chapter 6). Both agreements were considered to violate privacy and data protection EU laws, which led to the Safe Harbour Agreement being ruled invalid and the EU-Canada Agreement being rejected in its current format (European Court of Justice 2015, 2017). Similar problems could easily result in substantial delays in signing and ratifying the Withdrawal Agreement, which could thereby postpone the start of negotiations for any future UK-EU security agreement. Such delays could take place, for example, if either of the agreements is considered as not complying with the Charter for Fundamental Rights, which could trigger opposition from the European Parliament and rejection by the European Court of Justice rejection. Furthermore, it is also be important to consider elements beyond the content of the agreements that might contribute to delays, including diverging national interests and political opportunism. Given that the future security agreement would have to be unanimously agreed upon by all Member States, it would not be far-fetched to imagine a Member State blocking the process, even temporarily, because it either holds a different view on the matter, or wishes to draw attention to an unrelated grievance. The EU-Canada Comprehensive Economic and Trade Agreement (CETA), for instance, was delayed due to the Walloon Parliament considering that the agreement went against the interests of Wallonia's agricultural sector and that the proposed system for settling disputes was problematic (Rankin 2016).

Regarding the second possibility, even if the Withdrawal Agreement is signed and ratified in time for the UK's official exit from the EU, that still leaves a very limited amount of time to negotiate, sign and ratify an international security agreement, as the expected transition/implementation period has been stipulated to end in December 2020. From current and previous examples of comprehensive international negotiations, it is easy to have a glimpse of the challenge ahead. The EU-Canada Comprehensive Economic and Trade Agreement took seven years to be concluded, and the EU-Mercosur Agreement, which is now in its 32nd round of negotiations, has been on the negotiation table for eight years. Although it is possible to identify agreements that underwent a quicker process, such as the EU-Japan Economic Partnership Agreement, whose negotiation took only four years, these legal arrangements are often more limited in terms of scope. If, in addition to the experiences of previous negotiations, we consider that the UK might not be favourable to extending the transition/implementation phase, then it could be facing a cliff-edge Brexit, which would result in sudden cooperation disruption. Given the serious risk posed by an interruption in cooperation to law enforcement and judicial authorities' activities, it is therefore crucial to consider the different possible templates for the future UK-EU security relationship, including alternatives to the preferred option of a comprehensive agreement.

Alternative Models
to the Current UK-EU Relationship

Following a successful signature and ratification of the Withdrawal Agreement, the UK and the EU will be able to start making concrete progress on their future security relationship. As mentioned in the previous chapter, the UK wishes to maintain access to its current opt-ins, although there is currently no model of third country partnership that provides such a deep level of cooperation. In fact, the UK currently enjoys making use of EU instruments, to which third countries have either limited access to, or none at all. Therefore, the departing question currently is: which template has the potential to deliver the UK's justice and home affairs preferences? Such a question implies not only a scrutiny of existing EU agreements with third countries, but also a reflection on the most adequate legal format for the future relationship. Regarding this last point, there are a number of options on the table, even if they are not all equally advantageous: bilateral agreements between the UK and individual Member States, multiple UK-EU agreements on specific sectors/instruments, bilateral agreements with EU agencies and bodies, and, the currently preferred option, a comprehensive security agreement (HM Government 2017a).

Bilateral Agreements Between the UK
and Individual Member States

The UK could try to bypass the EU level by signing bilateral agreements directly with Member States on the basis of international instruments, such as the 1959 Council of Europe Mutual Legal Assistance Convention in Criminal Matters (including its Second Protocol) or the 1957 Council of Europe Convention on Extradition. This option is, however, not without its problems (see Mortera-Martinez, this volume, Chapter 6). Even if the UK were to identify with which Member States it would be most advantageous to sign bilateral agreements, not only would these instruments imply having multiple teams negotiating in parallel, but they would also not be able to deliver the same level of cooperation currently enjoyed by the UK. For instance, in the case of the Mutual Legal Assistance Convention, although this agreement has been ratified by all Member States, it does not offer the same extent of operational cooperation (namely, it does not cover such an extensive list of crimes). This limitation is partly due to numerous Member States issuing reservations to this instrument at the time of ratification.[2] Reservations mainly include the refusal to accept cross border observations, controlled deliveries and covert investigations (Niehuss et al. 2018). Furthermore, if we focus specifically on Joint Investigation Teams (JITs), a mutual legal assistance instrument that is foreseen in the Second Protocol to the European Convention, cooperation may become even more problematic. As not all Member States have ratified this legal instrument (it is the case of Greece, Italy, and Luxembourg), future bilateral agreements wishing to include JITs will vary from country to country and might require domestic legal change in the non-ratifying countries (Niehuss et al. 2018). Depending on the focus of the JIT, cooperation could also be based on specific United Nations (UN) conventions, namely the UN Convention against Transnational Organised Crime of 2000 (Article 19), the UN Convention against Illicit Traffic in Narcotic Drugs and Psychotropic Substances of 1988 (Article 9), and the UN Convention on Corruption of 2003 (Article 49). Their focus would, however, be considerably more limited than the current EU JIT instrument.

In the case of the Convention on Extradition, relying on this instrument would entail a much lengthier process (House of Lords 2016) and would not guarantee results, given that most Member States do not extradite their own nationals to non-EU countries (see Mortera-Martinez, this volume, Chapter 6). The refusal to extradite nationals is for many countries, not only inscribed in secondary legislation, but also in the Constitution itself, rendering any expectation of domestic change in those countries very unlikely (Niehuss et al. 2018). As an example, the United States' request in 2011 for the extradition of George Wright, a member of the Black Liberation Army convicted of murder, was denied by the Portuguese courts on the grounds that the person was a Portuguese citizen (BBC 2011). Hints of how strongly Member States feel about extradition can already been seen in Art 185 of the Withdrawal Agreement, as mentioned in the previous section of this chapter, with countries reserving the possibility of refusing European Arrest Warrant requests from March 2019 onwards.

---

[2]For a complete list of country reservations to the European Convention on Mutual Assistance in Criminal Matters please visit: https://www.coe.int/en/web/conventions/full-list/-/conventions/treaty/030/declarations.

In addition to bilateral agreements focusing on police and judicial cooperation, it is also important to mention bilateral agreements for border control purposes. As discussed in Chapter 3, there are three potentially problematic border crossings: Northern Ireland/Republic of Ireland, Dover/Calais, and Gibraltar/Spain (see Wolff; Orsini; Gomez Arana; Irrera, this volume, Chapter 8). Given their dissimilar political, economic and historical contexts, they will most likely require significantly different solutions. In the case of Gibraltar, border checks are already very thorough and unlikely to change with Brexit. The constant delays and the drug trafficking situation, however, could benefit from a bilateral agreement on border cooperation and law enforcement cooperation (see Osini; Gomez Arana, this volume, Chapter 8). The Dover/Calais border is similar to the Gibraltar border in terms of being a currently existing non-Schengen border, and hence more closely scrutinised. It already is the focus of a bilateral agreement between France and the UK on juxtaposed border controls, which enables the UK and France to cooperate on preventing illegal migrants and goods from circulating (see Wolff, this volume, Chapter 8). Following Brexit, the model of border control at this crossing is not expected to change dramatically, although some revisions to the bilateral agreement might be necessary in order to counter longer queues and the insecurity associated with it.

Regarding the Northern Ireland/Republic of Ireland border crossing, this is where most changes will be expected to occur, as it could potentially evolve from an open border to one that is strongly controlled (see Irrera, this volume, Chapter 8). Although both the UK and the EU agree that the achievements of the peace process must be protected and that, in order to do so, a hard border must be avoided, the solution proposed in the Protocol on Ireland/Northern ireland of the Withdrawal Agreement is perceived by numerous actors as being highly controversial. Following from the idea that Northern Ireland would need to maintain regulatory alignment with the rest of the EU in order to avoid the creation of a border (Negotiators of the EU and the UK Government 2017: 49 and 50), the March 2018 draft Withdrawal Agreement announced the establishment of a common regulatory area that would guarantee free circulation of goods (Art 3, Chapter III, Protocol on Ireland/Northern Ireland). In addition, this document also mentions that the UK and the Republic of Ireland are free to continue to operate the Common Travel Area, although the latter should not interfere with Ireland's obligations under Union Law (Art 2, Chapter II, Protocol on Ireland/Northern Ireland). The November 2018 final Agreement goes further than that and proposes that, from the end of the transition/implementation phase, the entire territory of the UK stays in a customs union with the EU until a more satisfactory arrangement can be found (Preamble, Protocol on Ireland/Northern Ireland).

Three main issues emerge from these border proposals: the first problem is that the Withdrawal Agreement stipulates that the UK will no longer be able to use its opt-in and opt-out arrangements once the transition starts (Article 122 (1) a), which means that the prospect of maintaining regulatory alignment might quickly disappear as EU Member States continue to move forward in their integration process, leaving the UK frozen in time with its current opt-ins. The second problem is that these different proposals (the maintenance of the Common Travel Area and the maintenance of a customs union) might simply not be compatible. Although the Common Travel Area predates the European Union, it would be difficult for the Republic of Ireland to currently maintain a common travel area with a country outside of the EU (so far, there is no common travel with a non-EU country that is not part of the Schengen area[3]). How would the circulation of European Economic Area citizens be controlled between Ireland and Northern Ireland, given that they can exercise their free movement rights in Ireland? The final problem is that the proposals for more definitive solutions have so far been very vague, lacking any detail about what the border could look like in practice, and how it could function beyond the Withdrawal Agreement's temporary solution. The former UK Secretary of State for Foreign Affairs, Boris Johnson, defended the possibility of withdrawing from the Customs Union and Single Market, while at the same time avoiding a new border being built through the usage of technological solutions (Hervey 2018). Although his example of the congestion charge system in London as a basis for a border solution was met with scepticism, it was representative of the UK's general interest in adopting a smart border for Northern Ireland (Karlsson 2017). In particular, the example of the Norway-Sweden border has often been hailed as a possible model, given its level of integration and low friction (Cellan-Jones 2017). When considering this possible solution, however, it is important to keep in mind that smart borders concern the quality of the collaboration and data exchange

---

[3] The Isle of Man and the Channel Islands constitute a special case, as they take part in the Common Travel Area, but are not in the European Union. As Crown Dependencies, their relation with the EU is governed by the UK's Treaty of Accession to the EU (they only participate in the free movement of goods and not in the free movement of people).

between the two sides, more than the technology itself. In this sense, technology alone does not constitute the answer that the UK is looking for, and the UK would still need to secure a good information exchange agreement either with the Republic of Ireland or the EU. Furthermore, a smart border, even if it has limited visibility, is still a border from a psychological perspective. This may be a self-evident observation, but it is an important one to keep in mind given the historical context of the Northern Ireland/Republic of Ireland border and the impact its change might have on collective identity (see Irrera, this volume, Chapter 8).

Bilateral UK-EU Sectoral Agreements

The UK could also attempt to replicate the UK opt-ins in separate bilateral sectoral agreements with the EU. This option would offer a pragmatic and tailor-made approach, which could be expanded according to the needs of both parties. It would also enable the UK to deviate from EU rules in areas where it does not have bilateral agreements, although its influence on EU decision-making would be very limited. The most well-known example of such an approach is most likely the EU-Switzerland relationship, although other countries such as Andorra, Monaco and San Marino have similar forms of agreements. The Swiss-EU bilateral agreement system emerged in the early '70s and currently has 20 main agreements and 100 subsidiary ones, which are based on EU law. Most agreements are independent from each other and can be terminated individually (Integration Office FDFA/FDEA 2009). Despite the flexibility offered by this system, it has also proved quite challenging. In addition to being slow moving (it took Switzerland over 40 years to develop its bilateral agreements), its main disadvantage is that it constitutes a cumbersome and fragmented basis for a relationship. This view has already led the EU to announce that the Swiss model has reached its limits and needs to be replaced by a new comprehensive framework (Council of the European Union 2014). According to the European Commission, the bilateral sectoral system has slowly shown that it is not capable of sustaining a coherent relationship or providing comprehensive solutions to the current problems faced both by the EU and its partners: 'the disadvantages of the sectoral approach include unmanageable complexity and legal uncertainty' (European Commission 2012: 16). On the basis of this track record, even if the UK were interested in exploring this model, it is unlikely that the EU would be willing to do so.

Bilateral Agreements with EU Agencies and Bodies

Let us now turn our attention to bilateral agreements with EU agencies and bodies. At the moment, third country access to most EU instruments is dependent on agreements to adopt and implement specific EU legislation, or in certain cases regulatory alignment. An agreement with Europol or Eurojust, for example, would allow the UK to continue to exchange information with these agencies. As mentioned in Chapter 3, however, and similarly to the other models discussed above, these bilateral agreements would constitute a step backwards for Britain, as they do not offer the same level of participation as EU membership (House of Lords 2016; see de Vries; Trauner, this volume, Chapter 7). Focusing again on Europol's example, the UK's access to data repositories and operational cooperation would not only take a few years to negotiate, but it would also be reduced in comparison to what it currently has. More specifically, the UK would still be able to ask Europol's operational centre for specific data from the Europol Information System, but it would no longer have direct access to the system itself (see Bossong and Rieger, this volume, Chapter 7). It is also important to mention that access to these instruments is dependent on maintaining regulatory alignment with the EU. If the UK choses to follow a different direction in the area of, for instance, data protection, it is likely that any future access would be curtailed (for a detailed discussion on data protection see Fahey, this volume Chapter 6; Trauner, this volume, Chapter 7). As mentioned in Chapter 4, however, regulatory alignment cannot simply be assumed because the Withdrawal Agreement specifies that the UK will no longer have the possibility of opting into new JHA measures during the transition/implementation period. Furthermore, it is important to bear in mind that regulatory alignment for AFSJ instruments would also require a degree of alignment with Single Market instruments (see Farrand; Porcedda, this volume, Chapter 7). As a result, we will most likely begin to see some degree of regulatory differentiation between the EU and the AFSJ from March 2019 onwards. Moreover, the option of bilateral agreements with EU agencies and bodies is rendered even more complicated by the fact that not all EU instruments are accessible to third countries (see Farrand, this volume, Chapter 7). This is the case, for instance of the European Criminal Record Information System (ECRIS), an EU-wide database enabling Member States to exchange information regarding individuals' previous convictions (House of Lords 2018). This does not mean that the legal challenges cannot be overcome, but rather that, if this is the chosen option, negotiations will require a great deal of imagination and flexibility.

UK-EU Comprehensive Security Agreement

Finally, a comprehensive agreement between the UK and the EU, covering most of the UK's current opt-ins, may be a challenge, but would probably be the most appealing option compared to other alternatives (see Mortera-Martinez, this volume, Chapter 6). A comprehensive treaty would demonstrate political commitment to the UK-EU relationship, which could compensate for the current perception of eroding trust (Stone 2017), and which would likely allow for greater flexibility when negotiating the inclusion of the UK's priority instruments.

ENFORCEMENT AND DISPUTE RESOLUTION

The desire to avoid the jurisdiction of the European Court of Justice (CJEU), which was one of the main elements at the beginning of the UK's request for derogations, continues to be at the heart of the country's position for a future agreement: 'in the future, the EU treaties and hence EU law will no longer apply to the UK. [...] the jurisdiction of the CJEU must end' (May 2018: 5; see Fahey, this volume, Chapter 6; Bossong and Rieger; Wilson and Carr, this volume, Chapter 7). According to the UK Government's position paper on enforcement and dispute resolution, the UK's exit from the EU will mark the end of CJEU jurisdiction over the UK, the supremacy of EU law and the doctrine of direct effect. In practice, this means that any legal acts stemming from the future UK-EU relationship would need to be implemented through the UK's domestic order (HM Government 2017b). This position is very much in line with the UK's 2014 decision to proceed with a mass opt-out from police and judicial cooperation (see Chapter 2), as it mainly stems from the desire to avoid CJEU jurisdiction in those areas. However, the extent of the government's red line on CJEU jurisdiction is not entirely clear, despite the fact that the importance of no longer needing to abide by CJEU rulings was frequently associated with the concept of sovereignty and repeatedly reiterated during the Brexit referendum campaign. Does it refer only to direct jurisdiction, or also to indirect involvement? The 2018 Government paper on the future relationship refers to mechanisms for resolving disputes, but the role of the CJEU remains vague: the 'CJEU would only have a role in relation to the interpretation of EU rules', and 'the court of one party cannot resolve disputes between the two' (HM Government 2018: point 42).

If, on the one hand, Theresa May has openly admitted that the UK must face up to the hard fact that CJEU decisions will continue to affect the UK post-Brexit (May 2018), she has on the other hand, been widely criticised for this stance and for allowing CJEU jurisdiction over the UK to continue during the expected transition/implementation period: 'if the CJEU still has jurisdiction, we will not have left the EU. It is perhaps the most important red line in ensuring the leave vote is honoured' (Rees Mogg cited in Stewart 2017).

If the red line refers to direct jurisdiction, the creation of a relationship that is not subject to CJEU jurisdiction would in itself be feasible given the EU has agreements with third countries that are not governed by CJEU legislation and decisions, but rather resort to independent arbitration (see Mortera-Martinez, this volume, Chapter 6). This is the case, for example, of the Europol agreements with Norway and with Switzerland that foresee arbitration tribunals, whose members are appointed by both parties (Article 17 in both agreements). It is important to mention, however, that the European Parliament has already stressed in its resolution on the framework of the future EU-UK relationship that it considers the proliferation of bilateral agreements and dispute settlement committees as an important shortcoming of the EU's relationship with third countries (in particular Switzerland), and that the EU and the UK should find another, more appropriate governance framework for their future relations (European Parliament 2018).

If, on the other hand, the red line refers also to indirect involvement, then the UK's objective may be more difficult to achieve or may even be unfeasible. Given that EU Member States would need to continue to comply with CJEU case law, they would not be able to sign a third country agreement that would fail to comply with the *acquis communautaire*, in particular with the Charter of Fundamental Rights. As the CJEU ensures that the Charter is applied to all areas of EU life, its indirect influence continues to be felt on countries outside of the EU (Woods 2017). The two recent cases of the agreements with Canada and the US are good examples of this kind of situation. As mentioned earlier in this chapter (in the section on Transitional Arrangements), the EU-Canada PNR agreement was considered to violate privacy and data protection EU laws; and in the EU-US safe Harbour agreement, the US government was considered to be compromising the essence of the fundamental right of respect for private life (see Bossong and Rieger, this volume, Chapter 7). As a consequence, both agreements have been prevented by the CJEU from entering into force. Naturally, neither Canada nor the US consider themselves to be under the jurisdiction of the CJEU. And yet, the court still has a considerable impact on them. This impact is particularly telling, given that the EU-US relationship is traditionally perceived as being asymmetric, with the EU usually assuming the role of norm importer (Argomaniz 2009). Therefore, even if the future EU-UK security agreement has a separate arbiter, it will still need to indirectly follow CJEU rulings (see Trauner, this volume, Chapter 7). Furthermore, if the UK leaves its current position of regulatory alignment when adopting new legislation post-Brexit or when it is no longer able to opt into new instruments, this connection to the CJEU will be a greater determinant of what kind of relation it can have with Member States. Still with regard to the indirect influence that the CJEU might have in the future, it is relevant to mention that this institution is not alone; various European bodies, such as the European data protection supervisor and the future European public prosecutor's Office, will continue to have a similar degree of indirect influence (see Trauner, this volume, Chapter 7).

THE UK's INFLUENTIAL POSITION IN EUROPEAN SECURITY

The last issue we would like to discuss in this chapter on political and legal considerations regarding the future UK-EU security relationship is that of the UK's influence over EU justice and home affairs decision-making and policies. Will the UK's current influence over security matters decline with Brexit? Will it be more isolated on the world stage (see Lavorgna, this volume, Chapter 7)? And how will the UK develop new strategies to influence EU politics and policies from outside? As mentioned previously, the UK has always held a leadership role in police and judicial cooperation in criminal matters, often being the source of new measures and serving as a model for other Member States (House of Lords 2016; see Ripoll Servent, this volume, Chapter 6). Examples of such deep influence include, among various initiatives:

1. The Passenger Name Records (PNR) Directive, whose European Parliament report was the responsibility of Lord Kirkhope of Harrogate (European Parliament 2016);
2. The EU Policy Cycle[4];
3. The European Criminal Intelligence Model (Gruszczak 2017; see Trauner, this volume, Chapter 7);
4. The Data Retention Directive, which was pushed by the UK Government while it held the presidency of the Council (Ripoll Servent 2015) (see Ripoll Servent, this volume, Chapter 6; MacKenzie, this volume, Chapter 7);
5. The direction of the EU counter-terrorism strategy (see MacKenzie, this volume, Chapter 7);
6. Specific elements within the EU's cybersecurity policy (see Porcedda; Lavorgna, this volume, Chapter 7). Especially, this was the case, with the European Network and Information Security Agency (ENISA)'s approach to information sharing, which was based on the UK's Centre for the Protection of National Infrastructure (Black et al. 2017);
7. Forensic bioinformation (see Wilson and Carr, this volume, Chapter 7). The UK has been a pioneer in the usage and promotion of bioinformation (fingerprints and DNA) in the context of the judicial system, currently holding the world's third—after China and the USA—largest forensic DNA database (UK Government Statistics 2018; BBC 2017; FBI 2018).

The extent to which the UK might maintain its level of influence over EU security was not the object of extensive discussion, although it was mentioned by both the Remain and Leave campaigns during the referendum. The Remain camp argued that Brexit would substantially decrease the UK's capacity to shape the EU's direction, and would even affect the UK's position in the world. In the words of Bill Hughes, former Director-General of the Serious Organised Crime Agency, 'the UK is seen as a major and leading partner. That will change'

---

[4]The EU Policy Cycle is a multi-annual policy-making process, which was adopted in 2010 and is aimed at fostering coherence, continuity and efficiency within EU serious and organised crime policies.

(Hughes cites in House of Lords 2016: paragraph 28). Once the UK leaves the European Union, it will no longer take part in European Council discussions, Council of Ministers' votes, nor will it sit on the management board of AFSJ agencies. As a result, it will have a considerably decreased capacity to shape policies and norms, which may affect it post-Brexit. If we consider that the security of the UK is very much dependent on the security of its closest neighbours, then this loss of influence has the potential to seriously impact the UK's internal security. Furthermore, this impact will most likely go beyond the UK-EU relationship, affecting the UK's cooperation with third countries. If these states perceive the UK's political position as changing from a useful insider to a country on the margins of the EU, then they may view the UK as less of a priority for their foreign policy (see MacKenzie, this volume, Chapter 7). As another element that could potentially decrease the UK's influence, it will be interesting to observe whether the current trade negotiations could have a spillover effect on the future security ones. Despite Jean-Claude Juncker maintaining that these will be separate negotiations and that cross-contamination needs to be avoided (Munich speech in February 2018), it is not unlikely that, after a lengthy and often frustrating negotiation process, the political goodwill will be impacted on both sides.

The Leave campaign, however, dismissed such a view by saying that the UK's international standing is independent from EU membership and that its influence would continue thanks to its renowned security capabilities (Menon et al. 2018), influential economy, and traditionally global foreign policy (Black et al. 2017). One could also argue that the UK has managed to exert its influence throughout the past two decades, despite its selective participation in Justice and Home Affairs. The UK was always considered a particularly awkward partner with respect to this area—not fully in, but not fully out either—and yet it still managed to find ways to deeply influence decision-making. Of course, an opt-out (or a decision not to opt-in) is not equivalent, in terms of effect, to non-membership. Still, it would not be surprising if the UK managed to find ways to continue to exert its influence, in particular through other international organisations which it is part of, such as NATO, the G8 and the Council of Europe. Until now, its influence was assured by being very pro-active and by leading by example. Given its track record, the UK could find innovative ways to continue to exert its power despite no longer being a member, as an engaged outsider. In fact, despite the approaching exit, the UK recently managed to gather international support, including from 19 EU Member States, to expel Russian diplomats in response to the poisoning of Sergei and Yulia Skripal, which took place in Salisbury, demonstrating that EU membership is only one of a number of elements influencing the UK's international standing (Armstrong 2018).

References

Argomaniz, J. 2009. When the EU Is the 'NormTaker': The Passenger Name Records Agreement and the EU's Internalisation of US Border Security Norms. *Journal of European Integration* 31 (1): 119–136.

Armstrong, M. 2018. Widespread Support for UK as Around 100 Russian Diplomats Are Expelled. *Euronews*, 27 March. Available from: http://www.euronews.com/2018/03/27/widespread-support-for-uk-as-around-100-russian-diplomats-are-expelled. Last accessed 27 May 2018.

BBC. 2011. *George Wright Wins US Extradition Case in Portugal*, 17 November. Available from: http://www.bbc.co.uk/news/world-us-canada-15778384. Last accessed 29 March 2018.

BBC. 2017. *Privacy Concerns as China Expands DNA Database*, 17 May. Available from: https://www.bbc.co.uk/news/world-asia-china-39945220. Last accessed 18 June 2018.

Black, J., A. Hall, K. Cox, M. Kepe, and E. Silversten. 2017. *Defence and Security After Brexit. RAND Corporation Europe*. Available from: https://www.rand.org/content/dam/rand/pubs/research_reports/RR1700/RR1786/RAND_RR1786.pdf. Last accessed 27 May 2018.

Cellan-Jones, R. 2017. Frictionless Borders: Learning from Norway. *BBC News*, 29 September. Available from: http://www.bbc.co.uk/news/technology-41412561. Last accessed 5 April 2018.

Council of the European Union. 2014. *Council Conclusions on a Homogeneous Extended Single Market and EU Relations with Non-EU Western European Countries*, General Affairs Council Meeting, 16 December.

European Commission. 2012. *Communication from the Commission to the European Parliament, the Council, the European Economic and Social Committee and the Committee of the Regions on EU Relations with the Principality of Andorra, the Principality of Monaco and the Republic of San Marino*, COM(2012) 680 Final.

European Commission. 2018. *Brexit Next Steps.* Powerpoint slide. Available from: https://www.parliament.uk/documents/lords-committees/eu-select/scrutiny-brexit-negotiations/Slide-1-brexit-next-steps.pdf. Last accessed 8 April 2018.

European Commission and HM Government. 2018. *Draft Agreement on the Withdrawal of the United Kingdom of Great Britain and Northern Ireland from the European Union and the European Atomic Energy Community.* Available from: https://www.gov.uk/government/uploads/system/uploads/attachment_data/file/691366/20180319_DRAFT_WITHDRAWAL_AGREEMENT.pdf. Last accessed 26 March 2018.

European Court of Justice. 2015. *The court of justice declares that the commission's US safe harbour decision is invalid*, Press Release N°117/15, 6 October, Luxembourg.

European Court of Justice. 2017. *The court declares the agreement envisaged between the European Union and Canada on the transfer of passenger name record data may not be concluded in its current form*, Press Release N°84/17, 26 July, Luxembourg.

European Parliament. 2016. Parliament Backs EU Directive on Use of Passenger Name Records. *European Parliament News*, 14 April. Available from: http://www.europarl.europa.eu/news/en/press-room/20160407IPR21775/parliament-backs-eu-directive-on-use-of-passenger-name-records-pnr. Last accessed 8 April 2018.

European Parliament. 2018. *European Parliament Resolution of 14 March 2018 on the Framework of the Future EU-UK Relationship*, 2018/2573.

FBI. 2018. *CODIS-NDIS Statistics.* Available from: https://www.fbi.gov/services/laboratory/biometric-analysis/codis/ndis-statistics. Last accessed 18 June 2018.

Gruszczak, A. 2017. The EU Criminal Intelligence Model-Problems and Issues. In *EU Criminal Law and Policy-Values, Principles and Methods*, ed. J. Banach-Gutierrez and C. Harding. London and New York: Routledge.

Hervey, G. 2018. Boris Johnson Compares Irish Border Post-Brexit to London Congestion Charge. *Politico*, 27 February. Available from: https://www.politico.eu/article/boris-johnson-compares-irish-border-post-brexit-to-london-congestion-charge/. Last accessed 5 April 2018.

HM Government. 2017a. *Security, Law Enforcement and Criminal Justice: A Future Partnership.* Available from: https://www.gov.uk/government/uploads/system/uploads/attachment_data/file/645416/Security__law_enforcement_and_criminal_justice_-_a_future_partnership_paper.PDF. Last accessed 22 March 2018.

HM Government. 2017b. *Enforcement and Dispute Resolution—A Future Partnership Paper*. Available from: https://assets.publishing.service.gov. uk/government/uploads/system/uploads/attachment_data/file/639609/ Enforcement_and_dispute_resolution.pdf. Last accessed 5 April 2018.

HM Government. 2018. *The Future Relationship Between the United Kingdom and the European Union*. Available from: https://assets.publishing.service.gov.uk/government/uploads/system/uploads/attachment_data/ file/725288/The_future_relationship_between_the_United_Kingdom_and_ the_European_Union.pdf. Last accessed 21 July 2018.

House of Lords. 2016. Brexit: Future UK-EU Security and Police Cooperation. *European Union Committee*, 7th Report of Session 2016–2017.

House of Lords. 2018. Brexit: The Proposed UK-EU Security Treaty. *European Union Committee*, 18th Report of Session 2017–2019, HL Paper 164, July. Available from: https://publications.parliament.uk/pa/ld201719/ldselect/ ldeucom/164/164.pdf. Last accessed 25 August 2018.

Integration Office FDFA/FDEA. 2009. *Bilateral Agreements Switzerland-EU*. SFBL: Bern.

Karlsson, L. 2017. Smart Border 2.0—Avoiding a Hard Border on the Island of Ireland for Customs Control and the Free Movement of Persons. *European Parliament, Directorate General for Internal Policies, Policy Department for Citizens' Rights and Constitutional Affairs*, November, PE 596.828.

May, T. 2018. *PM Speech on our Future Economic Partnership with the European Union*, 2 March. Available from: https://www.gov.uk/government/ speeches/pm-speech-on-our-future-economic-partnership-with-the-european-union. Last accessed 7 April 2018.

Menon, A., M. Chalmers, C. Macdonald, L. Scazzieri, and R. Whitman. 2018. A Successful Brexit: Three Foreign and Security Policy Tests. *The UK in a Changing Europe*, Available from: http://ukandeu.ac.uk/wp-content/ uploads/2018/02/77181-UKIN-A-Successful-Brexit-security-tests-.pdf. Last accessed 2 May 2018.

Negotiators of the EU and the UK Government. 2017. *Joint Report from the Negotiators of the European Union and the United Kingdom Government on Progress During Phase 1 of Negotiations*, 8 December. Available from: https:// ec.europa.eu/commission/sites/beta-political/files/joint_report.pdf. Last accessed 5 April 2018.

Niehuss, A., B. Farrand, H. Carrapico, and J. Obradovic-Wochnik. 2018. *European Union Member States' Judicial Cooperation Frameworks—A Focus on Extradition, Mutual Legal Assistance, and Joint Investigation Teams*. Report for the Home Office.

Rankin, J. 2016. Belgium Politicians Drop Opposition to EU-Canada Trade Deal. *The Guardian*, 27 October. Available from: https://www.theguardian.com/world/2016/oct/27/belgium-reaches-deal-with-wallonia-over-eu-canada-trade-agreement. Last accessed 28 March 2018.

Ripoll Servent, A. 2015. *Institutional and Policy Change in the European Parliament: Deciding on Freedom, Security and Justice*. Houndmills: Palgrave Macmillan.

Stewart, H. 2017. Brexit MPs Angry as Theresa May Accepts Continuing Rule of EU Court. *The Guardian*, 9 October. Available from: https://www.theguardian.com/politics/2017/oct/09/brexit-mps-angry-as-theresa-may-accepts-continuing-rule-of-eu-court. Last accessed 7 April 2018.

Stone, J. 2017. Brexit: David Davis Rushes to Repair Damage After Undermining Trust in Negotiations. *The Independent*, 12 December. Available from: https://www.independent.co.uk/news/uk/politics/brexit-david-davis-phoned-guy-verhofstadt-legally-binding-brexit-deal-a8105876.html. Last accessed 29 March 2018.

UK Government Statistics. 2018. *National DNA Database Statistics*. Available from: https://www.gov.uk/government/statistics/national-dna-database-statistics. Last accessed 18 June 2018.

Woods, L. 2017. Transfering Personal Data Outside the EU: Clarification from the ECJ? *EU Law Analysis*, 4 August. Available from: http://eulawanalysis.blogspot.co.uk/2017/08/transferring-personal-data-outside-eu.html. Last accessed 6 April 2018.

CHAPTER 6

Sectoral Views on Brexit and Future UK-EU Internal Security Relations

Abstract This chapter presents an array of short expert views on Brexit and future UK-EU relations with regard to internal security. It consisting of both Fichera's and Ripoll Servent's discussions of Brexit's impact on the future development of the Area of Freedom, Security and Justice (AFSJ); Mortera-Martinez's analysis of the two parties' negotiation stances shaping future cooperation; and Fahey's reflection upon how transatlantic relations can inform future UK-EU cooperation in internal security.

Keywords Brexit · The area of freedom, security and justice · Post-Brexit · Institutional governance · Stability · Transatlantic relations

The first chapter of sectoral views focuses on Brexit and the future Area of Freedom, Security and Justice (AFSJ) relations between the UK and the EU. In the opening contribution, Fichera summarises the potential impact of Brexit on the future development of the EU's AFSJ, as well as the consequences for the UK in terms of migration, asylum and borders legislation, and its decreased participation in police and judicial cooperation in the future. Ripoll Servent discusses these consequences further by showing the UK's deep involvement in the AFSJ through multiple instruments, institutions and agencies, and by alerting us to the loss of expertise that these platforms will experience as a result of Brexit.

© The Author(s) 2019
H. Carrapico et al., *Brexit and Internal Security*,
Palgrave Studies in European Union Politics,
https://doi.org/10.1007/978-3-030-04194-6_6

Mortera-Martinez provides a realistic view of the limitations of a potential EU-UK security agreement and how these may affect the future UK-EU relationship. She does this by analysing the negotiation preferences of both parties and the policy options on the table, looking specifically at extradition, access to law enforcement databases and partnerships with EU agencies. The final contribution in this chapter, by Fahey, reflects on transatlantic relations and how they inform future UK-EU relations, specifically with regard to external/internal security, the exposure of a lack of transparency in transatlantic relations, the possibility for the UK to replicate EU-US agreements, the importing of international norms and the UK becoming a rule-taker within the transition period set out in the Withdrawal Agreement (WA).

Brexit and the Area of Freedom, Security and Justice

Massimo Fichera

The AFSJ is a complex set of policies and legislation including key areas of cooperation, such as data protection, exchange of information and criminal justice. The participation of the UK in the AFSJ has always been characterised by a high degree of complexity. It should be borne in mind that, following the end of the transitional period pursuant to Protocol 36 of the Treaty of Lisbon, the provisions of what was once the Third Pillar ceased to apply to the UK, as of 1 December 2014. However, the UK has confirmed the applicability of 35 measures, mostly in the field of mutual recognition in criminal matters and legislation on Europol and Eurojust. Once Brexit has officially begun, even this piecemeal approach may be changed, which could add further complexity to the relationship between the UK and the EU.

The consequences of Brexit on the development of the AFSJ may be of a different nature and concern both the EU and the UK.

Concerning the EU, on the one hand, Brexit may increase the level of differentiated integration, especially in the field of police and judicial cooperation and immigration and asylum. Not only the coherence of the AFSJ, but also the principle of legal certainty could be affected: the UK would participate in mutual recognition measures, as it has done so far, but not in measures on the protection of the procedural rights of the defence (e.g. participating in the Framework Decision on the EAW, but not in the Directive on Access to a Lawyer). On the other hand, deeper integration in the EU may be facilitated in some areas of police and judicial cooperation and immigration and asylum, e.g. in terms of a move away from mutual recognition towards harmonisation of substantive criminal law or the strengthening of the European Public Prosecutor Office, and a move away from a resettlement towards a relocation approach in the field of immigration and asylum. At the same time, the effectiveness and level of cooperation between EU agencies and bodies could also be affected, such as in matters of data collection and retention. One important aspect could be the fate of data and information that have already been exchanged, or the question of how the rulings of the Court of Justice of the European Union in the AFSJ should be treated starting from the date of Brexit. Moreover, it is important to bear in mind that AFSJ, free movement and citizenship rules are strictly connected, so that the negotiations concerning the latter field inevitably affect the former. For example, one potential issue is how the "past conduct" of citizens who might be expelled from the country on the grounds of public policy or public security could be judged if it covers events both preceding and succeeding Brexit.

Concerning the UK, following Brexit, future governments risk being excluded from several components of the network of judicial and police cooperation, such as the exchange of criminal records and the establishment of joint investigation teams. In addition, the effectiveness of the activities of UK investigation and prosecution authorities may be undermined, and the UK could end up being affected by measures in the field of the AFSJ without being directly capable of participating in the development of the AFSJ. The EU will also lose the UK's expertise and input in AFSJ policy-making.

Finally, the UK currently only participates in part of the immigration, asylum and borders legislation, namely the Common European Asylum System, the Dublin Regulation and a few directives on minimum standards for the asylum system. As a result of Brexit, there is a danger that, first of all, the above standards will no longer be respected; and, second, that the exchange of information is compromised. The same is true of Eurodac, a biometric database which includes fingerprints of asylum seekers and irregular migrants.

The UK government seems to be at least in part aware of the shortcomings associated with Brexit. As indicated in the HM Government Technical Note on Security, Law Enforcement and Criminal Justice

(HM Government 2017), "a piecemeal approach to future cooperation, drawing on precedents for EU agreements with third countries on
individual measures (e.g. Europol) or functions (e.g. extradition) would
result in a limited patchwork of cooperation falling well short of current
capabilities and not deliver our shared objectives" (p. 1). Hence the proposal of a more comprehensive UK-EU Internal Security Treaty, possibly negotiated on the basis of Article 218 TFEU. Cooperation would
be promoted via three pillars: internal security, external security and
wider cooperation. However, it is not yet entirely clear what areas this
new Treaty would cover and in what it would be different from existing
arrangements between the UK and the EU.

THE IMPACT OF BREXIT ON THE INSTITUTIONAL GOVERNANCE
OF THE AREA OF FREEDOM, SECURITY AND JUSTICE

Ariadna Ripoll Servent

The UK has traditionally occupied an awkward position in the AFSJ.
This is partly the result of its opt-out/opt-in clauses, which have left
British governments with a large room to manoeuvre in decisions of
whether to participate in negotiations (and when to leave them). This
special position has become one of the most recognisable features of the
AFSJ and has made the governance of this policy particularly complex
(for a more detailed legal analysis, see Peers [2018]). One should not
forget, however, that UK participation is more complex than just the
official voice of the British government in the (European) Council. UK
members have had a strong say in the European Parliament (EP)—where
they have the right to vote on all issues related to the AFSJ—but also in
the growing number of EU agencies and the jurisprudence of the EU
through numerous cases originating in the UK. Therefore, Brexit could
have a much more far-reaching impact on the governance of the AFSJ
than many imagine.

The awkward role of the UK in this field has not only been characterised by its opt-out clauses, but also by its substantive contributions
to Justice and Home Affairs (JHA) integration. Traditionally, British
governments have clearly been in favour of intergovernmental forms
of cooperation, which is one of the reasons why JHA was only incorporated in the Maastricht Treaty as a separate pillar that did not follow
the decision-making rules of the single market (qualified majority voting

and participation of the EP). At the same time, British governments have been one of the major policy entrepreneurs in the field of JHA, coming up with new forms of cooperation and using the EU to bypass potential vetoes at the national level. This was the case, for instance, with the Data Retention Directive, a clear instance of presidential entrepreneurship, where the British government used its role as Council president to push an initiative to retain telecommunications data for law enforcement purposes that had failed to pass in the UK Parliament (Ripoll Servent 2015). Therefore, the UK has traditionally punched above its weight in the Council and European Council, shaping key JHA decisions by using the norms of consensus and compromise that prevail among Member States; despite its opt-out, the UK has been seen as a source of expertise and a constructive partner, and has been included in discussions and compromises to a greater extent than its legal position would suggest (Adler-Nissen 2009). This has put the UK in an advantageous position, particularly in issues related to criminal law and police cooperation, in which it has been the main advocate for further collection of personal data. In comparison, British governments have been more reluctant to opt into measures dealing with migration and border management (Weyembergh 2017; Peers 2018).

What does this mean for the future governance of the AFSJ after Brexit? Some might, of course, be happy to see the UK go, since the level of differentiation within the AFSJ may be reduced. Yet this largely depends on the deal reached on the Irish matter and how it affects the Common Travel Area between the UK and Ireland (Alegre et al. 2017). Some could also see Brexit as an opportunity to redress certain imbalances over security and liberty—a chance to recast the main discourse on how to tackle security challenges beyond the use of data processing and restrictive migration and border management measures (Mitsilegas 2017). At the same time, Brexit brings with it challenges for the EU institutions. Firstly, the UK's withdrawal will mean an important braindrain for the EU—one which has already begun. British representatives have been central to building the AFSJ beyond the British government, which they have done from a wide variety of political perspectives. For instance, in the EP, British members (MEPs) were essential in building the expertise and reputation of the committee specialising in civil liberties and justice and home affairs (LIBE). Building on their own experiences in British home affairs committees, they ensured that the LIBE committee perpetuated the role acquired by British committees in the accountability and transparency of home affairs policies. MEPs like Baroness Sarah Ludford (Liberal Democrats) or Jean Lambert (Greens) were essential in building up the expertise of the LIBE committee, a task which was continued by the current chair of the committee, Labour Claude Moraes. Some of those who have been at the forefront of the committee have already gone back to the national arena, notably Timothy Kirkhope, a conservative MEP ranked as the most influential British MEP in 2016 for his role as rapporteur of the EU-Passenger Name Record Directive and political coordinator of the European Conservative and Reformist (ECR) group in the LIBE committee. Also gone is the head of Europol, Rob Wainwright, one of the most influential British policy-makers in AFSJ and an important policy entrepreneur in furthering police cooperation (*Politico* 2018). A less visible loss of expertise may also be noticed in the longer term in the field of advocacy and social movements, since many of the most ardent critics of EU policies in this field come from British organisations, such as Statewatch or Liberty. It will therefore be interesting to see whether these organisations remain interested and active in EU affairs, or whether other EU actors rise to fill in the role of these and many other human rights activists that have been prominent in the UK, especially when it comes to bringing cases to national and European courts and supporting migrants in claiming the rights accorded to them by EU law.

However, there is also a second type of impact which Brexit might have and which could affect the very institutional structure of the EU. Contrary to the belief that Brexit might minimise the variable geometry of the AFSJ, it could actually help to further it. If anything is clear at the moment, it is that both the UK and the EU have a vested interest in maintaining some sort of cooperation in the area of internal security, especially in matters related to criminal law, police cooperation and law enforcement. Therefore, it would not be surprising to see that EU governments are willing to sacrifice the institutional coherence of the AFSJ for the sake of maintaining the cooperation with the UK alive—even if it means bypassing the EU treaties (and the wishes of the Commission) and furthering integration in an intergovernmental setting (Weyembergh 2017). This would be problematic for maintaining the coherence of the AFSJ and ensuring that EU law remains aligned and under the democratic control and accountability provided by EU institutional structures.

A Strong and Stable Partner?: What Are Britain's Negotiating Options for a Future Security Treaty?

Camino Mortera-Martinez[1]

Police and judicial cooperation in criminal matters has been difficult to agree on in the final Withdrawal Agreement between the UK and the EU. This suggests that a future deal on JHA will be no easier to negotiate than a deal on trade. The UK government wants a 'bespoke' treaty with the EU, going beyond any existing deals the bloc has with other third countries. However, the EU's main guiding principle for negotiations with the UK is 'no better out than in'. In JHA, this means that a non-EU, non-Schengen country cannot have more rights and fewer obligations than an EU Member State or a Schengen country. Both are opening positions in a negotiation, and are likely to evolve over time. But time is a luxury which neither the EU nor the UK has: once the expected transition period is over, in December 2020, London and Brussels will face a cliff-edge unless they have agreed how to keep Britain closely associated to EU police and judicial co-operation while respecting the UK's wish to 'take back control'. The UK hopes that, as negotiations proceed, the Member States will push the institutions to be more pragmatic in their thinking about future institutional ties. However, Britain's inability to come up with precise ideas does not help its cause.

The EU has built a network of cooperation channels with third countries on police and judicial cooperation. Given that much of this co-operation touches upon the EU's passport-free Schengen area, the EU distinguishes between partnerships with non-EU Schengen members, such as Norway and Switzerland, and arrangements with non-Schengen countries like the US and Canada. None of the EU's security partners has a perfect, all-encompassing relationship with the EU. Non-EU Schengen countries like Norway and Switzerland have better police and judicial co-operation with the EU, but in exchange they have abolished border controls and accepted the jurisdiction of the CJEU. Non-EU, non-Schengen countries such as Canada and the US are (relatively) free to do what they want because their

---

[1] This contribution is an excerpt from 'Plugging in the British: EU', a policy brief published by the Centre for European Reform on May 25th 2018 with the support of the Konrad-Adenauer-Stiftung (Mortera-Martinez 2018).

co-operation with the EU on extradition and databases is fairly loose. Then again, these countries are not on the EU's doorstep, and neither has previously been a member of the EU.

Both the British government and the EU have identified three main priority areas in the negotiations: extradition agreements, access to law enforcement databases, and partnerships with EU agencies like Europol.

On extradition, Britain is unlikely to convince its partners to replicate the EAW just for the UK. The biggest problem would be getting countries to lift constitutional bans on extraditing their own nationals, because this would require constitutional changes and even referendums in some EU countries. Germany and Slovenia, for example, would need to change their constitutions. In Slovenia, constitutional change can trigger a referendum. In fact, these constitutional bans will start to apply on Brexit day, in March 2019: Member States are allowed to refuse to extradite their own nationals to Britain after it formally leaves the EU, according to Article 185 of the Withdrawal Agreement (former Art. 168 in the March 2018 version).

After Brexit, Britain will have three options: first, it could seek bilateral agreements with the EU-27, like the US and Canada. However, a system of 27 bilateral treaties would be harder to negotiate and less efficient than a single, pan-European extradition treaty. Second, it could fall back on the 1957 Council of Europe Convention on extradition, a non-EU treaty, as Switzerland has done. Extradition under the Convention takes almost 20 times longer than it does with the EAW and is heavily dependent on the state of bilateral relations between countries. The least damaging and most realistic option for Britain would thus be to seek a surrender agreement similar to that which Norway and Iceland have with the EU. But even if the UK can begin negotiating a surrender agreement before it leaves the EU in March 2019, it will inevitably be faced with a delay before the new treaty enters into force, as the EP will need to approve it and EU countries may need to make some changes to their criminal laws. During this interim period it will have to revert to the inefficient 1957 Convention. The question is how long the interim period would last. Apart from time pressure, the biggest problem in negotiating a surrender agreement is likely to be the issue of judicial oversight. There are several options to solve this problem, none of which is perfect. First, the UK could try to replicate Norway and Iceland's dispute resolution mechanism for extradition with the EU. Second, the UK and the EU could devise a completely new EU-UK court with jurisdiction over extradition (and perhaps other EU JHA matters). This court could be built from scratch or be a separate part of the CJEU (Bárd 2018). While this would be attractive for the British Government, the EU is unlikely to agree to such a court as it would undermine the integrity of EU law (this court would have jurisdiction over intra-EU warrants). Finally, the UK could agree to accept the oversight of the CJEU over surrender procedures between Britain and the EU-27.

There is no legal basis in the EU treaties for a non-EU, non-Schengen country to access Schengen data. Britain is unlikely to retain direct access to Schengen's main law enforcement database, the Schengen Information System. After Brexit, the UK could ask Europol or a cooperative EU or Schengen country to run searches on its behalf, as the US and Canada do. It will be easier for the UK to stay plugged into non-Schengen databases containing fingerprints (the Prüm databases) or air passenger data (Passenger Name Record).

Britain should be able to have a good partnership with Europol, as the US does. This will allow the UK to post liaison officers to Europol, but not to have direct access to Europol's databases. Denmark, an EU country which left Europol in 2015, managed to negotiate a partnership deal with the EU but can no longer directly access the agency's databases.

The major obstacle to an agreement is that Britain's red lines (no European Court of Justice jurisdiction, and no acceptance of the EU Charter of Fundamental Rights) and its stated ambitions for the future security relationship are incompatible. To accelerate negotiations in this area, the EU and the UK should clarify what their future security partnership will cover, as well as its cost and shape. A future security treaty should include a dispute resolution mechanism which could be an entirely new court, an arbitration mechanism, or the CJEU. The treaty should be part of the wider Brexit deal to minimise the risk of it being voted down by the EP. This would also allow Britain and the EU to include a chapter on data protection that could apply to both trade and law enforcement.

On JHA, as in other parts of the Brexit conundrum, the solution is likely to be a half-way house. The future UK-EU security treaty could combine elements of existing models, but have a completely different shape. None of the EU's security partners has been part of the bloc before, and security is not a zero-sum game: if Britain and the EU fail to sign a security deal, the only winners will be criminals.

TRANSATLANTIC RELATIONS AND POST-BREXIT EU-UK SECURITY

Elaine Fahey

Transatlantic relations form an intricate but perhaps surprisingly insightful place to begin reflection upon UK-EU security going forward. Arguably, the Brexit negotiations and preparations of EU 27 in published documents (2018) indicate that the US is a privileged partner of the EU, perhaps enjoying a first-among-equals or *primus inter pares* status—a status to which the UK may eventually aspire to. Defining 'internal' 'security' in the post-Brexit era may be significantly less 'internal', and less 'secure', and less about security; or it may concern more external and securitised civil and criminal justice. In fact, a fundamental question for resolution going forward in the post-Brexit era will likely concern the depth of the effects of the 'external' upon the 'internal' and the separability of security from defence, foreign policy and justice.

Brexit has exposed many other elementary questions and one acutely thorny feature of transatlantic relations, namely its lack of transparency. For example, a debate has opened up regarding the disparity between the US State Department and EU Treaties Office on the definition of an agreement in transatlantic relations (Larik 2017). The numerical content of the two respective entities varies dramatically over precisely how much law is in force. Differences remain when counting agreements that are not yet in force, consolidated, amended or altered; acts in trade and security; and agreements annulled (e.g. as Passenger Name Records). This is an eye-opening exercise as to the transparency of transatlantic relations and the transparency of the rule of law between the two partners. This 'counting' exercise also heavily impinges upon the UK's capacity to perfectly replicate or grandfather laws, rules and standards here. No doubt significant rule of law and legitimacy expectation questions may ensue and the full scale of the challenges of deciphering these issues may arise in less than straightforward fashions or contexts (Larik 2017).

More generally, transatlantic relations in the realm of JHA has operated as a vibrant source of law-making (Fahey 2017). A huge proliferation of soft law in a diversity of fields has also been matched by a creeping institutionalisation in order to meet accountability, legitimacy and transparency considerations. For example, the EU-US Umbrella

Agreement is a good example of recent EU-US criminal justice cooperation with a shift towards soft institutionalisation (Fahey 2018). For example, the main accountability functions of the Agreement are set out in Article 14, which put an onus on authorities to act accordingly or risk considerable sanctions. It strives to develop a system to facilitate claims in the event of misconduct and thus constitutes some form of looser localised 'institutionalisation' if it can be called that. These developments will be very difficult for a third country partner to replicate or grandfather to any degree barring participation.

Current EU-US JHA cooperation spans extradition, mutual legal assistance, passenger name records, financial messaging, the death penalty, cybercrime, and security and information sharing. While all of these forms of cooperation have proven themselves to be useful diplomatic channels, sometimes merely legally replicating what existed at a bilateral level, at least three considerations threaten their existence going forward and in turn the UK's capacity to either replicate, grandfather or participate therein (see negotiation positions, this volume, Chapter 4). Firstly, existing EU-US JHA measures are still vulnerable to ECHR challenge, having largely remained free from scrutiny. The ratification of ECHR Protocol No. 16 by ten EU Member State courts for ECHR advisory jurisdiction may generate further lines of scrutiny going forward into EU-ECHR law (Council of Europe Treaty Series 2013). Secondly, existing EU-US JHA measures remain vulnerable to data protection challenges in the new post-*Schrems* (Court of Justice 2015), GDPR, *Opinion 1/15* era (Court of Justice 2017) of strict scrutiny of data transfer as a cross-cutting dimension of EU law in internal and external contexts. This era poses a significant brake upon the idea of UK diverging from EU law in any rights-based domain, arguably not limited to data protection. *Thirdly*, the era of rising significance of the 'autonomy of EU law' for the CJEU recently, particularly post- *Opinion 2/13* (Court of Justice 2014) and *Achmea* (Court of Justice 2018) is one, which threatens institutionalisation as a means to redress any of the foregoing. While the current red lines and avoidance of the CJEU ideologically dominate all analysis, it should be remembered that it impinges upon a deeper and more specialised relationship with the UK and formulations of good governance in the field of justice and security, which may arguably have an entirely different resonance with trade-based considerations (see, for example, House of Lords 2017).

Another significant factor, moving away from a court-centric view of EU law, is that the EU legislator has become an active and dynamic importer of external norms in its AFSJ in the post-Lisbon period (Fahey 2016). These developments provide important evidence of socialisation of the EU at an international level. Notably, transatlantic relations stand apart as one of the few areas of the AFSJ in which external norms are absent, that is, in which the EU is not a norm importer. Conversely, in the same time period, the CJEU has become increasingly devoted to the autonomy of EU law and its reification and no longer cites external norms (e.g. in the area of external migration law) (Moreno Lax 2017: 462). Will the UK be so eager to de facto and de jure converge with international norms? These developments pose important reflection points for understanding rule-takers and rule-makers in the international legal order going forward. The exceptionalism of transatlantic relations is a significant issue from which important lessons can be learned.

Looking forward, the WA (European Commission and HM Government 2018) in its March draft sets out in Part Four, at the time of writing, many important facets of the transition. During the transition period, the WA provides for the UK to become a rule-taker, where it no longer participates in the institutions of the EU and instead, continues to largely have the full force of EU law applied to it, while being subject to the jurisdiction of the CJEU. In particular, Article 122 thereof provides for the scope of the transition to the effect that all EU law remains applicable to the UK during the transition period. Notably, it provides in Article 122(1)(a) that Protocol No. 21 on the position of the UK and Ireland in respect of the AFSJ is not applicable during the transition (in the sense that the UK will no longer have the option to request new opt-ins into AFSJ legislation),[2] removing the flexibility rights that have surrounded the UK's participation in this field. This opt-in opt-out right has been exercised consistently by the UK as to EU-US relations and has not hindered its capacity to lead policy. For example, in the field of

---

[2] See Article 122(1)(a) 'Unless otherwise provided in this Agreement, Union law shall be applicable to and in the United Kingdom during the transition period. However, the following provisions of the Treaties and acts adopted by the institutions, bodies, offices or agencies of the Union shall not be applicable to and in the United Kingdom during the transition period: (a) ... Protocol (No. 21) on the position of the United Kingdom and Ireland in respect of the area of freedom, security and justice...'.

Passenger Name Records, the UK has spearheaded the internal dimension to an EU policy (on PNR), initially depicted as an external relations policy domain. This affords a useful reflection point on becoming a ruletaker in UK-EU relations going forward and, dare one say, on the potential insignificance of law in the realm of the transatlantic.

REFERENCES

Adler-Nissen, R. 2009. Behind the Scenes of Differentiated Integration: Circumventing National Opt-Outs in Justice and Home Affairs. *Journal of European Public Policy* 16 (1): 62–80.

Alegre, S., D. Bigo, E. Guild, E.M. Kuskonmaz, H. Ben Jaffel, and J. Jeandesboz. 2017. *The Implications of the United Kingdom's Withdrawal from the European Union for the Area of Freedom, Security and Justice.* Report to the Committee on Civil Liberties, Justice and Home Affairs. Available from: http://www.europarl.europa.eu/thinktank/en/document.html?reference=IPOL_STU(2017)596824. Last accessed 31 May 2018.

Bárd, P. 2018. *The Effect of Brexit on European Arrest Warrants.* Centre for European Policy Studies Paper in Liberty and Security in Europe, No. 2018-02, April.

Council of Europe Treaty Series. 2013. *No. 214. Protocol No. 16 to the Convention on the Protection of Human Rights and Fundamental Freedoms,* Strasbourg, 2.X.2013.

Court of Justice. 2014. Opinion 2/13 Opinion of the Court (Full Court) of 18 December 2014, EU:C:2014:2454.

Court of Justice. 2015. Case C-362/14 Schrems v Data Commissioner, EU:C:2015:650.

Court of Justice. 2017. Opinion 1/15 of the Grand Chamber ECLI:EU:C:2017:592 (EU-Canada PNR Agreement).

Court of Justice. 2018. C-284/16, Judgment ECLI:EU:C:2018:158, 6 March 2018.

European Commission and HM Government. 2018. *Draft Agreement on the Withdrawal of the United Kingdom of Great Britain and Northern Ireland from the European Union and the European Atomic Energy Community.* Available from: https://www.gov.uk/government/uploads/system/uploads/attachment_data/file/691366/20180319_DRAFT_WITHDRAWAL_AGREEMENT.pdf. Last accessed 26 March 2018.

Fahey, E. 2016. Joining the Dots: External Norms, AFSJ Directives and the EU's Role in the Global Legal Order. *European Law Review* 41: 105.

Fahey, E. 2017. The Evolution of Transatlantic Legal Integration: Truly, Madly, Deeply? EU-US Justice and Home Affairs. In *Routledge Handbook on Justice and Home Affairs,* ed. F. Trauner and A. Rippoll-Servent. Abingdon: Routledge.

Fahey, E. (ed.). 2018. *Institutionalisation Beyond the Nation State: Transatlantic Data Privacy and Trade Law*. Cham, Switzerland: Springer.

HM Government. 2017. *Security, Law Enforcement and Criminal Justice: A Future Partnership*. Available from: https://www.gov.uk/government/uploads/system/uploads/attachment_data/file/645416/Security__law_enforcement_and_criminal_justice_-_a_future_partnership_paper.PDF. Last accessed 22 March 2018.

House of Lords. 2017. Brexit: Judicial Oversight of the European Arrest Warrant. *European Union Committee*, 27 July.

Larik, J. 2017. Brexit and the Transatlantic Trouble of Counting Treaties. *EJIL Talk!* 6 December.

Mitsilegas, V. 2017. The United Kingdom in Europe's Area of Criminal Justice. The Triple Paradox of Brexit. *Criminology in Europe* 16 (2): 9–10.

Moreno-Lax, V. 2017. *Accessing Asylum in Europe: Extraterritorial Border Controls and Refugee Rights Under EU Law*. Oxford: Oxford University Press.

Mortera-Martinez, C. 2018. Plugging in the British: EU Justice and Home Affairs. *Policy Brief*, Centre for European Reform, May.

Peers, S. 2018. Differentiated Integration and the Brexit Process in EU Justice and Home Affairs. In *The Routledge Handbook of Justice and Home Affairs Research*, ed. A. Ripoll Servent and F. Trauner, 253–263. London: Routledge.

Politico. 2018. Europe's Terror Defenses Pass to Belgian Hands, 2 May. Available from: https://www.politico.eu/article/europol-europes-terror-defenses-pass-to-belgian-hands-eu-law-enforcement-agency-catherine-de-bolle/. Last accessed 22 May 2018.

Ripoll Servent, A. 2015. *Institutional and Policy Change in the European Parliament: Deciding on Freedom, Security and Justice*. Houndmills: Palgrave Macmillan.

Weyembergh, A. 2017. Consequences of Brexit for European Union Criminal Law. *New Journal of European Criminal Law* 8 (3): 284–299.

CHAPTER 7

Sectoral Views on Police and Judicial Cooperation

Abstract This chapter offers short expert views on different aspects of police and judicial cooperation, including De Vries' contribution on cooperation regarding counterterrorism and the fight against organised crime; Bossong and Rieger's exploration of future data sharing options for police cooperation; Trauner's piece on the negotiations regarding the UK's future participation in Europol; Wilson and Carr's discussion of future cooperation in Forensic Science; and MacKenzie's considerations on the UK's role in EU counter-terrorism policy. This chapter also encompasses a number of expert views that focus specifically on security threats, including Sergi's analysis of Brexit creating opportunities for transnational criminal networks; Farrand's exploration of Brexit's impact on combatting counterfeiting; and Porcedda's and Lavorgna's pieces on the consequences of Brexit for the UK and the EU in the area of cybersecurity.

Keywords Brexit · Police and judicial cooperation · Transnational organised crime · Terrorism · Cybercrime · Europol · Eurojust · Databases

The second sectoral views' chapter is composed of nine contributions revolving around police and judicial cooperation in criminal matters. In the first text, de Vries departs from the question of whether criminals taking back control as a consequence of Brexit can still be avoided.

© The Author(s) 2019
H. Carrapico et al., *Brexit and Internal Security*,
Palgrave Studies in European Union Politics,
https://doi.org/10.1007/978-3-030-04194-6_7

As a response, he outlines the manifold challenges to future cooperation on counter-terrorism and the fight against organised crime. Bossong and Rieger's contribution focuses on future data sharing for police cooperation, and suggests that decentralised mechanisms for information sharing could be an alternative to the UK's direct access to EU databases. Trauner also focuses his contribution on the future of police cooperation. He sketches out the crucial role of the UK in Europol and draws attention to the obstacles to future cooperation, differences in membership rights, and the implications of a UK-EU deal for third countries, showing that the negotiations regarding Europol will be a difficult trade-off between principles and efficiency. Equally important for the capacity of the UK's law enforcement in countering insecurity is the EU's track record in the domain of forensic science. Wilson and Carr point out the challenges regarding post-Brexit cooperation in this area and conclude that continued general access to the AFSJ forensic science initiatives is vital for forensic science in the UK and its role internationally. MacKenzie describes the UK's role in EU counter-terrorism policy and argues that both the EU and the UK will be negatively affected by Brexit when it comes to counter-terrorism, labelling the negotiations as an exercise in damage-control.

The following four pieces focus their attention on the relationship between Brexit and specific aspects of insecurity, including terrorism, organised crime, and cyber insecurity. Sergi takes on the myth of 'taking back control' of borders as a way to keep potential terrorists and transnational organised criminals out of the UK, showing how Brexit will lead to a weaker and more isolated Great Britain. In a similar vein, Farrand considers the impact of Brexit on combatting counterfeiting and argues that it could lead to a considerable loss of expertise, information, and best practices offered to the UK by the EU, and a loss of trust, on the side of the EU, in the UK's ability to address counterfeiting. Porcedda and Lavorgna's contributions focus specifically on cybersecurity. Porcedda points out that the EU's tools for countering cybercrime include not only AFSJ investigative and prosecution-related instruments, but also preventative legal instruments rooted in the internal market. Lavorgna's piece argues that Brexit will negatively impact police cooperation and access to data for law enforcement between the UK and the EU, the regulatory harmonisation, and the ability of the UK to remain attractive for tech talents and cybersecurity companies.

A Hard Brexit Will See Criminals Take Back Control

Gijs de Vries[1]

What price Brexit? Whatever it takes, as Brexiteers would have it? A hard Brexit would see Britain crash out of dozens of EU agencies, instruments and data systems. Criminals would be taking back control, in Britain as in the rest of Europe. Conflicts around Europe would become more difficult to manage; Russia and China would expand their power at Europe's expense. Can such a scenario be avoided?

Perhaps it still can. Recent developments suggest that common sense, historically associated with British policy-making, may be enjoying something of a revival. In her most recent speeches Theresa May has adopted a tone designed to sound more constructive than before. The change from hectoring is welcome. Atmospherics are no substitute for policy, but they do matter.

Fortunately there have been changes in substance, too, including in the area of security. Less than a year ago Mrs May issued a thinly veiled threat to the EU: work with Britain or face the consequences in terms of (your) security. Britain's Article 50 letter to the EU was widely regarded as a crude attempt to blackmail the EU (Asthana et al. 2017). According to the renowned former British ambassador to the EU, Sir Stephen Wall, the letter originally contained even tougher language and had to be toned down (Payne 2017).

A different Mrs May, it seemed, took the floor at the February Munich Security Conference (May 2018). Barbs against presumed EU ideology aside, the speech contained much that was constructive and sensible. The Prime Minister called for the two sides to consult each other regularly, to coordinate and deliver operationally on the ground, and to work together on developing the capabilities—in defence, cyber and space—to meet future threats. The UK, Mrs. May said, was open to contributing to EU mechanisms, including development programmes, post-Brexit. And when participating in EU agencies such as Europol the UK would respect the remit of the European Court of Justice.

While this went down well in the rest of Europe, other sections of the speech raised eyebrows. There would need to be an EU-UK treaty

[1]This contribution was originally published in the LSE Brexit Blog on the 12th of March 2018. For the original, please visit: http://blogs.lse.ac.uk/brexit/2018/03/12/a-hard-brexit-will-see-criminals-taking-back-control/.

which offered "a principled but pragmatic solution to close legal cooperation [...] to respect our unique status." The UK demanded "a future relationship" with the European Defence Fund and the European Defence Agency, whose budget the UK has long fought to curtail. And the UK wanted "an open and inclusive approach to European capability development – that fully enables British defence industry to participate." Cake, anyone?

That said, the speech signals a growing recognition in London that, in terms of its security, the UK needs the EU as much as the EU needs the UK—and an implicit rebuff to the many pundits who cleave to the opposite point of view. One such opinion-leader, former MI6 head Sir Richard Dearlove dismissed continental intelligence agencies as "the leakiest ships of state." The European Arrest Warrant, too, was pretty useless: "few would note its passing" (Slack and Cohen 2016). A similar sense of English superiority can occasionally be caught wafting through the corridors of Whitehall. Mrs May, to her credit, does not regard it a sound basis for policy.

However, renegotiating the UK's security relationship with the EU will prove a formidable undertaking. Politicians as well as journalists still tend to underestimate what Brexit will mean for policing, judicial cooperation and counter-terrorism. They also fail to appreciate the amount of work needed to stave off the threat.

Post Brexit, the UK will lose influence. Its police forces and intelligence services also risk losing access to information. Continued access to information will come at a price.

Of course, bilateral intelligence cooperation between the UK and other EU countries is not regulated by the EU and would continue as of old. The UK would also stay a member of the Counter-Terrorist Group, which brings together the intelligence and security services of the EU Member States, Norway and Switzerland, and of the 'SIGINT Seniors' (the UK, Canada, Australia, New Zealand, the USA, plus Belgium, Denmark, France, Germany, Italy, the Netherlands, Spain and Sweden). However, Britain will lose access to IntCen, the EU's Brussels-based centre for strategic intelligence analysis.

Were the UK to leave Europol British police forces would lose access to Europol's Information System, the Bomb Data System, the EU Internet Referral Unit and other much-needed information. The National Crime Agency, Britain's Financial Intelligence Unit, would lose access to the EU's network of FIUs, which is based at Europol.

This would serve neither Britain's interests nor those of its European partners. So, the UK's wish to stay involved is well-understood. But as a non-EU country Britain would no longer be entitled to a seat on the Management Board. At best, it may have to settle for non-voting observer status. British police officers could no longer expect to lead Europol teams.

Eurojust coordinates criminal investigations and prosecutions, including into terrorism, where it supported 74 cases in 2017. Post Brexit the UK will lose its seat in the college, but will it request to appoint a liaison officer like Norway, Liechtenstein and other countries? The Government's policy paper on security cooperation offers little clarity (HM Government 2017a).

The UK may also wish to renegotiate its role in the European Union Agency for Network and Information Security (ENISA), which is responsible for cybersecurity, including protection from state-sponsored cyber-attacks and espionage, and cyber crisis management. As a third country, the UK could participate in the work but would not be represented on the Management Board.

The European Global Navigation Satellite Systems Agency (GNS) manages Galileo, the EU's global satellite system, which provides securely encrypted services, including the Public Regulated Service for security operators (police, border control, and others) in EU Member States. The Galileo Satellite Security Monitoring Centre, currently located in Swanwick (UK), will move to Madrid. As it leaves the EU, Britain will lose the senior positions it currently holds in GNS. Does it still see a role for itself?

At the end of the transition period, the Commission warns, the UK will no longer have access to any EU network, any information system, and any database. These include SIS II, which gives police forces access to information about people (some 35,000 wanted on a European Arrest Warrant) and stolen property such as cars, passports, and firearms. ECRIS, or the European Criminal Records Information System, let countries share criminal records in Europe. For example, if a British person is convicted of a crime in Spain, then the Spanish authorities will send details of that crime to the UK where they will be stored on the local criminal records system. FADO allows for the rapid sharing between EU countries of images of genuine, false and forged passports, visas, driving licences and other documents, as well as information on forgery techniques and national false document alerts. Will British police forces retain access to European Passenger Name Record data (PNR)? What about access to DNA profiles stored in other European countries (Prüm System)? How does London intend to limit these consequences of Brexit?

Some issues may be relatively easy to solve, such as continued British membership of the EU Internet Forum, an informal alliance of EU Member States, Europol, EU experts and private companies, or British participation in the Radicalisation Awareness Network (RAN) and the European Strategic Communications Network (ESCN), which share best practice on countering violent extremism. Should it wish to remain part of the criminal justice response to radicalisation through the European Judicial Training Network, the UK will have to pay into the EU budget.

Other nuts will be more difficult to crack. To tackle terrorism and other forms of cross-border crime the UK will have to renegotiate its status under a slew of criminal law instruments, such as the European Investigation Order, under which EU countries exchange information in criminal cases. For example, if the UK is tracking terrorist suspects in Belgium, it can request the Belgian authorities to interrogate witnesses or conduct house searches on its behalf. The UK has suggested that it would like to continue using the European Arrest Warrant. What about the European Protection Order, which allows court protection orders made in criminal cases in one Member State to be enforced in another? What about, for example, the Framework Decisions on mutual recognition of financial penalties, custodial sentences, supervision measures, and confiscation orders? Each of these legal instruments, which apply to EU Member States, will have to be changed—a complicated, time-consuming process.

To protect British security, the UK will need to stay closely connected to EU institutions and instruments. But even this soft Brexit will come at a price. The UK will lose both power and influence. It will no longer have a voice in EU legislation and decision-making on terrorism, crime, foreign policy or security. Furthermore, to the extent that it wants access to EU agencies, instruments and data systems, the UK will still be required to share sovereignty and accept the jurisdiction of the European Court of Justice. It will also have to pay up. This is what a soft Brexit implies: a degree of taxation without full representation.

In the end, this bric-a-brac may just about enable security cooperation between the UK and the rest of Europe to continue. But make no mistake: cooperation will become more cumbersome and messy, and a predictable source of mutual acrimony. Britain will trade security for the semblance of sovereignty.

Neither a hard nor a soft Brexit will benefit public security. The clock is ticking. How long will it take for reality to sink in?

EU-UK Internal Security Cooperation After Brexit

Raphael Bossong and Steffen Rieger

The EU and its Member States should aim for flexible solutions to meet the UK's demand for a continued close security partnership. Admittedly, the equitable treatment of Denmark or—in broader terms—the coherence of the EU's complex and differentiated legal order in the Area of Freedom, Security and Justice poses significant problems. Yet to avoid a return to a mutually damaging negotiation pattern, whereby the UK considers using its security capacities as a bargaining chip in the wider Brexit negotiation process, the EU should be ready to think creatively—at least in the comparatively narrow field of police and criminal justice cooperation. The two most commonly discussed stumbling blocks are the jurisdiction of the Court of Justice and the maintenance of data protection standards. The latest preliminary agreement on the rights of EU citizens in the UK suggests that the role of the Court could be partly depoliticized by reference to transitional periods and limited scope conditions. As concerns the general regulatory alignment on data protection, one should bear in mind that since May 2018 the Article 29 Working Party has been upgraded to the so-called 'European data protection board'. Even if this board is currently limited to the new EU data protection regulation, which does not cover national police and internal security affairs, this strengthened institutional infrastructure might be used for a comprehensive regulatory dialogue, possibly also with third countries. This could support the general adequacy assessment on data protection by the Commission.

However, this brief contribution focuses on a third major concern for the UK, namely maintaining access to EU databases for police cooperation. No country outside the EU or the Schengen zone has full access to the SIS or the analytical databases at Europol. This basic limitation will have to apply to the UK as well and will mainly result in a numerical decrease of data exchanges and queries for mainstream policing purposes by and with the UK. This loss must be accepted as a consequence of Brexit, but may be limited as far as possible. An obvious alternative to EU databases is an intensified use of decentralised mechanisms for information-sharing, as for instance under the Prüm Treaty. Yet aside from the well-known limitations of these systems, the EU is currently investing in new centralized information infrastructures to allow for 'interoperability' between all EU databases for police cooperation, border and migration control. This gives rise to the question whether currently decentralized data-exchange mechanisms—such as under the Prüm treaty, PNR and API data exchanges, Fiu.net for financial intelligence, or the European Criminal Record System—should be transformed into centralized systems over the medium term. It is, therefore, essential to secure the UK's permanent participation in all currently available decentralized information-systems, even though they may evolve in the future. And while the EU will increasingly work on centralized infrastructures for interoperability, the UK should continue to work on activities that support the effectiveness of decentralized networks (training, capacity-building, technical standardization of data). The further roll-out of 'hit/no-hit' queries across all European police data-systems may potentially serve as bridge between these parallel work streams, especially with regard to the future project of a 'European police records' system.

At the same time, the future role of the UK within Europol should also be approached with an open mind. While an official governance role and direct database access will be lost, the scope and capacities of a future UK liaison office at Europol to enable indirect access remain to be defined. The existing US liaison office within Europol deserves more attention in this regard than the recent arrangement with Denmark. Already now, the UK has the largest contingent of seconded officers at Europol, which could be expanded further across different security branches like the US liaison office. From the side of EUROPOL, the decentral SIENA network may also be used to maintain a close UK alignment, possibly in a special user-group as has already been created for counterterrorism purposes. Furthermore, the growing data processing powers of Europol could, in conjunction with the creation of interoperability, bridge the time-gap between direct and indirect data access. For instance, could a UK liaison bureau member ask Europol staff to use the new 'single search interface' or even 'batch searches' to reach across all EU databases? At least on the basis of a 'hit/no-hit' notification, the UK could then direct a quick bilateral follow-up request at the respective Member State that entered, or holds more, data on a particular suspect. Last but not least, the UK should remain associated as far as possible with Europol-led Joint Investigation Teams, and related flexible structures in the fight against cybercrime (such as J-CAT). All these concessions to the UK may be balanced by the new inter-parliamentary scrutiny body for EUROPOL, where one could conceive of the UK as a remaining associated or observing partner.

Finally, the broader European landscape of information-exchange for internal security must be maintained. Rather than seeing EU-channels and historically older professional networks as competitors, the emphasis should be on maximum complementarity. This applies, for instance, to the Police Working Group on Terrorism or INTERPOL, which should continue to deepen its partnership with Europol. Large EU Member States, such as Germany, should secure long-term alignment, so that core data sets (e.g. terrorist-watch lists) are synchronized across platforms as far as possible. This is also of critical importance for the growing contacts between the EU (especially the Counterterrorism Centre at Europol) and the Counterterrorism Group (CTG) of European domestic intelligence services. In fact, domestic intelligence services should be an area of deepening European cooperation, irrespective of Brexit. This requires, on the side of the UK, a willingness to accept a greater role of the EU—such as through a closer alignment with EUROPOL and EU databases for border management—, and on the side of the remaining Member States and EU institutions, a differentiated stance on the intelligence capacities of the UK. It is unlikely that the position of the UK on global signals intelligence partnerships (Five Eyes) will change anytime soon, while there are bound to be further legal disputes over the scope of EU data protection laws and the mass collection of telecommunications data as practiced in the UK (see the debate over Data Retention and Investigatory Powers Act 2014). For all other intelligence services, however, there could be space for new European initiatives that build on growing successes of the CTG and which would underline the mutual commitment of the UK and the EU to a deep and strategic security partnership.

THE UK's FUTURE RELATIONSHIP WITH EUROPOL: UNDERSTANDING THE TRADE-OFFS

Florian Trauner

Founded by the Europol Convention in 1995, the European Police Office, Europol, has come to take a central place in the EU's policy-making on internal security. Located in The Hague and staffed with around 1000 men and women, Europol is a hub for the pooling, exchange and analysis of information on organised crime and counter-terrorism at EU level. While having no coercive powers of its own, it also coordinates joint investigations and operations of national police authorities. Europol no longer only relies on the information provided by police agencies at Member State level but also gathers its own data, for instance on cybercrime. It has become a 'high tech organisation' (Robert 2016) pooling a variety of EU and national databases and developing new analytical approaches to make sense of the 'big data' it gathers on security risks and threats in Europe.

The UK has played a pivotal role for Europol's development and day-to-day operations. The UK relies on this agency 'more than almost any other country' (own assessment of the UK government quoted in Carrapico et al. 2017). The UK is an active member of all 13 of the EU's current law enforcement priority projects (HM Government 2017a: 6). The British government is among the top four contributors to Europol Information System and Europol's director until May 2018 was a former British MI5 analyst, Rob Wainwright. The UK has also used the agency to influence other Member States and the EU's policy-making process. A case in point has been the UK's efforts to 'Europeanise' its national model of intelligence-led policing through Europol. By pushing Europol to base its Organised Crime Threat Assessments (OCTA) on the British model, the UK was able to shape Europol's work and influence the Council's strategic priorities in the area of fighting organized crime (Carrapico and Trauner 2013).

Given this context, it comes as no surprise that the UK government has been keen to maintain the status quo. British officials believe that Brexit should have 'no impact whatsoever' on the UK's relations with Europol (*The Telegraph* 2017). The UK government plans to adopt a new UK-EU Security Treaty allowing the UK to maintain membership rights with Europol (HM Government 2017a). The UK and the EU both have an interest in not disrupting the existing cooperation on internal security matters. The UK expertise and intelligence capabilities—in particular on counter-terrorism—is appreciated by other Member States. Moreover, organised crime networks should not become capable of developing within the UK or of using it as a base for operations in the EU's territory following to a lack of EU-UK law enforcement cooperation. At first glance, therefore, a realization of the UK's plan seems realistic.

Yet the negotiations on the UK's future relations with Europol will be difficult. Three issues are particularly complex: (1) judicial scrutiny; (2) membership rights; and (3) implications of a Brexit deal for other third countries. Regarding the first, the Court of Justice of the EU (CJEU) plays the ultimate arbiter in relation to litigation involving Europol's handling of data and privacy rules. A continued UK membership is therefore likely to depend on the acceptance of the role of the CJEU— one of the red lines defined by the UK government—and the EU's data protection rules (while it will no longer participate in the adoption of these rules). The UK hopes for an alternative dispute resolution mechanism that would allow the UK to remain outside the remit of the jurisdiction of the CJEU (HM Government 2017a: 14). An acceptance of such an 'alternative' court for maintaining the status quo will be a difficult pill to swallow for Member States.

The second issue concerns membership rights. The UK is not satisfied with having a future relationship that resembles one of Europol's current external relations (HM Government 2017a: 11). Other non-EU-Member States such as Norway and Switzerland have operational agreements with Europol. These agreements allow for law enforcement cooperation and data exchange but they do not provide direct access to Europol's databases. Information must be requested through liaison officers posted in The Hague. Direct access is a right preserved for Member States, as are voting rights in Europol's board meetings. The UK wants more than this: 'the UK and the EU need to look beyond existing third country precedents, designing instead comprehensive arrangements that reflect the exceptionally broad and deep security relationship that exists today' (HM Government 2017a: 16). Put differently, the UK desires a status that is comparable to what it has at present while being formally out of the EU.

If the EU accepts such a blurring of the rights and privileges between non-EU-Member States and Member States, this will have implications for Europol's other external relations (the third issue mentioned before). Other law enforcement authorities are also interested in accessing the millions of shared files on European internal security issues. If the UK is granted access to these files as a non-EU Member State, what is the justification for not giving the same rights to the USA? After all, the US is also a central partner for the EU in the fight against international terrorism. This kind of concern features prominently when talking to senior staff in the EU's institutions.

Overall, the case of Europol highlights how difficult it will be to realise UK Prime Minister Theresa May's objective, that 'Brexit [should be] a success for everyone' (quoted in *Daily Mail* 2017). The EU-UK negotiations on Europol will target damage control and will have to make difficult trade-offs between principles and efficiency. Even if the status quo is appreciated and *efficient*, the *principles* defined in the EU law or publicly announced by the UK government—such as no more legal scrutiny by an EU court or a clear distinction of membership rights for member and non-Member States—may trump such a functional perspective.

AREA OF FREEDOM, SECURITY AND JUSTICE AND FORENSIC SCIENCE

Tim J. Wilson and Sophie Carr

A major success within the Area of Freedom, Security and Justice (AFSJ) has been the enhancement of forensic science's contribution to criminal justice and security. This is seen very clearly in faster and more efficient forensic biometric information sharing within what a leading MP has described as the EU 'system' for international criminal justice and security cooperation (Neil 2017). AFSJ initiatives have not equalled the scale and reach—particularly in research—of US government and bioscience commercial activity (Wilson 2016). EU membership, however, has critically counterbalanced the neglect of forensic science by successive UK governments. Involvement in AFSJ-funded projects has reduced the risk of professional isolation for British experts and protected earlier public investment in forensic bioinformation, especially DNA databases. The benefits of AFSJ participation extend beyond cross-border crime and offending (Wilson 2015), with improvements also in the probative power of forensic sciences in British criminal proceedings and anti-terrorist/security activities that lack an international dimension.

Successful EU achievements in this domain reflect the power to pool—through comitologically managed implementation processes—the problem-solving capabilities of Member States and institutions (Wilson 2018). This overcomes 'cooperation asymmetry': 'governments remain extremely reluctant to cooperate on security matters [...], terrorists have cooperated in networks since the onset of modern day terrorism' (Sandler 2006). The algorithmically-enabled comparison of huge volumes of scientifically standardised data has commoditised forensic biometric cooperation. Such transformations have enhanced public protection through increased effectiveness and with greater efficiency (Wilson 2016), for example, at approximately €27 for each Dutch international forensic DNA match (Taverne and Broeders 2015).

For reliable, prompt, large-scale and efficient forensic biometric cooperation, there is no alternative post-Brexit to seeking continued access to the AFSJ system. This can be seen from comparisons of the scale of forensic biometric data sharing possible through the EU and Interpol systems (Soleto Muñoz and Fiodorova 2014; Wilson 2016). The huge differences such comparisons reveal not only reflect technical choices and project delivery capabilities. Strong national control over data under EU criminal law, confidence in EU data protection law, a tendency to search for information within the EU/Schengen area first and above all mutual trust between Member States, compared with the context in which the Interpol system operates, all account for the comparatively greater success of the AFSJ system for sharing DNA data (Soleto Muñoz and Fiodorova 2014). Particularly with the emphasis on the Charter of Fundamental Rights and the Court of Justice (CJEU) within the EU 'system', it can be seen why the Prime Minister's 'red lines' on these aspects of the acquis were questioned early in the Brexit process (House of Commons 2017b).

Sharing information is only the beginning of the story. The results of the comparative analysis have to be scientifically valid and interpreted accurately within a context determined by the totality of the evidence in any particular criminal case.

The first objective can be achieved both more reliably and cost-effectively through scientific standardisation. Over the last decade, great strides have been made in forensic DNA multiplex convergence. The analysis (via multiplex kits) of only a few loci (markers) from the human genome can determine whether cellular material recovered from a crime scene matches reference material donated by a known individual ('source attribution'). The UK, as a major partner in the EU-funded research and an influential innovator in this process, benefited considerably from what became global convergence in selected multiplex loci (markers) (development through in effect a tri-continental process with parallel changes in the USA and China) towards this country's core biochemical standards (illustrated in Table 7.1).

The risk for the UK in this process was that new multiplex loci (markers) could have deviated significantly from the earlier UK loci selection. This would have made much of the data on its forensic DNA database

Table 7.1 The international convergence of DNA multiplexes

Year	Multiplex	Number of markers	Overlap with UK multiplex at that time		Overlap with USA multiplex at that time	Overlap with China multiplex at that time
			England and Wales	Scotland		
1995	UK SGM	7		N/A	N/A	N/A
1998	USA original CODIS	13		6	N/A	N/A
1999	UK SGM+	11		N/A	8	N/A
2010	China Sinofiler	15		9	11	N/A
2014	UK (England and Wales) DNA-17	17	N/A	11	8	10
2015	UK (Scotland) DNA-24	24	17	N/A	13	14
2017	USA CODIS core loci	20	15	20	N/A	14

Source Wilson, T. 2015. The Global Perspective. In *Annual Report of the Government Chief Scientific Adviser 2015: Forensic Science and Beyond: Authenticity, Provenance and Assurance: Evidence and Case Studies*, ed. M. Peplow. London: Government Office for Science

Table contains public sector information licensed under the Open Government Licence v3.0: http://nationalarchives.gov.uk/doc/open-government-licence/version/3/

increasingly obsolete for international cooperation purposes. The advantages for the UK—in terms of improving the discriminatory power of scientific results in investigations with no international dimensions—is that participation in EU-sponsored multiplex research facilitated the introduction of multiplexes that improve scientific reliability when the recovered cellular material is either degraded or low in volume. The pending next generation of forensic DNA analysis will require the same EU and international cooperation.

The second objective (assessing probative value) can be much more challenging. This is because, contrary to traditional binary conceptions (e.g. a fingerprint analysis presented as an 'identification' or not), evidential reliability needs to be conceptualised within a continuum, particularly when scientific advances have enabled greater analysis of poor quality or quantity source material. Areas of questionable reliability may then be characterised as 'liminal zones': areas of transition where heightened scrutiny may be required. This is very much work in progress that requires further policy development to enhance evidential reliability, including devising standardised formats, assessments and terminology for expert reports and refining interpretational protocols (Carr et al., forthcoming). The forensic disciplines are international; universal adoption cannot be achieved by British forensic scientists working in isolation.

The UK pioneered the use of forensic bioinformation during the last century, implementing both fingerprint and DNA comparison methods. Mistakes during the marketization of forensic science were compounded by deep cuts in funding, inadequate research and the failure to develop a national strategy for forensic science (House of Commons 2011 and 2013). The increased fragility and fragmentation of the UK forensic science research and investigative capabilities have been partly counterbalanced by the active participation, including in multiplex research projects, by British forensic scientists in European Network of Forensic Science Institutions (ENFSI) (Kjeldsen and Nueteboom 2015). Many initiatives to improve forensic science begin within regular scientific fora such as the working groups of ENFSI, but professional implementation within national criminal justice systems often require support from Eurojust and Europol, and funding from the Commission. Thus, continued general access to AFSJ forensic science initiatives is vital for the well-being and critical trust in forensic science in the UK and its continued international role.

The UK, EU, and Counter-Terrorism

Alex MacKenzie

The UK has made at least three important contributions to the development of the EU's counter-terrorism policy. Firstly, it has helped provide direction to the area. This is clear in the EU's Counter-Terrorism Strategy, which was agreed on in 2005 during the British Presidency and closely resembles the UK's strategy from the time (European Parliament 2017). Secondly, the UK has often managed to upload and drive measures in line with its preferences to the supranational level. Evidence of this can be found in the controversial Data Retention Directive (DRD) and EU Passenger Name Records (EU-PNR), which were adopted in the EU in 2006 and 2016 respectively (Ripoll Servent and MacKenzie 2017).[2] Finally, the UK has been an enthusiastic and active promoter of counter-terrorism cooperation with third states. Agreements on PNR data and the Terrorism Financing and Tracking Programme (TFTP) are some of the most high-profile products of EU cooperation with third states, but examples of technical assistance also span the globe (Ripoll Servent and MacKenzie 2012). These three themes form the basis of the discussion on the future EU-UK counter-terrorism relationship below. Ultimately, I stress that, although there are a number of obstacles, the UK and EU must recognise the level of their interdependence and remain as close as possible. EU-UK security negotiations are an exercise in damage-control, and the erosion of trust and opening up of grey areas must be avoided.

Despite the claims of some in the 'Leave' campaign during the EU referendum, exiting the EU will probably not make the UK more secure.[3] An estimated 5000 European citizens travelled from their home countries to Iraq and Syria to join Islamic State (IS), with perhaps thirty percent returning by 2016 (International Centre for Counter-Terrorism 2016: 4). Unexpectedly, many have stayed in the region even after the defeat of the group, although concern remains that they might yet return home—a challenge shared by many EU Member States (International Centre for Counter-Terrorism 2018). Jihadist terrorism is a transnational

---

[2]The DRD was invalidated by the Court of Justice of the European Union (CJEU) in 2014.

[3]Ian Duncan Smith, for example, warned that remaining in the EU would expose the UK to the possibility of Paris-style attacks (those from 13 November 2015) (BBC 2016).

problem and tackling it requires complicated and sensitive cooperation between actors. The real danger is that Brexit may damage co-operation by reducing trust and opening up grey areas, thereby blinding both sides to threats. The history of terrorism shows that terrorists take advantage of gaps in co-operation between actors.

The three themes mentioned above will now be considered in turn. Firstly, whereas in the past the UK was seen as influential in EU counter-terrorism, it will now have to find ways to try to influence the policymaking process from outside. If it does not do so, counter-terrorism may go down the EU's agenda, making co-operation less of a priority and more difficult as a result. Further difficulties for both will be keeping their priorities aligned and finding ways to cooperate with each other even when domestic obstacles emerge. Ultimately, new arrangements, closer than those currently in place between the EU and US, will need to be decided on and introduced to facilitate cooperation.

Secondly, the UK will find it difficult to stay involved in the EU's security apparatus and even more so to upload measures compatible with its interests and systems. The UK has already stated that it wants data to flow in the same way as it does at present (HM Government 2017b). The UK is, currently, plugged into several EU databases (e.g. the Schengen Information System or SIS II), but it will become a third state at some point in the near future and access to these will be terminated (European Commission 2017a). The UK also wants access to Europol's assets and databases after Brexit, but no non-Member State has the same level as the Member States. On the UK side, there are considerable political obstacles to ensuring continued data transfer because it will likely have to seek an 'adequacy' decision from the European Commission (of data protection legislation), meaning that limits may be placed on how far it can diverge from EU legislation after Brexit (House of Lords 2017). Similarly, the supposed red line on the CJEU poses problems for UK involvement in EU agencies and measures, such as the European Arrest Warrant (EAW). On the EU side, Member States will be keen to avoid conceding much more to the UK than current arrangements with other non-EU states, such as the US. The EU has a difficult balancing act ahead of it, but it is the UK that wants more for less from an organisation that it has chosen to leave. In both direction and substance, the EU-UK relationship will be asymmetrical in favour of Brussels and, as the weaker party, the UK will have little leverage over it. Nonetheless, both sides must recognise the dangers of not cooperating and find an arrangement as close as possible to the current status quo.

Thirdly, the external dimension of EU counter-terrorism should not be forgotten; it is essential for internal security. It is not yet clear how Brexit will affect the UK's ability to share data and negotiate its own security agreements, although the arrangements it reaches with the EU will likely place some limits on its freedom to do so (House of Commons 2017a). Also, while intelligence co-operation takes place outside of EU structures and the UK is part of the 'Five Eyes', Washington arguably derives at least some of the value of the UK-US relationship from the UK's involvement in the EU (Inkster 2016). Brexit could cause a weakening of transatlantic relations and harm all three actors in the process. The UK has already suggested that it may take part in Common Security and Defence Policy (CSDP) missions in the future, but many likely exaggerate the capabilities of the UK outside of the EU (House of Lords 2018). The UK is no more than a middle power and the EU will be diminished by Brexit, with this having repercussions beyond Europe.

Overall, the negotiators face a number of obstacles and the negotiations are really about damage-control. The UK's departure from the EU will complicate counter-terrorism cooperation, not make the UK more secure, while the EU faces losing perhaps its most important Member State in this area. Both sides should seek the closest possible arrangements, even closer than those between the EU and US in recognition that they are heavily interdependent whether they like it or not. However, a future of close EU-UK co-operation is far from inevitable given current technical, legal, and political obstacles.

'Not in My Backyard': Brexit and the Myths of Transnational Organised Crime

Anna Sergi[4]

Brexit is fast approaching and the language of security—with words like risk, threat and harm floating around in political discourses on justice and border control (Falvey 2017)—complicates an already confused scenario on what exactly Great Britain will look like without the EU. In particular, the language of security is made to echo immediacy and a sense of urgency in solving a problem that is going to affect all of us and

---

[4]This text was originally published in the BSC Blog on the 1st of March 2018. For the original text, please see https://thebscblog.wordpress.com/2018/03/01/not-in-my-backyard-brexit-and-the-myths-of-transnational-organised-crime/.

with potentially alarming consequences (McDonald 2008). In the midst of political confusion in terms of what Brexit will mean for the UK's shores—especially in terms of agreements for cooperation and border control—the old adage that sees migration as a quintessential contribution to insecurity can easily resurface (Huysmans 2006). In other words, the idea that, by closing our borders, we will keep out potential terrorists and transnational drug traffickers, is tempting and apparently intuitive. And yet it is a superficial and incorrect concept, as it is based on mistaken premises.

The assumptions on the links between terrorism—international terrorism—and migration from Islamic countries has been proven wrong by recent events: terror attacks in Paris and London in the past years have confirmed that perpetrators, even when they are of Islamic faiths, are usually born and bred in the country and radicalised at a later stage (Dearden 2017). Thus, even in the public domain, the fear and the following stigmatisation of Muslim migrants, current and future, seem today easier to dispute. This, however, is also the result of the visibility of terrorism, when events like the London Bridge attack of 3 June 2017, which counted 8 deaths in total, dominated the news for weeks, offering the public all the details about the offenders' past and actions. This visibility, instead, does not complement the news on much more frequent criminal activities—of serious, often transnational, and organised crime, such as drug or human trafficking, counterfeiting and/or smuggling. Organised criminal groups, however, not only benefit from this lack of visibility (Sergi 2017)—as they arguably appreciate being under the radar—and will benefit from Brexit the most.

Indeed, myths can be debunked when it comes to organised crime and the impending exit of the UK from the European Union. The first myth relates to cross-border crime, and, as seen before, relies on the argument that with stricter border control and isolation we can disrupt trafficking and smuggling activities. This could be partially true if we were in a situation in which trafficking and smuggling only happened because of the porosity of borders. This assumption, however, is not true, as organised crime activities are heavily dependent, amongst other things, on market rules of supply and demand. Therefore, the border—and the overcoming of border controls—is factored into the business risk (Sidharth 2011). This is why isolation and increased border controls only make the business risk grow—by making it more difficult to cross the border unchecked—and the cost of an increased business risk are not born by the traffickers/smugglers but by the clients or the victims. In other words, in a cocaine trafficking scenario, cocaine will end up costing more on the streets because traffickers have to match the increased risk of shipping it into an isolated country, where demand is unlikely to decrease. By learning from the experience of other countries—namely Australia, for example (Winstock 2015)—an option to avoid the inflation of drug costs on the street is to ship lower quality drugs or developing drugs locally produced. On all accounts, however, the increased business risk paired with the usual demands leads to the possibility of increased profits: if cocaine is going to be more expensive in the UK, but demand does not decrease, then the UK will become an attractive place to do business. In this sense, Brexit will not only not decrease the availability of (transnationally-shipped) drugs but will also increase profits for organised crime groups (*The Economist* 2018). Great Britain needs to be able to work with partners towards international cooperation in policing—which Brexit also threatens—in order to understand how criminal networks work across global routes and how best to intervene to disrupt them.

There is another myth which relies on the nature of contemporary organised crime, as a threat to national security, in the form of transnational networks and not so much as a local issue. While it is obvious that some (organised) crimes are transnational, the nature of organised crime in Great Britain is certainly not only transnational, as, arguably, it has always been highly localised instead (Treadwell and Ayres 2014). Organised crime networks in different parts of the UK can be both 'heavy' organisations, which are structured and 'organised', but also 'lighter' organisations, which are based on opportunistic network ties occasional cooperation and easier involvement for willing participants (Sergi 2018; Treadwell 2012). If we consider organised crime as a socio-behavioural model of doing crime (Sergi 2017), that is rooted in networks and (sub)cultural values, then it follows that, together with fighting networks which operate cross border, policies must consider how organised crime activities and actors are closely linked to local environments, changes and structures, and social, economic and cultural levels. This line of thinking re-establishes organised crime as a very British problem (National Crime Agency 2017), that isolation and border control are not likely to affect (i.e. by reducing it) in the way certain political factions would like.

With concerns linked to the City of London becoming the 'laundry of choice' of different criminal groups (Talani 2013), both local

(Gelder 2017) and foreign (LLB 2017), political parties have repeatedly called for a review of regulations (Davies and Burke 2017). With the advent of Brexit, and with the possible changes in transparency regulations now established by the EU, this concern becomes even more real. When it comes to understanding and policing organised crime, together with many other threats which the UK considers a national security concern, we must therefore conclude that Brexit would only make for a weaker and more isolated Britain. This translates into more opportunities for profit and investments for transnational criminal networks—and will be a nightmare for national law enforcement agencies.

Brexit and Counterfeiting: EU-UK Relations and Anti-counterfeiting Policies in the AFSJ

Benjamin Farrand

An aspect of intellectual property law and policy that acts as an intersection between trade policies and security policies concerns the counterfeiting of goods, in which illegitimate goods bearing logos or identifying marks identical to those sold in the EU by legitimate undertakings, such as Nike, Pfizer or Gucci, with the intention of free-riding on the quality and reputation of those brands. The EU has had a consistent anti-counterfeiting policy, underpinned by regularly updated Regulations concerning the prohibition of import and sale within the EU of counterfeit goods, the most recent of which is Regulation 608/2013 concerning customs enforcement of intellectual property rights.

As well as being considered an issue of economic importance due to economic harms attributable to losses to legitimate sellers from this free-riding, counterfeiting of products such as medicines, tobacco, foodstuffs and children's toys may result in serious physical harm, to the extent that anti-counterfeiting policies are as much part of the Area of Freedom, Security and Justice as they are of the Single Market and Customs Union. However, the EU has quickly found that implementing legislation is insufficient in combatting this form of criminal activity, which has historically been subject to criticisms of a lack of verifiable data (Organization for Economic Cooperation and Development 2008), as well as a lack of cohesive policies concerning the identification and seizure of goods upon their entry to the EU and of trends in terms of transit routes, countries of origin and final intended destinations within the EU (Farrand 2018). For this reason, recent initiatives in this field have focused on developing best practices, and facilitating information sharing between national customs and police authorities, in addition to working closely with the private sector in order to gather empirical data and provide for a knowledge-based approach to anti-counterfeiting activities. The most important development in this approach was the establishment of the European Observatory on Infringements of Intellectual Property Rights, which is now based in the EU Intellectual Property Office (EUIPO, an EU agency). While not being an agency traditionally associated with AFSJ, the Observatory has nevertheless contributed to it through its cooperation and coordination activities. It has produced significant amounts of data identifying trends and routes for counterfeit goods, and works closely with Europol to coordinate anti-counterfeiting initiatives (Europol and European Union Intellectual Property Office 2017), and regularly brings private sector right-holders and national authorities together to develop best practices and provide training for law enforcement, judiciaries and customs officials. This work has resulted in the development of several tools for national authorities and stakeholders, including the Enforcement Database, ACIST (the Anti-Counterfeiting Intelligence Support Tool, which provides information on the counterfeited and pirated goods detained at all EU Member States' borders) and ACRIS (the Anti-Counterfeiting Rapid Intelligence System which allows EU-based companies affected by IP infringements in countries outside the EU to gather information on these cases by local authorities).

The first, and most obvious impact of the UK's withdrawal from the EU is a likely loss of access to these agencies. While some form of agreement with Europol similar to that concluded with Norway may be possible, the House of Lords European Select Committee made clear, however, that this process is highly technical and that negotiations are lengthy, 'being measured in years, not months' (House of Lords 2016: 17). Furthermore, and unlike Europol, under Regulation 2017/1001 on the European Union trade mark (which establishes the EUIPO), there is no provision made for non-EU states for obtaining EUIPO membership. It is worth noting at this juncture that despite cooperation in other areas, the EEA states and Switzerland are not party to the EU trade mark or the EUIPO, and by extension the Observatory. UK customs officials may therefore lose the ability to participate in the Observatory's meetings on customs enforcement and anti-counterfeiting, and UK authorities are likely to lose access to the information repositories contained in the Enforcement Database, ACIST and ACRIS. As a result, a valuable source of information, expertise and identification of best practices will be lost.

The second impact will be on relations of trust and confidence between EU and UK authorities. The UK is already regarded in some areas as being a weak link in the Customs Union, based on the EU's Anti-Fraud Office (OLAF) concluding as a result of Operation Octopus that the UK was the most significant hub for fraudulent traffic involving the avoidance of customs duties and VAT, resulting in losses to the EU of more than €3.2 billion in the period 2013–2016 (OLAF 2017: 19). Poor existing customs enforcement, combined with concerns expressed in the House of Commons Northern Ireland Committee over the ability of UK officials to monitor goods moving between Northern Ireland and the Republic of Ireland (House of Commons 2018), combined with media reports that the UK is ill-equipped to manage its customs affairs at major ports such as Dover (Blitz 2017) gives rise to concerns that the UK will be a potentially attractive transit point for sellers of counterfeit goods. If the UK is unable to prevent the import of counterfeit goods into the country, which could then be transported into the EU through Northern Ireland, the UK will become a potential security threat for the EU. In order to avoid such a scenario, the EU may mandate significant requirements upon the UK in order to prevent it becoming a transit point for goods destined for the EU coming from countries such as China and India, imposing obligations on it under its Action Plan for Intellectual Property Rights Enforcement in Third Countries (for more on these policies see European Commission 2018b).

In conclusion, in the field of anti-counterfeiting policies, as a result of the UK leaving the EU, two distinct but related impacts will be felt: the first, a loss of expertise, information and best practices limiting the capacity of national authorities to effectively counter the importation of counterfeit goods into the UK; and the second, a loss of trust in the UK's capability, capacity and competence to act to combat counterfeiting, resulting in the EU perceiving it as a potential transit route for illicit goods, rather than a partner in anti-counterfeiting actions.

BREXIT, CYBERCRIME AND CYBER SECURITY: FROM 'BLOCK OPT-OUT' TO 'CREATIVE OPT-INS' IN THE AFSJ AND THE INTERNAL MARKET?

Maria Grazia Porcedda[5]

In order to tackle common cybercrime and cyber security challenges, EU member states recently agreed on a suite of legal instruments that engender several forms of cooperation (European Commission and High Representative of the European Union for Foreign Affairs and Security Policy 2013). Brexit begs the question as to how new arrangements are going to affect the UK's ability to fight against cybercrime and achieve cyber security, and therefore whether continued operational cooperation is compelling.

Given the UK's advanced cyber capabilities (Bada et al. 2016),[6] Brexit may seem to come at greater expense to the remaining Member States than the UK. The EU-27 may find continued operational cooperation with the UK on cyber security matters extremely valuable (MacAskill and Boffey 2018), and therefore open to negotiation. The latest White Paper published by the Department for Exiting the Union (2018) highlights the desire for continued cooperation in cyber security and the fight against cybercrime. Yet, the National Cyber Security Strategy (HM Government 2016) sees the EU as a multilateral organization upon which the UK can exercise influence to achieve common goals, rather than a vital partner with whom to develop common strategies.

The devil, as usual, is in the details. EU law on cyber security and related mechanisms of cooperation concern both the AFSJ and the Internal Market, which are functionally interconnected in cyber security. As a result, different forms of Brexit would have different impact on the achievement of cyber security. After illustrating the functional interconnection between the AFSJ and the Internal Market, this contribution appraises how different forms of Brexit would affect the response to cybercrime and the broader achievement of cybersecurity.

---

[5] All views expressed in this piece remain mine and do not reflect in any way the views of the EPSRC. I wish to express my gratitude to Helena Farrand-Carrapico and Martyn Egan for the insightful comments that helped improving this text.

[6] The 1990 Computer Misuse Act was passed long before the Budapest Convention. For a comparative legal historical perspective on cybercrime, see https://www.coe.int/sv/web/octopus/countries (accessed 22 June 2018).

The Functional Interconnection Between the AFSJ and the Internal Market

The common fight against cybercrime draws immediately to mind instruments with a legal basis in the AFSJ (2010) opted-into by the UK. First, Directive 2013/40/EU on attacks against information systems, which lays down substantive provisions on computer-related crimes, giving teeth to the Budapest Convention on Cybercrime (2001).[7] Thanks to the common rules agreed upon, Member States can confiscate and recover the illegal assets yielded by cybercrime throughout the EU by means of the Proceeds of Crime Directive 2014/42/EU, as well as issue a European Arrest Warrant (Council Framework Decision 2002/584/JHA) to apprehend wanted cybercriminals on the run. The European Investigation Order (Directive 2014/41/EU) obliges EU member states to assist each other in collecting evidence within set time limits, which is crucial in investigations of computer-related crime. The criminal justice response to cybercrime across EU member states is strengthened by the European Cybercrime Centre (EC3) within Europol (Regulation 2016/794/EU), as well as Eurojust (Wall 2016).[8]

The AFJS-based rules obviously act as a deterrent to crime, in the form of criminal convictions and possible custodial sentences, but are triggered only when preventative measures rooted in the Internal Market fail. Those measures address Network and Information Security (NIS), a policy sub-area that aims to create positive and negative incentives for organizations to maintain their networks and information systems secure, thus supporting the prevention of cybercrime. They include technical and organizational security measures, rules on liability and accountability, the burden of proof and uptake of insurance, rules to minimize the impact of security incidents and avoid harming individuals who can be identified on the basis of data.

Data and security breaches are a case in point: they are criminalized across the EU—as illegal access and data interference—pursuant to the Directive on attacks against information systems (with varying degrees of harmonization [European Commission 2017b]),[9] but rules trying to

---

[7] To which it is bound by means of clear connection clauses (Porcedda and Wall 2018). On connection clauses, see Cremona (2016).

[8] Wall (2016) also adds issues of common research under EU funding.

[9] In the UK, for instance, the definition of 'computer misuse' does not include the notion of data.

pre-empt breaches are based on the Internal Market (Porcedda 2018). Preventative efforts are pursued by sectorial (vertical) instruments, such as the e-Privacy Directive (2002/58/EC) and the Framework Directive (2002/21/EC) to be replaced by the European Electronic Communications Code (European Commission 2016) which address the security of Telecommunications infrastructure and confidentiality of communications thereof; the Electronic Identification and Assurance Services Regulation (Regulation 2014/910/EU, hereafter eIDAS Regulation), which develops a secure interoperable system of e-government and assurance services; and the Payment Services Directive 2 (2015/2366/EU), which contains measures for the security of financial transactions. Other measures are found in broader-scoped (horizontal) instruments, such as the General Data Protection Regulation (Regulation 2016/679/EU, hereafter GDPR), which has a strong focus on information security and risk assessment/management as a way of protecting personal data and information therein, and the (partly horizontal) Network and Information Security Directive (2016/1148/EU), which aims to secure essential services and information society services across the EU (Porcedda 2018). Coordination of NIS-related multinational efforts is (mostly) overseen by the European Network and Information Security Agency, whose remit is currently being extended (European Commission 2017b).

The importance of preventative legislation is highlighted by the UK National Cyber Security Strategy. Apart from the GDPR, which is hoped to function as a lever "to drive up standards of cyber security and protect citizens" (HM Government 2016), the Strategy plans for measures to 'defend' cyberspace akin to those pursued under EU law, without however mentioning them explicitly. These include securing e-government, as laid down by the eIDAS Regulation, cooperating with industry and protecting critical national infrastructure as currently ruled by the NIS Directive. The document also refers to the standardization and the collection of e-evidence; similar initiatives were planned at EU level before the issuing of the national Strategy (European Commission 2015) and are currently being translated into legal instruments (European Commission 2018a).

In sum, instruments on cybercrime (based in the AFSJ) and on NIS (based in the Internal Market) need to be seen as complementary, because the AFSJ instruments address the gaps in laws pursuing NIS, and vice versa. To understand what is at stake with Brexit, it is therefore important to assess the interplay between these functional interconnections and the scenarios of 'soft' and 'hard' Brexit, and other solutions that may be pursued as part of the Agreement on the Future Relationship.

The Functional Interconnection, 'Soft' and 'Hard' Brexit

The two classic scenarios of so-called 'soft' and 'hard' Brexit would impact continued cooperation on the fight against cybercrime differently. Soft brexiting alludes to leaving the EU, but maintaining access to either the Internal Market, the customs union, or both, thus remaining under the jurisdiction of the Court of Justice of the European Union (hereafter CJEU). Access to the Internal Market may be achieved by re-joining the 1960 EFTA Convention and either signing the 1994 European Economic Area Agreement, or signing ad hoc access agreements to selected areas of the Internal Market, similarly to the approach of Switzerland. Membership of the customs union would place the UK in a situation akin to that of Turkey. 'Hard' brexiting alludes to giving up EU membership *tout court*, that is giving up existing cooperation taking place under the auspices of the Treaties (without a withdrawal agreement and subsequent deal on the future relationship).

Should the UK opt for a 'soft', Internal Market-based Brexit, it would implement NIS-related instruments that are part of the EEA agreement,[10] with several advantages. One advantage consists in the (sought after) opportunity (Department for Exiting the Union 2018) for continued participation in the national regulatory authorities and bodies set up through NIS-related legal instruments, the networks they form, and the exchange of information they have led to. Another advantage is legal approximation, which brings about greater legal certainty for organizations and individuals, and enables Member States to act like a block and impose on multinational tech behemoths (and industrial complexes) the cutting-edge measures necessary to prevent cyber threats. A 'soft' Brexit without access to the Internal Market would not automatically bring about the advantages just illustrated. *A fortiori*, it is questionable whether it would be possible at all to impose ambitious preventative measures mentioned in the 2016 Cyber Security Strategy in a hard Brexit scenario.

---

[10] See http://www.efta.int/eea-lex.

Clearly, a hard Brexit would entail leaving the Internal Market (and customs union) altogether. Some scholars rightly note that, even if the UK chose a hard Brexit, it would enjoy a high level of harmonization because all Internal Market legislation currently under negotiation within the EU institutions is likely to be adopted before the final cut-off date. This could be conducive, for instance, to the UK swiftly obtaining a desired adequacy decision for personal data flows with the EU (Department for Exiting the Union 2018). However, regulatory divergence will eventually loom large, unless the UK makes the effort to maintain regulatory alignment.

Whether soft or hard, brexiting will preclude the UK from opting-in to impending instruments adopted in the AFSJ after 29 March 2019 (European Commission 2018c). This includes the e-evidence legislation (European Commission 2018c), which is expected to address an important part of the fight against cybercrime and possibly give further teeth to the Budapest Convention on Cybercrime, and which the UK has currently not opted into. Moreover, it will raise complex legal questions as to how to retain cooperation currently structured by AFSJ-related instruments (European Commission 2018c, EU and UK 2018), and, as Wall (2016) has noted, the intelligence this produces. Indeed, the AFSJ was designed for the perusal of Member States only; continued access to the EU databases set up within the AFSJ would expose the UK to judicial review by the Court of Justice of the European Union (European Parliament 2018: point 28); this would challenge one of Brexit's main pillars, namely abandoning the jurisdiction of the CJEU. Cooperation within Europol and Eurojust could be maintained, but only under the auspices of an international partnership (European Parliament 2018).

For those who believe that some form of compromise may be possible, the European Economic Area does not offer a viable model. Ongoing attempts to devise ad hoc security cooperation with EEA partners by means of international cooperation have proven cumbersome and inconclusive thus far (see Chapter 5, this volume). Therefore, allowing the UK to 'opt back in to' instruments of the AFSJ after Brexit will require legal creativity as well as political willingness on both sides. Such willingness was manifested in early 2018 (May 2018) but later faltered (MacAskill and Boffey 2018).

As said, a no-deal, hard Brexit would completely sever the UK from pending and future initiatives addressing NIS, which are fundamental for the successful prevention of cybercrime—and with it the pursuit of cybersecurity—across both sides of the Channel.

Legal Creativity: The 'Third Way' of Association Agreements?

The European Parliament-backed 'third way', whereby the UK could sign an association agreement with the EU (European Parliament 2018), may offer the opportunity to exercise legal creativity (within the limits set in point 4 of the Resolution). The European Parliament's resolution refers to negotiating ad hoc thematic agreements, including in the areas of internal security and security cooperation. The resolution touches briefly but explicitly on cooperation in cyber security (points 24 and 36). The idea of signing ad hoc association agreements was adopted in the UK Government's White paper (Department for Exiting the Union 2018), which however rejects the full jurisdiction of the CJEU (a very challenging caveat from the perspective of EU law, and a likely dealbreaker).

Both the Resolution and the White paper mention continued access to databases established within the AFSJ, as well as continued cooperation in the development of Galileo, a satellite navigation system which, once fully operational, will supposedly rival the US-backed GPS, and which has clear relevance for cyber security (and signals intelligence). As an Internal Market-based project with clear relevance for the AFSJ,[11] Galileo constitutes a significant example of the functional interplay between different areas of EU law, areas which cannot be addressed separately.

The level of involvement of the UK in Galileo has been at the heart of disagreements over the future of cooperation in security (much like continued access to AFSJ databases) (MacAskill and Boffey 2018). Resolution of such single issues could act as an important litmus test of the political willingness to explore legally creative solutions to continue cooperating in the fight against cybercrime. However, from the perspective of jointly achieving cyber security, any Brexit solution can only be inferior to the legal and operational status quo.

---

[11] For documents concerning Galileo, see http://ec.europa.eu/growth/sectors/space/galileo/documents_en.

BREXIT AND CYBERSPACE: IMPLICATIONS FOR CYBERSECURITY

Anita Lavorgna

Criminal opportunities in cyberspace are top concerns for both the British public and policymakers, with cybercrime being included in the national security agenda because of its seriousness and sophistication (Lavorgna and Sergi 2016). Traditionally, the UK has been a key actor in cybersecurity at the EU level and has driven many of its developments (Wall 2016), not only through its contribution to the EU budget, but also and foremost providing intelligence and expertise. While the departure of the UK from the EU is very likely to entail a series of negative effects in terms of cybersecurity from both sides, it is probable that the UK will suffer the most in the unfortunate outcome of a more isolated position towards its neighbouring countries.

First, Brexit is likely to have a negative impact on police cooperation and access to data for law enforcement purposes. Over the years, institutionalised forms of cross-border exchange of information as well as of law enforcement and judicial cooperation (ENISA, Europol and Eurojust *in primis*) have gained a central role in preventing and countering cybercrimes at the EU level and beyond, becoming an essential instrument for internal security. If a trend can be identified, it is the formation of increasingly close networks of information and intelligence sharing across the EU and with EU Member States (Hillebrand 2017). Emblematic in this regard is the creation of the European Cybercrime Centre (EC3) at Europol, launched in January 2013 to strengthen the law enforcement response to cybercrime in the EU, and specifically to contribute to faster reactions in the event of online crimes. EC3 aims to support Member States and the European Union's institutions in building operational and analytical capacity for investigations and cooperation with international partners in particularly serious areas of cybercrime, such as large-scale online frauds, online child sexual exploitation, and crimes affecting critical infrastructures and information systems in the EU. Despite the fact that, because of its 'opt-out' privileges, the UK is already an odd player in the area of UK-EU cooperation (Carrera et al. 2016) and that both the UK and the EU are likely to wish to maintain collaboration in such a crucial internal security area, the UK will lose influence and access to full transnational cooperation following its departure from the EU. Consequently, EU-UK cooperation will become more fragile and less accountable (Hillebrand 2017). The UK, for instance, could join

Europol as a non-EU law enforcement partner to remain somehow part of it, but this move will not compensate for Britain's exclusion from the full agency's membership.

Second, Brexit is likely to negatively affect regulatory harmonisation. The lack of such harmonisation may have a detrimental effect for many forms of cybercrimes, with offenders enjoying easier ways to exploit legislative loopholes and asymmetries: it is a well-researched fact that gaps in substantive and procedural law, which depend on different national legal traditions, create a fertile ground for offenders that can simply move across international borders to make investigation and prosecution extremely difficult, a challenge that is deepened and broadened by the inherently borderless nature of cyberspace. In any case, for many cyber-related issues and also as regards future regulatory developments that will most probably occur and expand already in the near future (think, for instance, of regulations concerning cryptocurrencies, smart goods, and artificial intelligence), harmonisation may simply remain the only option for the UK. Considering how deeply interwoven the UK and EU economies already are, and the fact that the UK may wish to somehow maintain access to the internal market, the UK may have to adopt EU (or EU-like) regulations in many cases. In this hypothetical future, however, the UK will have lost the possibility to shape and influence regulatory frameworks. Paradoxically, the UK may have to accept more EU law than it currently does as a EU Member State in order to fully comply with the EU *acquis* (including the protection of fundamental rights), and also in cases where it is now not bound as a result of its 'opt-outs' privileges (Mitsilegas 2017).

Third, Brexit is likely to have a significantly negative impact on the ability of the UK to remain an attractive hub for tech talents and cybersecurity companies, which will have an impact on the UK's cyber-abilities and, consequently, the level of protection available (Sharf 2016). Cyber-skills shortage and mobility is a major problem in cybersecurity, and policies aimed at discouraging immigration, as well as the increased perception of the UK as a less open and welcoming country, could have adverse consequences in recruiting skilled cyber-security professionals. The cybersecurity industry is already lamenting the shortage of well-prepared and talented professionals; the UK has been traditionally a destination of choice for young talents, but a weaker pound, political uncertainty and lack of easy access to the European (job) market may move preferences towards other options in the continent.

To summarise, the need to renegotiate many data and intelligence sharing procedures in a context where information exchange between agencies is so important will remain a pivotal aspect in any possible post-Brexit scenario. The loss of international influence and soft power in the area of cybersecurity is likely to entail serious negative effects in the prevention of cyber-attacks, their investigation and prosecution, and cyber resilience on different levels. Whether the UK is heading towards hard or soft Brexit, cybersecurity will remain an increasingly complex and high stakes problem for which cooperation between States will always be essential.

References

Asthana, A., D. Boffey, H. Stewart, and P. Walker. 2017. Don't Blackmail Us Over Security, EU Warns May. *The Guardian*, 30 March. Available from https://www.theguardian.com/politics/2017/mar/29/brexit-eu-condemns-mays-blackmail-over-security-cooperation. Last accessed 27 May 2018.

Bada, M., I. Arreguín-Toft, I. Brown, P. Cornish, S. Creese, W. Dutton, M. Goldsmith, E. Ignatuschtschenko, L. Pace, L. Pijnenburg Muller, T. Roberts, S. Von Solms, and D. Upton. 2016. *Cyber Security Capacity Review of the United Kingdom*. Oxford: Global Cyber Security Capacity Centre, University of Oxford.

BBC. 2016. *Staying in EU 'Exposes UK to Terror Risk', Says Iain Duncan Smith*, 21 February. Available from: http://www.bbc.co.uk/news/uk-politics-eu-referendum-35624409. Last accessed 30 April 2018.

Blitz, J. 2017. Why Dover Is Braced for Customs Gridlock After Brexit. *Financial Times*, 18 October. Available from: https://www.ft.com/content/7ff7c97c-b33c-11e7-a398-73d59db9e399. Last accessed 19 May 2018.

Carr, S., A. Gallop, E. Piasecki, G. Tully, and T.J. Wilson. (forthcoming). Clarifying the "Reliability" Continuum and Testing Its Limits: Biometric (Fingerprint and DNA) Expert Evidence. In *Forensic Science Evidence and Expert Witness Testimony: Reliability Through Reform?* ed. R. Roberts and M. Stockdale. Cheltenham: Edward Elgar.

Carrapico, H., and F. Trauner. 2013. Europol and Its Impact on EU Policy-Making on Organised Crime. *Perspectives on European Politics and Society* 14 (3): 357–371.

Carrapico, H., C. Berthélemy, and A. Niehuss. 2017. Better Safe Than Sorry? Brexit and Internal Security. *Report for the UK in a Changing Europe Funding Initative*. Birmingham: Aston University.

Carrera, S., E. Guild, and N. Chun Luk. 2016. What Does Brexit Mean for the EU's Area of Freedom, Security and Justice? *CEPS Commentary*. Available from: https://www.ceps.eu/system/files/What%20does%20BREXIT%20mean%20for%20the%20EU.pdf. Last accessed 28 March 2018.

Cremona, M. 2016. A Triple Braid: Interactions Between International Law, EU Law and Private Law. In *Private Law in the External Relation of the EU*, ed. M. Cremona and H.-W. Micklitz, 33–55. Oxford: Oxford University Press.

Daily Mail. 2017. Prime Minister Theresa May: How I Will Make Brexit a Success for Everyone, 6 September 2017. Available from: http://www.dailymail.co.uk/news/article-4856216/How-ll-make-Brexit-success-EVERYONE.html. Last accessed 28 March 2018.

Davies, R., and J. Burke. 2017. Labout Demands Review into City of London Role in Money Laundering. *The Guardian*, 19 October. Available from: https://www.theguardian.com/business/2017/oct/19/labour-demands-review-uk-banking-role-money-laundering-gupta-south-africa. Last accessed 15 May 2018.

Dearden, L. 2017. London Terror Attack Suspect Was British-Born and Previously Investigated by MI5 Over Extremism, May Confirms. *Independent*, 23 March. Available from: https://www.independent.co.uk/news/uk/home-news/london-terror-attack-suspect-identity-british-born-citizen-mi5-investigate-extremism-islamist-a7645331.html. Last accessed 15 May 2018.

Department for Exiting the Union. 2018. *The Future Relationship Between the United Kingdom and the European Union*. Available from: https://www.gov.uk/government/publications/the-future-relationship-between-the-united-kingdom-and-the-european-union. Last accessed 12 July 2018.

European Commission. 2015. *A Digital Single Market Strategy for Europe*. COM (2015) 192 final. Brussels.

European Commission. 2016. *Proposal for a Directive Establishing the European Electronic Communications Code*, (Communication) COM (2016) 590 final, 2016/0288 (COD).

European Commission. 2017a. *Position Paper Transmitted to EU27 on the Use of Data and Protection of Information Obtained or Processed Before the Withdrawal Date*, TF50 (2017) 14. Available from: https://ec.europa.eu/commission/sites/beta-political/files/use-data-protection-information_en.pdf. Last accessed 18 December 2017.

European Commission. 2017b. *Proposal for a Regulation of the European Parliament and of the Council on ENISA, the "EU Cybersecurity Agency", and Repealing Regulation (EU) 526/2013, and on Information and Communication Technology Cybersecurity Certification ("Cybersecurity Act")*, COM (2017) 495 final.

European Commission. 2018a. *Proposal for a Regulation on European Production and Preservation Orders for Electronic Evidence in Criminal Matters*, COM (2018) 225 final 2018/0108 (COD).

European Commission. 2018b. *Report on the Protection and Enforcement of Intellectual Property Rights in Third Countries*, SWD (2018) 47 final.

European Commission. 2018c. *Draft Agreement on the Withdrawal of the United Kingdom of Great Britain and Northern Ireland from the European Union and the European Atomic Energy Community, as Agreed at Negotiators' Level on 14 November 2018*, TF50 (2018) 55. Available from: https://ec.europa.eu/commission/sites/beta-political/files/draft_withdrawal_agreement_0.pdf. 14 November 2018.

European Commission and High Representative of the European Union for Foreign Affairs and Security Policy. 2013. *Cyber Security Strategy: An Open, Safe and Secure Cyberspace*, (Joint Communication) JOIN (2013) 01 final.

European Parliament. 2017. The European Union's Policies on Counter-Terrorism Relevance, Coherence and Effectiveness. *LIBE Committee*. Available from: http://www.europarl.europa.eu/RegData/etudes/STUD/2017/583124/IPOL_STU(2017)583124_EN.pdf. Last accessed 18 December 2017.

European Parliament. 2018. *European Parliament Resolution of 14 March 2018 on the Framework of the Future EU-UK Relationship*, 2018/2573.

Europol and European Union Intellectual Property Office. 2017. *2017 Situation Report on Counterfeiting in the European Union*.

European Union and United Kingdom. 2018. *Joint Report from the Negotiators of the European Union and the United Kingdom Government on the State of Play of the Negotiations Under Article 50 TEU on the Withdrawal of the United Kingdom of Great Britain and Northern Ireland from the European Union and the European Atomic Energy Community*, TF50 (2018) 54, 14 November 2018.

Falvey, D. 2017. 'Borders at Risk' After 'Inadequate' Home Office Planning Could Leave 'Brexit in Jeopardy'. *Express*, 16 November. Available from: https://www.express.co.uk/news/uk/880172/Brexit-news-eu-illegal-immigration-home-office-borders-uk-parliament-select-committee. Last accessed 15 May 2018.

Farrand, B. 2018. Combatting Physical Threats Posed via Digital Means: The European Commission's Developing Approach to the Sale of Counterfeit Goods on the Internet. *European Politics and Society* 19 (3): 338–354.

Gelder, S. 2017. Tommy Adams Jailed: Brother from Notorious Islington Crime Family Gets Seven Years for Money Laundering. *Islington Gazette*, 2 November. Available from: http://www.islingtongazette.co.uk/news/crime-court/tommy-adams-jailed-brother-from-notorious-islington-crime-family-gets-seven-years-for-money-laundering-1-5263470. Last accessed 15 May 2018.

Hillebrand, C. 2017. With or Without You: The UK and Information and Intelligence Sharing in the EU. *Journal of Intelligence History* 16 (2): 91–94.

HM Government. 2016. *National Cyber Security Strategy 2016–2021*. Available at: https://assets.publishing.service.gov.uk/government/uploads/system/uploads/attachment_data/file/567242/national_cyber_security_strategy_2016.pdf.

HM Government. 2017a. *Security, Law Enforcement and Criminal Justice: A Future Partnership*. Available from: https://www.gov.uk/government/uploads/system/uploads/attachment_data/file/645416/Security__law_enforcement_and_criminal_justice_-_a_future_partnership_paper.PDF. Last accessed 22 March 2018.

HM Government. 2017b. *The United Kingdom's Exit from and New Partnership with the European Union*. Available from: https://www.gov.uk/government/uploads/system/uploads/attachment_data/file/589189/The_United_Kingdoms_exit_from_and_partnership_with_the_EU_Print.pdf. Last accessed 18 December 2017.

House of Commons. 2011. The Forensic Science Service. *Science and Technology Committee*, 2nd Report of Session 2010–12, HC 855.

House of Commons. 2013. Forensic Science. *Science and Technology Committee*, 2nd Report of Session 2013–14, HC 610.

House of Commons. 2017a. EU-Canada Agreement on Passenger Name Record Data. *European Scrutiny Committee*. Available from: https://publications.parliament.uk/pa/cm201719/cmselect/cmeuleg/301-i/30131.htm. Last accessed 30 April 2018.

House of Commons. 2017b. Implications of Brexit for the Justice System. *Justice Committee*, 9th Report of Session 2016–17, HC 750.

House of Commons. 2018. The Land Border Between Northern Ireland and Ireland. *Northern Ireland Affairs Committee*. Available from: https://publications.parliament.uk/pa/cm201719/cmselect/cmniaf/329/329.pdf. Last accessed 14 May 2018.

House of Lords. 2016. Brexit: Future UK-EU Security and Police Cooperation. *European Union Committee*, 7th Report of Session 2016–2017.

House of Lords. 2017. Brexit: The EU Data Protection Package. *European Union Committee*. Available from: https://publications.parliament.uk/pa/ld201719/ldselect/ldeucom/7/7.pdf. Last accessed 18 December 2017.

House of Lords. 2018. Brexit: Common Security and Defence Policy. *European Union Committee*, 16th Report of Session 2017–19. Available from: https://publications.parliament.uk/pa/ld201719/ldselect/ldeucom/132/132.pdf. Last accessed 27 May 2018.

Huysmans, J. 2006. *The Politics of Insecurity: Fear, Migration and Asylum in the EU*. London and New York: Routledge.

Inkster, N. 2016. Brexit, Intelligence, and Terrorism. *Survival* 58 (3): 23–30.

International Centre for Counter-Terrorism. 2016. *The Foreign Fighters Phenomenon in the European Union Profiles, Threats & Policies*. Available from: https://www.icct.nl/wp-content/uploads/2016/03/ICCT-Report_Foreign-Fighters-Phenomenon-in-the-EU_1-April-2016_including-AnnexesLinks.pdf. Last accessed 18 December 2017.

International Centre for Counter-Terrorism. 2018. *The Homecoming of Foreign Fighters in the Netherlands, Germany and Belgium: Policies and Challenges.* Available from: https://icct.nl/publication/the-homecoming-of-foreign-fighters-in-the-netherlands-germany-and-belgium-policies-and-challenges/. Last accessed 30 April 2018.

Kjeldsen, T., and W. Nueteboom. 2015. *20 Years of Forensic Cooperation in Europe: The History of ENFSI 1995–2015.* The Hague: ENFSI.

Lavorgna, A., and A. Sergi. 2016. Serious, Therefore Organised? A Critique of the Emerging "Cyber-Organised Crime" Rhetoric in the United Kingdom. *International Journal of Cyber Criminology* 10 (2): 170–187.

London Loves Business (LLB). 2017. *Money Launderers Paid £1.8m into London Banks in Two Weeks.* Available from: http://www.londonlovesbusiness.com/business-news/money-launderers-paid-18m-into-london-banks-in-two-weeks/18879.article. Last accessed 15 May 2018.

MacAskill, E., and D. Boffey. 2018. Brexit Row: GCHQ Chief Stresses UK's Role in Foiling European Terror Plots. *The Guardian.* Available from: https://www.theguardian.com/politics/2018/jun/19/barnier-uk-will-lose-access-to-eu-security-databases-after-brexit. Last accessed 19 June 2018.

May, T. 2018. *PM Speech at Munich Security Conference: 17 February 2018.* Available from: https://www.gov.uk/government/speeches/pm-speech-at-munich-security-conference-17-february-2018. Last accessed 24 March 2018.

McDonald, M. 2008. Securitization and the Construction of Security. *European Journal of International Relations* 14 (4): 563–587.

Mitsilegas, V. 2017. The United Kingdom in Europe's Area of Criminal Justice. The Triple Paradox of Brexit. *Criminology in Europe* 16 (2): 9–10.

National Crime Agency. 2017. *National Strategic Assessment of Serious and Organised Crime.* Available from: http://www.nationalcrimeagency.gov.uk/publications/807-national-strategic-assessment-of-serious-and-organised-crime-2017/file. Last accessed 15 May 2018.

Neil, R. 2017. HC Deb, 18 January 2017, vol. 619, cols. 956–957.

OLAF. 2017. *The OLAF Report 2016.* Available from: https://ec.europa.eu/anti-fraud/sites/antifraud/files/olaf_report_2016_en.pdf. Last accessed 15 May 2018.

Organization for Economic Cooperation and Development. 2006. *The Economic Impact of Counterfeiting and Piracy.* OECD.

Organization for Economic Cooperation and Development. 2008. *The Economic Impact of Counterfeiting and Piracy.* Available from: http://apps.who.int/medicinedocs/documents/s19845en/s19845en.pdf. Last accessed on 24 April 2018.

Payne, A. 2017. Theresa May's 'Blackmail' Security Threat to the EU Had to Be 'Toned Down'. *Business Insider,* 20 April. Available from: http://nordic.

businessinsider.com/mays-article-50-brexit-letter-to-eu-had-to-be-toned-down-2017-4/. Last accessed 27 May 2018.

Porcedda, M.G. 2018. Patching the Patchwork: Appraising the EU Regulatory Framework on Cyber Security Breaches. *Computer Law and Security Review* 34 (5): 1077–1098.

Porcedda, M.G., and D.S. Wall. 2018. Data Science, Data Crime and the Law. In *Research Handbook on Data Science & Law*, ed. V. Mak, E. Tjong Tjin Tai, and A. Berlee. London: Edward Elgar.

Ripoll Servent, A., and A. MacKenzie. 2012. The European Parliament as a 'Norm Taker'? EU-US Relations After the SWIFT Agreement. *European Foreign Affairs Review* 17 (2/1): 71–86.

Ripoll Servent, A., and A. MacKenzie. 2017. Eroding Germany's Commitment to Data Protection: Policy Entrepreneurs and Coalition Politics in EU Passenger Name Records. *German Politics* 26 (3): 398–413.

Robert, A. 2016. Big Data Revolutionises Europe's Fight Against Terrorism. *EurActiv.com*, 23 June. Available from: https://www.euractiv.com/section/digital/news/big-data-revolutionises-europes-fight-against-terrorism/. Last accessed 28 March 2018.

Sandler, T. 2006. Recognizing the Limits to Cooperation Behind National Borders: Financing the Control of Transnational Terrorism. In *The New Public Finance: Responding to Global Challenges*, ed. I. Kaul and P. Conceiçao. New York: Oxford University Press.

Sergi, A. 2017. *From Mafia to Organised Crime: A Comparative Analysis of Policing Models*. Cham, Switzerland: Palgrave Macmillan.

Sergi, A. 2018. What's Really Going on in London's Organised Crime Scene: According to a Criminologist. *Independent*, 24 January. Available from: https://www.independent.co.uk/news/uk/crime/mcmafia-london-gangs-crime-accuracy-what-is-it-like-real-life-kray-twins-a8173726.html. Last accessed 15 May 2018.

Sharf, E. 2016. Information Exchanges. Regulatory Changes to the Cyber-Security Industry After Brexit: Making Security Awareness Training Work. *Computer Fraud & Security* 7: 9–12.

Sidharth, K. 2011. Supply and Demand: Human Trafficking in the Global Economy. *Harvard International Review* 33 (2): 66–71.

Slack, J., and T. Cohen. 2016. Quitting EU Would Make Britain Safer, Says Former MI6 Chief: Sir Richard Dearlove Suggests Brexit Would Make It Easier to Deport Terrorists and Control Our Borders. *The Daily Mail*, 23 March. Available from: http://www.dailymail.co.uk/news/article-3506991/UK-safer-Europe-says-former-MI6-chief-Sir-Richard-Dearlove-suggests-Brexit-make-easier-deport-terrorists.html. Last accessed 27 May 2018.

Soleto Muñoz, H., and A. Fiodorova. 2014. DNA and Law Enforcement in the European Union: Tools and Human Rights Protection. *Utrecht Law Review* 10 (1): 149–162.

Talani, L.S. 2013. London: The Laundry of Choice? Money Laundering in the City of London. In *Dirty Cities: Towards a Political Economy of the Underground in Global Cities*, ed. L.S. Talani, A. Clarkson, and R.P. Pardo. Basingstoke, Hampshire and New York: Palgrave Macmillan.

Taverne, M.D., and A.P.A. Broeders. 2015. *The Light's at the End of the Funnel!: Evaluating the Effectiveness of the Transnational Exchange of DNA Profiles Between the Netherlands and Other Prüm Countries*. Zutphen: Paris Legal Publishers.

The Economist. 2018. Gangster's Paradise: Brexit Presents New Opportunities for Organised Crime, 24 January. Available from: https://www.economist.com/news/britain/21735569-crooks-stand-benefit-new-lines-business-smuggling-goods-and-people-brexit. Last accessed 15 May 2018.

The Telegraph. 2017. Exclusive: Brexit Should Have No Impact 'Whatsoever' on Links with Europol, Says Anti-slavery Commissioner. www.telegraph.co.uk, 28 August. Available from: https://www.telegraph.co.uk/news/2017/08/28/brexit-should-have-no-impact-whatsoever-links-europol-says-anti/. Last accessed 28 March 2018.

Treadwell, J. 2012. From the Car Boot to Booting It Up? eBay, Online Counterfeit Crime and the Transformation of the Criminal Marketplace. *Criminology and Criminal Justice* 12 (2): 175–191.

Treadwell, J., and T. Ayres. 2014. Talking Prada and Powder: Cocaine Use and Supply Among the Football Hooligan Firm. In *Football Hooliganism, Fan Behaviour and Crime*, ed. M. Hopkins and J. Treadwell. Basingstoke, Hampshire and New York: Palgrave Macmillan.

Wall, D.S. 2016. Policing Cybercrime in the EU: Shall I Stay or Shall I Go? *British Society of Criminology Newsletter* 78 (Summer).

Wilson, T. 2015. The Global Perspective. In *Annual Report of the Government Chief Scientific Adviser 2015: Forensic Science and Beyond: Authenticity, Provenance and Assurance: Evidence and Case Studies*, ed. M. Peplow. London: Government Office for Science.

Wilson, T.J. 2016. Criminal Justice and Global Public Goods: The Prüm Forensic Biometric Cooperation Model. *The Journal of Criminal Law* 80 (5): 303–326.

Wilson, T.J. 2018. The Implementation and Practical Application of the European Investigation Order in the United Kingdom: An Academic Perspective. In *Los avances del espacio de Libertad, Seguridad y Justicia de la UE en 2017: II Anuario de la Red Española de Derecho Penal Europeo (ReDPE)*, ed. Á. Gutiérrez Zarza. Madrid: Wolters Kluwer edit.

Winstock, A.R. 2015. *What Did We Learn from GDS2015? An Overview of Our Key Findings*, Global Drug Survey 2015. Available from: http://www.globaldrugsurvey.com/the-global-drug-survey-2015-findings/. Last accessed 5 May 2018.

CHAPTER 8

Sectoral Views on Migration and Border Cooperation

Abstract This chapter contains short expert views on migration, asylum and border cooperation. Roos shows how the end of freedom of movement in the UK could lead to EU migrants coming into the country illegally or slipping into semi-legality or illegality post-entry, and Wolff explores Brexit's impact on asylum seekers in the UK, arguing that an extensive and generous asylum and migration policy is crucial for the UK to remain a global player. Regarding border governance, Orsini compares current and possible future cooperation at the borders of Dover and Gibraltar; Gomez Arana calls for pragmatism and identity politics being taken into account to manage the border of Gibraltar in the future; and lastly, Irrera warns that Brexit could interrupt the peace process in Northern Ireland, to which the EU has contributed.

Keywords Brexit · Migration · Asylum · Border management · Human rights

Following the focus of Chapter 7 on police and judicial cooperation, the present chapter turns our attention to another important area of Justice and Home Affairs: migration, borders and asylum. In the first contribution, Roos draws on migration studies to show how terminating freedom of movement could lead to EU migrants coming to the UK illegally or slipping into semi-legality or illegality post-entry, making them more vulnerable to commit or become victims of crime. On this basis, he calls on

H. Carrapico et al., *Brexit and Internal Security*,
Palgrave Studies in European Union Politics,
https://doi.org/10.1007/978-3-030-04194-6_8

the UK to take these considerations into account when designing a new migration policy for EU migrants. Wolff continues to explore the impact of Brexit on individuals, in particular on asylum seekers in the UK. By highlighting issues around refugee protection, border controls and the UK's ability to return migrants, she argues that an extensive and generous asylum and migration policy is crucial if the UK is to remain a global player.

The remaining contributions focus specifically on the way Brexit could change border governance. Orsini's piece compares two of the main UK borders: Dover/Calais and Gibraltar. He argues that the bilateral and trilateral agreements governing border controls at the English Channel may change with the transforming relations between Britain and the EU, and that the unofficial cooperation between Gibraltarian and Spanish law enforcement at the land and maritime border between Spain and Gibraltar may decrease or even stop, leading to the consideration of a humanitarian crisis-like scenario for Gibraltar. Gomez Arana also focuses her contribution on Gibraltar, providing an overview of the territory's geopolitics and border politics between Spain and Britain. She calls for both pragmatism and identity politics to be taken into account in the future management of this border, as the outcome of the Brexit negotiations will constitute a significant example for other parts of Europe with regional tensions. Lastly, Irrera analyses how the EU has contributed to creating the conditions that allowed for a successful peace process in Northern Ireland to take place and warns that Brexit could interrupt this transformation, which could have very dangerous consequences.

MULTIPLE INSECURITIES: POTENTIAL IMPLICATIONS OF TERMINATING FREEDOM OF MOVEMENT IN THE UK

Christof Roos

The security implications which the termination of freedom of movement could bring about have not yet received much attention. This briefing is concerned with the potential insecurities emanating from the withdrawal agreement for EU citizens and British society. If not defined otherwise in future EU-UK trade relations, migrants with a EU passport will be subject to immigration control. The following sections identify likely security implications of these developments, foremost the issue of migrant illegality. Hypotheses derived from migration studies on the nexus between migrant illegality, insecurity and crime inform the respective conclusions.

On 8 December 2017, after months of deadlock, the EU and the UK managed to agree on commitments in order to secure the acquired rights of the 3.2 million EU citizens in the UK and the 1.2 million UK citizens in the EU. Those were considered "sufficient" by European Council President Tusk who agreed to the opening of the second phase of negotiations.

Given a withdrawal agreement will be signed and ratified by 29 March 2019, all EU citizens that have moved to the UK by this cut-off date will maintain their right to residency according to the conditions of the EU's citizenship directive (2004/38/EU). This cut-off date will be delayed by 21 months to 31 December 2020, after a transition period comes to an end. Equivalent to the directive, EU citizens that resided in the UK for five years at cut-off date will have the right to apply for permanent residency, those that arrived later and do not meet this threshold can apply for a temporary residence permit for later application to permanent residency. In fact, all EU citizens that lived in the UK at the time of the withdrawal will still enjoy the coverage of EU rights and the respective jurisdiction of the Court of Justice of the EU (CJEU) for another eight years (European Commission 2017: 6). The two-phased negotiation process leading to Brexit discussed these issues first in order to give citizens of the EU and the UK legal certainty on their respective status living abroad.

While the commitments provide for "[...] key guarantees ensuring many aspects of acquired rights" (Peers 2017), a few elements of the agreement motivated criticism from NGOs that represent mobile Europeans such as 'the3million' and 'British in Europe'. They expressed concern with regard to the possibility of an order to leave following an unsuccessful application for permanent or temporary residency with the British Home Office or the proposed time restrictions on CJEU litigation.[1] As the UK leaves the EU, free movement rights will cease to apply reciprocally to UK citizens, a right many Britons rely on, working across Europe. The concerns are indeed legitimate for people that, at withdrawal date, will miss the full coverage and advantages of EU freedom

---

[1] https://www.the3million.org.uk/publications, Last accessed on 20 May 2018; https://britishineurope.org/category/media-coverage/, Last accessed on 20 May 2018.

of movement. Regarding the security implications for the UK, situations should be anticipated in which EU citizens are denied the right to an immigrant status due to incomplete paper work or a criminal record (Peers 2017). This implies loss of status and the execution of an order to leave by the Home Office. EU citizens that face this situation may slip into illegality rather than leave the country. This brings us to the second part of this contribution, the likely increase in illegal immigration and illegal stay of EU citizens post-Brexit.

Illegality and Insecurity

The Withdrawal Agreement covers the rights of people who have exercised their free movement rights at the cut-off date but remains silent on the conditions for those who have the intention to move in the future. Whether a migration agreement for future movers between the UK and the EU will be part of future negotiations is uncertain. After all, free movement was among the issues that many in British society, media, and politics meant to terminate by leaving the EU (Roos 2018). During the last four decades, distinct migration patterns evolved due to free movement that established transnational labour markets as well as cross-border networks of migrants including their families in the country of origin. Reflecting these patterns, the present UK government is well aware that "[…] free movement will end but migration between the UK and the EU will continue" (HM Government 2017). Therefore, the replacement of EU freedom of movement with a UK migration policy for Europeans begs certain questions regarding the likely consequences of such a fundamental shift in policy.

Potential of Increase in Persons with No or Semi-Legal Status

On the assumption that the UK maintains its liberal economy we can predict persistent demand for low- and high-skilled foreign labour in various sectors, such as care, hospitality, agriculture and education (Paul 2015). The government's announcement of a reintroduction of migration control with a focus on migrant skills (HM Government 2017) could restrict entry options, in particular for the low-skilled. Immigration restrictions, however, are no guarantee for the decrease of actual migration. As the pull for migrant labour of various skill levels is likely to persist, people may find informal ways to enter and stay

(Cornelius and Tsuda 2004). In consequence, illegal migration and stay could increase as a result of re-established migration control. Indicative of this relationship between policy restrictions and continued migratory movements is the research on the U.S. migration relations with Mexico. The outcome of heightened U.S. border enforcement and immigration restrictions was the transformation of circular flows of workers towards a pattern of settlement and family reunification in the US. Instead of reducing illegal immigration, increasing efforts on control enforcement effectively reduced return migration to Mexico and incentivized settlement (Massey et al. 2016). If we applied this observation to the UK, we could expect the restriction of formerly legal channels of migration for the low-skilled to have similar effects on promoting illegal immigration and stay. It is also expected that family reunification will become more onerous for Europeans residing in the UK after Brexit (Peers 2017). If entry conditions are difficult to meet, irregular family reunification may be the alternative choice. If people who try to enter as workers or family members are not easily granted a leave to remain, we can assume that some EU citizens will enter as tourists, overstay and eventually start working illegally.

In Europe, it is estimated that most illegal migrants arrived legally and overstayed their tourist visa (Finotelli 2007; Cvajner and Sciortino 2010). Along these lines, Ruhs and Anderson discovered that migrant status in the UK defies a straight categorisation of legal or illegal. In fact, whether migrants comply with migration law is flexible and can shift between legal, illegal and semi-legal status. For example, students from third-countries may exceed the hours they are legally allowed to work per week and thus enter semi-legal situations within their working relationship (Ruhs and Anderson 2006). With Brexit, the constraints of compliance with the respective immigration status will apply to migrant workers and students from the EU as well. From the perspective of migration research, it seems very likely that these new conditions will impact in terms of promoting illegal or semi-legal status.

Illegality, Vulnerability and Crime

Migrants who live in illegality usually try to keep a low profile, avoiding the attention of authorities. This attitude is due to a fear of disclosure and eventual deportation. While life in the shadows may be barely visible to the authorities, the individuals concerned are more vulnerable to commit or become victims of crime. Illegal migrants are susceptible to sexual and labour exploitation. For fear of being detected they do not seek protection from law enforcement. Having to cope with these circumstances, people without status are also more likely to be victims of drug and other abusive behavior (Alt 2003: 166–167). Interestingly, research from the Netherlands shows that "[…] the legal construction of illegality by the state and the measures being taken to combat illegality more effectively stimulate the involvement of specific groups of irregular immigrants into criminal activities" (Engbersen and Broeders 2011: 180). Next to the obvious offence of illegal residence, most of the crimes reported in the Netherlands were minor offences such as shoplifting, theft, and burglary. In fact, an increase in these 'subsistence crimes' could be measured during the implementation of a policy against illegality. Thus, the application of restrictive policies contributed to the exclusion from the formal labour market and the social system which fed into a rise in subsistence crimes (Engbersen and Broeders 2011: 179–180).

These insights into the dynamics of illegality, vulnerability and crime should be considered and anticipated in designing a new migration policy for the UK. The call for terminating freedom of movement can be taken up in a restrictive or permissive way. EU rights for entry and residence for all EU citizens may be revoked but this does not preclude a scheme for EU workers and students that grants access to the UK labour market with a low entry threshold. Restrictive access conditions will almost certainly increase the illegality and insecurity of EU migrants in the country. The side effects of such a policy were described and, for the sake of internal security of the country, should be avoided.

REVISING THE UK's ASYLUM AND GLOBAL MIGRATION POLICY AFTER BREXIT

Sarah Wolff

During the campaign for Brexit, immigration was one of the main battle horses of the 'Leave' campaign, which argued that Europe had brought too many migrants to the UK. The objective is to reduce net immigration to 100,000 individuals per year. So far, the Withdrawal Agreement negotiations mostly focused on EU citizens' rights in the UK and Britons' rights in Europe on the day Britain will leave the EU. However, little thought has been given to the impact of Brexit on irregular migrants and asylum-seekers.

Although the UK has negotiated an opt-out from EU immigration policy for many years, it is also a semi- 'engaged outsider' (Adam et al. 2016) when it comes to cooperation in the field of asylum. The UK has in fact partially adopted EU law with the first wave of EU directives on qualification, reception and procedure that it decided to opt in to in 2004. Although it has not opted in to the recast wave of these directives, once the UK leaves the EU it will no longer be bound to this first wave of EU asylum law. This means, for instance, that the concept of subsidiary protection, which is granted to people who do not qualify as refugees under the 1951 Geneva convention, would no longer be a possibility for refugees in the UK anymore (Jeney 2016). This is why many NGOs have emphasized the need to strengthen refugee protection after Brexit.

The UK, with its opt-out from the common European asylum policy, has been largely unaffected by the so-called 'refugee' crisis. However, accordingly, there could be some impact on family reunification rights for refugees once the UK leaves the EU. During the crisis, the UK has not been the most generous country, since it initially accepted to resettle only 166 Syrian refugees from camps in Jordan and neighbouring countries between June 2014 and June 2015 (Harding et al. 2015). One of the channels through which the UK has resettled Syrian refugees has been through 'the Vulnerable Children's Resettlement Scheme (VCRS)'. So far, 566 children and families have been resettled; though the objective, according to the Home Office, is to reach the resettlement of 3000 children and their families from the MENA by 2020 (Home Office 2018).

Another issue will consist in defining how the UK will return migrants back to their home countries. The UK is indeed party to the Dublin Regulation, which organises the return of irregular migrants back to the country through which they initially entered the EU. NGOs consider this system as 'unfair and inefficient' because it, for instance, delays 'torture survivors' asylum claims and increases risk of detention' (Van Tiem 2016). In order to achieve a similar agreement post-Brexit, it would necessarily require the UK to negotiate bilateral agreements with EU countries, as well as with safe third countries. The UK would also lose access to the Eurodac directive and thus to the fingerprints of irregular migrants which provide evidence of the first country of entry. This will mean that law enforcement authorities will no longer be able to have access to this data since the regulation forbids any data sharing with a third country 'in order to ensure the right to asylum and to safeguard applicants for international protection from having their data disclosed to a third country' (European Parliament and Council of the EU 2013). As rightly outlined, 'the government may find itself in the extraordinary position of not only being unable to identify irregular migrants who have travelled through the EU to the UK, but also lacking the mechanism via to which to return them' (Hulme 2017).

Brexit implies that the UK will no longer take part in Frontex' operations. Following the court case UK vs. Council in 2007, the UK obtained the right to take part in operations of the agency even though, as it is not a member of Schengen, it cannot vote in its decision-making. Again, here some bilateral agreements may be negotiated in the future if the UK wants to take part in operations. The UK will also have to renounce to EU readmission agreements, which organise the return of irregular migrants to their home countries, as well as the return of third country nationals who have transited through a third country with a readmission agreement with the EU. This will probably lead to new bilateral negotiations between the UK and third countries.

Finally, the Touquet agreement between France and the UK is likely to remain and to continue as a bilateral agreement. Once the UK leaves the EU, it will need to assess the asylum-seekers' request under the UK's international protection law. But the treaty signed in 2003 by Nicolas Sarkozy offering juxtaposed controls is likely to remain. Currently, immigration entry checks, conducted by the French Border Police or the Belgian Border Police when departing from Brussels, happen before boarding the Eurostar to the UK, in the Schengen Area, rather than on arrival in the UK. The same happens with French Border Police controls in the UK before departure by train or ferry. Although Emmanuel Macron had planned to renegotiate the Touquet agreement during the presidential election, the latest meeting of January 2018 with Theresa May has in fact led to an expansion of the Touquet agreements. The text, which must still be adopted by the two national parliaments, includes an accelerated procedure by the British authorities when it comes to asylum-seekers' applications of unaccompanied minors and those who are eligible for family reunification. Accordingly, Macron has adopted the line of his predecessor Francois Hollande, thinking that moving the controls to Dover may actually increase the flow of refugees to Calais (Bernard 2018).

The future of refugees and irregular migrants is thus quite uncertain in the absence of a reform in UK law. At the moment this issue is at the bottom of the list of the UK's priorities. And yet, if the UK wants to remain a global player, providing extensive protection to refugees, and a more generous immigration policy, may be key to its future negotiations of trade agreements or other bilateral agreements with non-EU countries such as India. The future of the UK asylum and migration policy is thus crucial to its future as Global Britain. The UK has indeed so far attracted important numbers of international migrants. In 2014, the UK registered the highest inflow number of non-British nationals moving to the UK with 534,000 people recorded according to the Migration Observatory. Working and studying in the UK are the main drivers for legal migrants to come to the UK. The foreign-born population in the UK has been on the rise, with an increase from about 3.8 million in 1993 to over 8.7 million in 2015, according to the same source. The UK also has the fifth-largest immigrant population in the world with a population which is quite diverse, originating mostly from India, Poland and Pakistan (Connord and Krogstad 2016).

POST-BREXIT BORDER AND MIGRATION CONTROL IN THE UK: A LOOK AT TWO MARITIME BORDERS— THE ENGLISH CHANNEL AND THE STRAIT OF GIBRALTAR

Giacomo Orsini

Brexit was often discussed as a necessary step for the UK to 'take back control of the borders' (Reuteurs 2017). However, a close look at the mechanics of border and migration management in Britain unavoidably questions such a perspective. Not only it is unclear how leaving the EU could increase UK authorities' ability to control national frontiers and restrict the entrance of unauthorized people. Brexit might even endanger the already limited capacity to effectively control the British borders. Based on fieldwork and desk research, here I concentrate on the English Channel and the Strait of Gibraltar rather than the much-debated land border of Northern Ireland. Before moving to the discussion of both cases, however, I contextualize contemporary border and migration control in Britain.

Empirical analysis suggests that no border can effectively be secured (Pusterla and Piccin 2012). In the words of Vladimír Šimonák—Head of the Home Affairs Unit of the Permanent Representation of the Slovak Republic to the EU: "no border can be secured unless [authorities] can shoot unauthorized people crossing it".[2] Data which I collected over a series of fieldworks conducted along the EU external border[3] prove it unfeasible to effectively patrol borders—even less, maritime ones—since there are countless ways to cross them undetected, and no technologies available to prevent such a practice (Orsini 2016).

Moreover, despite a major political emphasis on border control to tackle unauthorized residence, in the UK as in the rest of the EU (Morehouse and Blomfield 2011), the great majority of unauthorized residents have entered with a regular permit and then overstayed (Vollmer 2011). Since Britain has never joined the Schengen space of free movement of people—with border controls which have thus applied equally to EU and non-EU citizens—it is unclear how leaving the EU will increase British forces' ability to control unauthorized entrance and residence in Britain. Moving the focus to the English Channel, the opposite seems to be rather the case.

As for the branch of sea separating Britain from continental Europe, major political and societal anxieties have historically concentrated on the thousands of non-EU citizens waiting to cross to the UK, in the so called 'Calais Jungle' and other more or less improvised camps (Reinish 2015). Based on a series of bilateral and trilateral agreements signed between Britain, France and Belgium, since 1994, juxtaposed border controls apply to the *Eurotunnel* and the ferries crossing the English Channel. Border controls are carried out before embarking or entering the tunnel by both British and Belgian or French authorities on both sides of the border, mainly 'to frustrate irregular migration to the United Kingdom, and the making of asylum claims there' (Mitsilegas and Ryan 2010). While thousands of undocumented migrants and asylum seekers cross the English Channel to enter the UK unauthorized, only a few—if any—do the same in the opposite direction to enter Belgium or France.

---

[2]Vladimír Šimonák was among the panellists of the Policy Forum 'The border and the wall. How to tackle migration control at the EU external border' organised by Professor Christof Roos at the Institute for European Studies of the Vrije Universiteit Brussel, on May 31, 2017.

[3]Between 2008 and 2017 I conducted fieldwork research in the Spanish enclave of Melilla and Morocco, in Malta, on the Italian and Spanish border islands of Lampedusa and Fuerteventura, and in the Strait of Gibraltar. Collaborating at distance with the Immanuel Kant University of Kaliningrad, in 2010 I also conducted a study of the functioning of the EU border separating the Russian enclave of Kaliningrad from Poland and Lithuania.

While the EU has no direct competence on these agreements, as already proved during the UK-France summit of the 18th of January of 2018,[4] such arrangements could change parallel to the transforming relations between Britain and the rest of Europe (*Politico* 2017).

Moving the attention to Gibraltar, Brexit seems to invite more alarming scenarios. The tiny British Overseas Territory, which has never joined the EU, shares a land and a maritime border with Spain. Yet, a long-standing international dispute between the British and Spanish governments—and, partly, the Moroccan one—complicates the issue, as the three countries recognize different jurisdictions over the waters of the Strait (Suárez de Vivero 2009). Officially, there is scarce if no cooperation at all between Spanish and Gibraltarian law enforcement agencies to control the shared border. However, observations and interviews conducted in the enclave show a different situation.

In fact, Gibraltarian and Spanish forces seem to collaborate rather closely at sea (Gibraltar Police Authority 2014). As I was told off the record by Gibraltarian law enforcement officials, if a migrants' boat enters Gibraltarian waters and is quickly detected by Gibraltarian forces, it is usually pushed back into the Spanish waters where Spanish officials take charge of them and land them in Spain. In case boat migrants are detected too close to the Gibraltarian shores, then migrants are landed on the Rock to be immediately transferred to Spain across the land border. To support such informal accounts there is one hard fact: despite the Strait of Gibraltar being one of the main entrances for undocumented border crossings into the EU (Spijkerboer 2007), almost no arrival has been recorded in Gibraltar. If, following Brexit, Spain will stop collaborating, undocumented migrants could reach the Rock and apply for asylum. This would potentially create the conditions for humanitarian crises to unfold in the British detached territory. Even more considering that Spain operates on the Strait the world's most sophisticated maritime border control apparatus—Integrated Exterior Surveillance System (Carling 2007). To rely on this system would potentially become impossible if no cooperation with Spain and the EU is put in place.

---

[4] An official report of the summit is available here: https://assets.publishing.service.gov.uk/government/uploads/system/uploads/attachment_data/file/674880/2018_UK-FR_Summit_Communique.pdf.

Justice and Home Affairs: The Case of Gibraltar

Arantza Gomez Arana[5]

Until the referendum on the UK leaving the European Union, Gibraltar managed to keep a distinctive political agenda and identity while being part of a planned and intentional political and economic integration process on the continent. A strong defence of nationalism at domestic level while being part of a supranational project can be challenging enough, while in the case of Gibraltar, considering its geographic location, it may be even more difficult. However, considering the result of the referendum—in which Gibraltarians voted to stay in the EU (96%) -, its future has become part of a complex negotiation process where border politics have a direct impact on them on a daily basis.

Geopolitics of Gibraltar

The importance of Gibraltar from a geopolitical point of view explains why different states over time have tried to have political control over it. It is part of an area that is used to surveil the entrance of the Mediterranean, which helps to manage the security agenda of Western countries.

Cooperation between Spain and the UK in relation to Gibraltar has been difficult in the twentieth century. When Gibraltar approved its constitution in 1969, Franco reacted by closing the border between Gibraltar and Spain (Witte 2017), which was only fully re-opened in 1985 when Spain joined the European Union, following the signing of the Brussels Agreement in 1984. The UK requested a normalization of relations between Spain and Gibraltar opening the border before the Spanish accession to the European Union (Remiro Brotons 2004). It was clear that the UK could veto this adhesion, but thanks to

---

[5] The text 'Justice and Home Affairs: the case of Gibraltar' has been partially published as a blog post for the Birmingham City University Centre for Brexit Studies. The original, which was published on 8th February 2018, can be found at: https://centreforbrexitstudiesblog.wordpress.com/2018/02/05/brexit-borders-negotiations-gibraltar-and-spanish-and-british-politics-on-sovereignty/. The author is also finishing a book on Gibraltar and Brexit that will be published by Emerald.

the Declaration of Lisbon of 1980 and the above-mentioned Brussels Agreement UK Spain relations improved considerably in relation to Gibraltar (Remiro Brotons 2004). However, in this agreement the UK also confirmed its willingness to discuss the sovereignty of Gibraltar (Martín y Pérez de Nanclares 2017). Spain has since then recurrently tried to explore that possibility with the UK (Galaz 2011).

Border Politics

The negotiations of a border between the Republic of Ireland and Northern Ireland will have a direct impact on the border-solution for Gibraltar. The weight of Gibraltar within the British negotiating team is difficult to analyse due to a lack of clear information. However, in the case of the European Union, the positions are clear. The same way that the Republic of Ireland has had a significant influence over the negotiations of its border with Northern Ireland, Spain seems to have a similar weight in relation to Gibraltar (Macdonald and Aguado 2017). The impact of implementing a similar border in Ireland and Gibraltar, should be similar from a pragmatic point of view. However, at a political level its impact may be different if we take into consideration the way the tension has been dealt with, politically speaking in Ireland and Gibraltar over the last couple of decades.

The UK and Spain have had several clashes linked to border politics and the division of rights in relation to a number of areas, including: Spanish fisheries (in 2012), Spanish surveillance of the Strait to detect human smuggling and drug trafficking activities (in 2015), problematic checks at the borders of a political nature between Spain and Gibraltar (in 2013), and the clash of a submarine and a merchant ship (in 2016) (Gonzalez and Guimon 2016; *El Pais* 2015; Romaguera 2013). In relation to money laundering, the decision of the European Court of Justice over the lack of cooperation of the Jyske Bank Gibraltar with Spain (European Court of Justice 2013) demonstrates other aspects of this difficult relationship. The Spanish Minister of Finance, publicly requested in 2015 that Gibraltar be considered a fiscal paradise by the European Union (Pellicer 2015). After the referendum, this obvious tension was finally publicly noticed at EU and British levels, which demonstrates the degree of identity politics surrounding this border. After Brexit, it is likely that it will become more difficult to create cooperation in either of these areas between Spain and Gibraltar.

Identity Politics in Gibraltar

As a way of resolving these issues between Spain and the UK, the countries agreed in 2002 to offer a referendum to Gibraltar, which produced an outcome of 99% of votes in favor of staying under the supervision of the UK (Witte 2017). However, after the outcome of the referendum on Brexit, in February 2017 a survey conducted in Gibraltar demonstrated that 75% of those aged 16–18 years old would contemplate the idea of leaving Gibraltar if there were problems with the border (Jain 2017). It is perhaps then not surprising, that in a survey of 16–18-year-olds conducted in February 2017, three quarters confirmed they would consider leaving Gibraltar if the border was shut or difficult to cross.

The day after the referendum on Brexit, Spain's Foreign Minister—Jose Manuel Garcia Margallo, openly explained his hopes after the outcome: "It's a complete change of outlook that opens up new possibilities on Gibraltar not seen for a very long time. I hope the formula of co-sovereignty - to be clear, the Spanish flag on the Rock - is much closer than before" (Badcock 2016). The reaction of Gibraltar was immediate; the Chief Minister of Gibraltar, Fabian Picardo, explained that they would not discuss this option (Nazca 2016). Three months later, the same politicians attended the UN General Assembly and at its 4th Commission—*Special Political and Decolonization and Committee* (see United Nations 2018)—Picardo responded to the latest comments of Garcia Margallo with a clear "No way, Jose!...[Spain] will never get its hands on our Rock" (*El Pais* 2016).

The tension reached its highest level when in April 2017, after Article 50 was triggered by the UK, the European Union seemed to offer Spain a veto power over the future of the relationship between the European Union and Gibraltar (Macdonald and Aguado 2017). This provoked a list of comments on the British side that compared the case with the 1982 Falklans/Malvinas situation and demonstrated how sensitive the status of Gibraltar is for some members of the political sector (Asthana 2017).

Mr. Grieve, the chair of the Intelligence and Security Committee of Parliament discussed those words: "That said, it is right to point out that with all our overseas territories, and that includes Gibraltar, if they were ever to be attacked we would go to war. That is stated United Kingdom Government policy" (Asthana 2017). A year later, a change of government took place in Spain, following a "confidence vote over a corruption case"[6] against the minority government. The implications for the negotiations could be significant.

Final Remarks

As in the case of Ireland, the way the negotiations take place with Gibraltar, as well as the final outcome, will be seen as significant examples for other parts of Europe where there are regional tensions: Scotland, Catalonia, Kosovo, etc.; or may even create new ones, as in the case of Ceuta and Melilla and Morocco. Considering that, in recent years, Westphalian arrangements seem to be less obvious/clear, that there are more coalitions or minority governments in several European countries representing a more heterogeneous view of politics than in the last few decades (Spain, UK, Iceland, The Netherlands, Germany, etc.), and that there is a rise of different types of nationalism within Europe feeding each other and creating a sort of "momentum", any outcome from Brexit that pretends to be successful in the European continent will have to take into consideration both identity-politics and pragmatism, instead of taking just one side. Justice and Home Affairs officials would benefit from considering the type of politics that European societies are creating and how susceptible they are to identity politics, in order to successfully cooperate with both national and transnational security issues.

THE EU, UK AND NORTHERN IRELAND—
THE RISK OF LOSING A GUARANTEE

Daniela Irrera

On 10 April 2018, the Good Friday Agreement celebrated its 20th anniversary. Europe will have to remember the end of one of its most difficult, enduring and bloody internal conflicts in its modern history, as well as a difficult and sophisticated power-sharing arrangement. Unionists and Nationalists decided to decommission, leave extremist positions and start jointly managing local government. Scholars and media almost unanimously maintain that the US special envoy was the most relevant

---

[6]Socialist chief Pedro Sanchez set to become Spain's Prime Minister By Julien Toyer May 31, 2018. https://uk.reuters.com/article/uk-spain-politics/socialist-chief-pedro-sanchez-set-to-become-spains-prime-minister-idUKKCN1IW0U0.

external actor to mediate the conflict, while the EU's influence was only secondary and more focused on the economic impact. However, the great visibility of the US's role is mainly the result of the special relationship between the two respective political leaders (President Clinton and Prime Minister Blair) and the fact that it was essential to have a formal commitment of all the parts. The EU's participation produced its effects on multiple sectors over the long-term period and in a variety of ways.

The EU has surely contributed to the development of the Ulster region, including the border counties, allowing all parts to access specific funds and allocating definite resources to an International Fund, which was the result of transatlantic cooperation. This intervention, which has been the most analysed and emphasised, only complements more important and broader dimensions.

The EU has widely contributed to making the so-called North–South dimension (which has been at the core of the peace process) a tangible space for dialogue and convergence. In particular, through special bodies and agencies created specifically for Northern Ireland, all actors involved, including the Irish and the UK Government, have been pushed to identify those policy areas in which North and South have common interests and preferences. This has helped to transform the conflict and to turn its potential into something productive.

Lastly, in doing so, the EU has also shaped conflicting identities. This was a slow and gradual process that mainly took place through local political parties and their work within the European parliament. The initial resistance of local politicians to the EU dimension has gradually turned into a process of socialization, which is not always easy but is certainly productive. Such a process has changed the parties' discourses, leaving fear and revenge in the past and moving towards the promotion of present opportunities. This evolution has had an additional side effect, contributing to changing the patterns of communication among the two communities.

Therefore, the EU was and is absolutely necessary in Northern Ireland. The main impact of Brexit on Northern Ireland is expected to be the fear of the possible reunification, or the more technical issues related to the Irish border. This is certainly true, but what is sustained here is that the EU has created the conditions which allowed the peace process to be successful and has guaranteed, over the years, the stability of the agreement, including the economic investments in Northern Ireland. One of the effects of Brexit would be to interrupt such guarantee, dangerously stopping a conflict transformation process which is essential for everyone in Europe.

REFERENCES

Adam, I., J. Berg, F. Trauner, M. Tuley, and L. Westerveen. 2016. The UK in Justice and Home Affairs: The Engaged Outside. *Policy Brief*, Issue 2016/6Institute for European Studies, Vrije Universiteit Brussel.

Alt, J. 2003. *Leben in der Schattenwelt. Problemkomplex "illegale" Migration*. Karlsruhe: von Loeper Literaturverlag.

Asthana, A. 2017. Theresa May Would Go to War to Protect Gibraltar, Michael Howard Says. *The Guardian*, 2 April. Available from: https://www.theguardian.com/politics/2017/apr/02/britain-and-eu-worse-off-without-brexit-deal-says-michael-fallon. Last accessed 29 March 2018.

Badcock, J. 2016. Spain Says 'Closer to' Controlling Gibraltar After Brexit Vote. *The Telegraph*, 24 June. Available from: https://www.telegraph.co.uk/news/2016/06/24/spain-proposes-shared-sovereignty-over-gibraltar-after-brexit-vo/. Last accessed 28 March 2018.

Bernard, P. 2018. Celebree par Theresa May et Emmanuel Macron, la Cooperation Franco-britannique a l'epreuve du Brexit. *Le Monde*, 18 January. Available from: http://www.lemonde.fr/europe/article/2018/01/18/celebree-par-theresa-may-et-emmanuel-macron-la-cooperation-franco-britannique-vit-a-l-epreuve-du-brexit_5243239_3214.html?xtmc=touquet&xtcr=7. Last accessed 18 May 2018.

Carling, J. 2007. Migration Control and Migrant Fatalities at the Spanish-African Borders. *International Migration Review* 41 (2): 316–343.

Connor, P., and J.M. Krogstad. 2016. *5 Facts About Migration and the United Kingdom, Factank*, Pew Research Centre, 21 June. Available from: http://www.pewresearch.org/fact-tank/2016/06/21/5-facts-about-migration-and-the-united-kingdom/. Last accessed 18 May 2018.

Cornelius, W.A., and T. Tsuda. 2004. Controlling Immigration: The Limits of Government Intervention. In *Controlling Immigration: A Global Perspective*, ed. W.A. Cornelius, T. Tsuda, P.L. Martin, and J.F. Hollifield, 3–48. Stanford: Stanford University Press.

Cvajner, M., and G. Sciortino. 2010. Migration Careers and Their Development Paths. *Population, Space and Place* 16: 213–225.

El Pais. 2015. Diez puntos calientes en el conflicto entre Gibraltar y España desde 2005, 11 August. Available from: https://politica.elpais.com/politica/2015/08/11/actualidad/1439288228_477478.html. Last accessed 28 March 2018.

El Pais. 2016. Spanish Flag Will Fly in Gibraltar "Sooner Than Chief Minister Thinks", 6 October. Available from: https://elpais.com/elpais/2016/10/06/inenglish/1475762366_981489.html. Last accessed 28 March 2018.

Engbersen, G., and D. Broeders. 2011. Fortress Europe and the Dutch Donjon: Securitization, Internal Migration Policy and Irregular Migrants Counter Moves. In *Transnational Migration and Human Security*, ed. T.D. Truong, and D. Gasper, vol. 6. Hexagon Series on Human and Environmental Security and Peace. Berlin and Heidelberg: Springer.

European Commission. 2017. *Joint Report from the Negotiators of the European Union and the United Kingdom Government on Progress During Phase 1 of Negotiations Under Article 50 TFEU on the United Kingdom's Orderly Withdrawal from the European Union*, 8 December, Brussels.

European Court of Justice. 2013. *EU law does not preclude Spanish legislation which requires credit institutions, operating in Spain without being established there, to forward directly to the Spanish authorities information necessary for combatting money laundering and terrorist financing*. Luxembourg. Press release N 54/13, 25 April.

European Parliament and the Council. 2013. Regulation (EU) No. 603/2013 of the European Parliament and of the Council of 26 June 2013 on the establishment of 'Eurodac'. *OJ* L180: 1–30.

Finotelli, C. 2007. *Illegale Einwanderung, Flüchtlingsmigration und das Ende des Nord-Süd-Mythos: Zur funkionalen Äquivalenz des deutschen und des italienischen Einwanderungsregimes*. Münster: LIT Verlag.

Galaz, M. 2011. Zapatero reitera ante Carlos de Inglaterra que hay que buscar solución al conflicto de Gibraltar. *El Pais*, 31 March. Available from: https://elpais.com/elpais/2011/03/31/actualidad/1301554130_850215.html. Last accessed 28 March 2018.

Gibraltar Police Authority. 2014. *Annual Report of the Gibraltar Police Authority*. Available from: http://gpasurvey.com/images/publications/Annual_Reports/GPA_Annual_Report_2013-2014.pdf. Last accessed 27 November 2017.

Gonzalez, M., and Guimon P. 2016. El Reino Unido pide disculpas a España por el accidente de un submarino nuclear en Gibraltar. *El Pais*, 21 July. Available from: https://elpais.com/internacional/2016/07/21/actualidad/1469083210_393273.html. Last accessed 28 March 2018.

Harding, L., P. Oltermann, and N. Watt. 2015. Refugee Welcome? How UK and Germany Compare on Migration. *The Guardian*, 2 September. Available from: https://www.theguardian.com/world/2015/sep/02/refugees-welcome-uk-germany-compare-migration. Last accessed 18 May 2018.

HM Government. 2017. *Policy Paper. The United Kingdom's Exit from the European Union: Safeguarding the Position of EU Citizens Living in the UK and UK Nationals Living in the EU*, 26 June 2017. Available from: https://www.gov.uk/government/publications/safeguarding-the-position-of-eu-citizens-in-the-uk-and-uk-nationals-in-the-eu/the-united-kingdoms-exit-from-the-european-union-safeguarding-the-position-of-eu-citizens-living-in-the-uk-and-uk-nationals-living-in-the-eu. Last accessed 14 December 2017.

Home Office. 2018. *Over 10,500 Refugees Resettled in the UK Under Flagship Scheme*, 22 February. Available from: https://www.gov.uk/government/news/over-10000-refugees-resettled-in-the-uk-under-flagship-scheme. Last accessed 18 May 2018.

Hulme, B. 2017. Could Brexit Be a Boom to Human Smuggling? *Open Democracy*. Available from: https://www.opendemocracy.net/benjamin-hulme/could-brexit-be-boon-to-human-smuggling. Last accessed 18 May 2018.

Jain, K. 2017. Brexit Causes Anguish on Gibraltar. *The Conversation*, 14 March. Available from: https://theconversation.com/brexit-causes-anguish-on-gibraltar-74426. Last accessed 28 March 2018.

Jeney, P. 2016. The European Union's Area of Freedom, Security and Justice without the United Kingdom: Legal and Practical Consequences of Brexit. *ELTE Law Journal* 1: 117–139.

Macdonald, A., and J. Aguado, 2017. EU Offers Spain Veto Right Over Gibraltar in Brexit Talks. *Reuters*, 31 March. Available from: https://www.reuters.com/article/us-britain-eu-gibraltar/eu-offers-spain-veto-right-over-gibraltar-in-brexit-talks-idUSKBN1722AS. Last accessed 28 March 2018.

Martín y Pérez de Nanclares, J. 2017. Brexit Y Gibraltar: la soberanía compartida como posible solución de la controversia. In *El Brexit y Gibraltar: Un reto con oportunidades conjuntas*, ed. M.M. Martín Martínez and J. Martín y Pérez de Nanclares, Colección escuela diplomática ministerio de asunto exteriores y de cooperación, September. Available from: http://www.exteriores.gob.es/Portal/es/Ministerio/EscuelaDiplomatica/Documents/coleccion%20ED%2023_para%20web.pdf. Last accessed 18 May 2018.

Massey, D.S., J. Durand, and K.A. Pren. 2016. Why Border Enforcement Backfired. *American Journal of Sociology* 121 (5): 1557–1600.

Mitsilegas, V., and B. Ryan. 2010. *Extraterritorial Immigration Control: Legal Challenges*. Leiden: Brill.

Morehouse, C., and M. Blomfield. 2011. *Irregular Migration in Europe*. Washington: Migration Policy Institute.

Nazca, J. 2016. Spain Seeks to Jointly Govern Gibraltar After Brexit. *Reuters*, 24 June. Available from: https://www.reuters.com/article/us-britain-eu-gibraltar/spain-seeks-to-jointly-govern-gibraltar-after-brexit-idUSKCN0ZA184. Last accessed 28 March 2018.

Orsini, G. 2016. Securitization as a Source of Insecurity: A Ground-Level Look at the Functioning of Europe's External Border in Lampedusa. *Studies in Ethnicity and Nationalism* 16 (1): 135–147.

Paul, R. 2015. *The Political Economy of Border-Drawing: Arranging Legality in European Labour Migration Policies*. New York: Berghahn Books.

Peers, S. 2017. The Beginning of the End? Citizens' Rights in the Brexit 'Sufficient Progress' Deal. *EU Law Analysis*, 9 December 2017. Available from: http://eulawanalysis.blogspot.it. Last accessed 14 December 2017.

Pellicer, L. 2015. Montoro dice que Gibraltar debe estar en la lista de paraísos fiscales de la UE. *El Pais*, 19 June. Available from: https://elpais.com/economia/2015/06/19/actualidad/1434739565_185828.html. Last accessed 27 March 2018.

Político. 2017. Macron Is Bad News for Britain's Borders. Available from: https://www.politico.eu/article/emmanuel-macron-bad-news-for-britain-border-dover-calais/. Last accessed 10 December 2017.

Pusterla, E., and F. Piccin. 2012. The Loss of Sovereignty Control and the Illusion of Building Walls. *Journal of Borderlands Studies* 27 (2): 121–138.

Reinish, J. 2015. 'Forever Temporary': Migrants in Calais, Then and Now. *The Political Quarterly* 86 (4): 515–522.

Remiro Brotons, A. 2004. Regreso a Gibraltar: acuerdos y desacuerdos hispano-británicos, Universidad Autónoma de Madrid, ISSN: 1575-720X. *Revista Jurídica* 10: 133–182. Available from: https://repositorio.uam.es/bitstream/handle/10486/3063/14295_10RJ132.pdf?sequence=1&isAllowed=y. Last accessed 18 May 2018.

Reuteurs. 2017. Whole of the UK Needs to Take Back Control of Borders and Cash from EU, Johnson Says. Available from: https://www.reuters.com/article/uk-britain-eu-johnson/whole-of-the-uk-needs-to-take-back-control-of-borders-and-cash-from-eu-johnson-says-idUSKBN1E11M8. Last accessed 13 December, 2017.

Romaguera, C. 2013. La verja de Gibraltar registra retenciones de más de siete horas. *El Pais*, 28 July. Available from: https://elpais.com/ccaa/2013/07/28/andalucia/1375033236_246363.html. Last accessed 28 March 2018.

Roos, C. 2018. The (De-)Politicization of EU Freedom of Movement: Political Parties, Opportunities, and Policy Framing in Germany and the UK. *Comparative European Politics*, 1–20. https://doi.org/10.1057/s41295-018-0118-1.

Ruhs, M. and B. Anderson. 2006. Semi-compliance in the Migrant Labour Market, Centre on Migration, Policy and Society. Working Paper No. 30, Oxford: University of Oxford.

Spijkerboer, T. 2007. The Human Cost of Border Control. *European Journal of Migration and Law* 9: 127–139.

Suárez de Vivero, J.L. 2009. *Aguas Jurisdiccionales en el Mediterráneo y el Mar Negro*. Brussels: European Parliament.

United Nations. 2018. *Special Political and Decolonization (Fourth Committee)*. Available from: http://www.un.org/en/ga/fourth/. Last accessed 18 May 2018.

Van Tiem, B. 2016. What Brexit Could Mean for Refugee Protection in Britain. *Open Democracy*, 8 August. Available from: https://www.opendemocracy.net/britte-van-tiem/what-brexit-could-mean-for-refugee-protection-in-britain. Last accessed 18 May 2018.

Vollmer, B. 2011. *Irregular Migration in the UK: Definitions, Pathways and Scale.* Available from: http://www.migrationobservatory.ox.ac.uk/wp-content/uploads/2016/04/Briefing-Irregular_Migration.pdf. Last accessed 9 December 2017.

Witte, G. 2017. As Brexit Tremors Ripple, the Rock of Gibraltar Shudders. *Washington Post*, 14 January. Available from: https://www.washingtonpost.com/world/europe/as-brexit-tremors-ripple-the-rock-of-gibraltar-shudders/2017/01/14/f86c0b70-d764-11e6-a0e6-d502d6751bc8_story.html?utm_term=.b540d29cd10f. Last accessed 28 March 2018.

CHAPTER 9

Conclusion—Priorities and Considerations for the Future UK-EU Security Relationship

Abstract This chapter summarises the complex current relationship between the UK and the EU in the area of internal security and the direct and indirect consequences that Brexit could have for different aspects of this field. There is little doubt that the risks of breakdown in cooperation vastly outweigh the security opportunities that Brexit presents. The reflections this book offers have not only revealed the importance of maintaining a strong relationship between the two negotiating parties, but also provided a glimpse of how politically and legally challenging, as well as technically complex, security negotiations will be, especially as internal security is closely intertwined with other policy fields, namely the Internal Market.

Keywords European union · Brexit · Justice and home affairs · Political and legal consequences

This book sought to provide information and guidance on the future relationship between the United Kingdom (UK) and the European Union (EU) in the policy area of internal security for both the general public and policy-makers, in particular those involved in the negotiations between the UK and the EU, while contributing to the growing academic literature on the EU's Area of Freedom, Security and Justice. The volume was organised in two distinct parts, with Chapters 2–5 discussing the current UK-EU internal security arrangements, Brexit's consequences in this area for both parties, their emerging negotiation positions, and some of the challenges to future cooperation that derive from these positions. The second part of the book, Chapters 6–8, provided experts' views on a wide range of issues related to the future UK-EU security relationship that address some of the ambiguity and uncertainty that currently dominates discussions on this relationship.

As Chapter 2 showed, internal security has evolved into one of the most dynamic and prioritised policy fields of the EU. The UK's unique opt-in and opt-out arrangements with the EU in this field have enabled it to selectively participate in measures which it perceives to be in its national interest, contributing to the field's complex differentiated integration. However, the UK has deeply shaped the AFSJ, with its involvement having benefitted both the UK and the EU, leading to Brexit potentially having a deep impact on the internal security of both parties. Chapter 3 explored this possible impact, which, it is argued, will be most severe for police cooperation, the area in which the UK's leading role considerably contributed to both parties' security. Additionally, despite the UK's limited participation in judicial cooperation and migration and asylum policies, there are manifold potential consequences of Brexit in these areas, with the chapter concluding that Brexit holds both positive and negative consequences for the EU in these fields while damaging the UK's internal security and involving a number of challenges for future cooperation. As Chapter 4 demonstrated, the emerging negotiation position of the UK regarding future cooperation in internal security with the EU is characterised by a largely unsubstantiated expectation that little will change in this area of cooperation for the sake of collective security, while the EU has signalled that it wants a partnership beneficial for both sides, but has also pointed out various challenges to future cooperation and voiced frustration with the UK's vague position and the lack of progress in the negotiations—feelings that, the authors warn, could reduce the political will necessary to reach a substantive agreement. Some of the political, legal, and constitutional challenges to such an agreement were explored in Chapter 5. In particular, the authors analysed transitional arrangements, discussing the possibilities of substantial delays in—or the no conclusion of—a security agreement, alternative models to the UK-EU relationship, dispute resolution and enforcement mechanisms in light of the UK Government's red line on CJEU jurisdiction, and the UK's potentially reduced influence on the EU's future internal security.

The second part of the book, Chapters 6–8, offered a diverse range of detailed accounts of the different challenges ahead for the UK's and the EU's internal security as a consequence of Brexit, authored by some of the leading academics and practitioners in the field. Chapter 6 focused on Brexit and future UK-EU relations with regard to internal security, consisting of both Fichera's and Ripoll Servent's discussions of Brexit's impact on the future development of the AFSJ; Mortera-Martinez's analysis of the two parties' negotiation stances shaping future cooperation; and Fahey's reflection upon how transatlantic relations can inform future UK-EU cooperation in internal security. Chapter 7 offered views on different aspects of police and judicial cooperation, including De Vries' contribution on cooperation regarding counterterrorism and the fight against organised crime; Bossong and Rieger's exploration of future data sharing options for police cooperation; Trauner's piece on the negotiations regarding the UK's future participation in Europol; Wilson and Carr's discussion of future cooperation regarding Forensic Science; and MacKenzie's considerations on the UK's role in EU counter-terrorism policy. It also included expert views on specific forms of insecurity, namely Sergi's analysis of Brexit creating opportunities for transnational criminal networks; Farrand's exploration of Brexit's impact on combatting counterfeiting; and Porcedda's and Lavorgna's pieces on the consequences of Brexit for the UK and the EU in the area of cyber crime and cybersecurity. Finally, in Chapter 8 on migration, asylum and border cooperation, Roos showed how the end of freedom of movement in the UK could lead to EU migrants coming into the country illegally or slipping into semi-legality or illegality post-entry, and Wolff explored Brexit's impact on asylum seekers in the UK, arguing that an extensive and generous asylum and migration policy is crucial for the UK to remain a global player. Regarding border governance, Orsini compared current and possible future cooperation at the borders of Dover and Gibraltar, Gomez Arana called for pragmatism and identity politics being taken into account to manage the border of Gibraltar in the future; and lastly, Irrera warned that Brexit could interrupt the peace process in Northern Ireland, to which the EU has contributed. In sum, the various contributions of this part of the book show the manifold potential direct and indirect consequences of Brexit on various policy areas and aspects of internal security, both for the UK and the EU, and point out various challenges to future cooperation in internal security between the two parties.

However, this book not only discussed the complex current relationship between the UK and the EU in the area of internal security and the direct and indirect consequences that Brexit could have for different aspects of this field, but also constitutes an important reflection on what European security is, how it is achieved and what role the UK plays in this policy context. There is little doubt that the risks of breakdown in cooperation vastly outweigh the security opportunities that Brexit presents. Such a reflection has not only revealed the importance of maintaining a strong relationship between the two negotiating parties, but also provided a glimpse of how politically and legally challenging, as well as technically complex, security negotiations will be, especially as internal security is closely intertwined with other policy fields, namely the Internal Market. The book has identified numerous challenges that need to be overcome in the negotiations in order to shape the future security relationship in a way that ensures the security of both the UK and the EU. The UK is faced with having to develop new forms of cooperation with its neighbours to fight ever more transnational security threats, as well as new strategies to maintain its leading role as an international security actor. As we enter one of the most challenging periods in the history of contemporary security in Britain, we hope that this book has contributed to a better understanding of the political, legal and technical trials ahead.

References

Adam, I., J. Berg, F. Trauner, M. Tuley, and L. Westerveen. 2016. The UK in Justice and Home Affairs: The Engaged Outside. *Policy Brief*, Issue 2016/6. Institute for European Studies, Vrije Universiteit Brussel.

Adler-Nissen, R. 2009. Behind the Scenes of Differentiated Integration: Circumventing National Opt-Outs in Justice and Home Affairs. *Journal of European Public Policy* 16 (1): 62–80.

Alegre, S., D. Bigo, E. Guild, E.M. Kuskonmaz, H. Ben Jaffel, and J. Jeandesboz. 2017. *The Implications of the United Kingdom's Withdrawal from the European Union for the Area of Freedom, Security and Justice*. Report to the Committee on Civil Liberties, Justice and Home Affairs. Available from: http://www.europarl.europa.eu/thinktank/en/document.html?reference=IPOL_STU(2017)596824. Last accessed 31 May 2018.

Alt, J. 2003. *Leben in der Schattenwelt. Problemkomplex "illegale" Migration*. Karlsruhe: von Loeper Literaturverlag.

An Garda Siochana and Police Service of Northern Ireland. 2016. *Cross Border Organised Crime: Threat Assessment 2016*.

Argomaniz, J. 2009. When the EU Is the 'NormTaker': The Passenger Name Records Agreement and the EU's Internalisation of US Border Security Norms. *Journal of European Integration* 31 (1): 119–136.

Armstrong, M. 2018. Widespread Support for UK as Around 100 Russian Diplomats Are Expelled. *Euronews*, 27 March. Available from: http://www.euronews.com/2018/03/27/widespread-support-for-uk-as-around-100-russian-diplomats-are-expelled. Last accessed 27 May 2018.

© The Editor(s) (if applicable) and The Author(s),
under exclusive license to Springer Nature Switzerland AG,
part of Springer Nature 2019
H. Carrapico et al., *Brexit and Internal Security*,
Palgrave Studies in European Union Politics,
https://doi.org/10.1007/978-3-030-04194-6

Asthana, A. 2017. Theresa May Would Go to War to Protect Gibraltar, Michael Howard Says. *The Guardian*, 2 April. Available from: https://www.theguardian.com/politics/2017/apr/02/britain-and-eu-worse-off-without-brexit-deal-says-michael-fallon. Last accessed 29 March 2018.

Asthana, A., D. Boffey, H. Stewart, and P. Walker. 2017. Don't Blackmail Us Over Security, EU Warns May. *The Guardian*, 30 March. Available from: https://www.theguardian.com/politics/2017/mar/29/brexit-eu-condemns-mays-blackmail-over-security-cooperation. Last accessed 27 May 2018.

Bada, M., I. Arreguín-Toft, I. Brown, P. Cornish, S. Creese, W. Dutton, M. Goldsmith, E. Ignatuschtschenko, L. Pace, L. Pijnenburg Muller, T. Roberts, S. Von Solms, and D. Upton. 2016. *Cyber Security Capacity Review of the United Kingdom*. Oxford: Global Cyber Security Capacity Centre, University of Oxford.

Badcock, J. 2016 Spain Says 'Closer To' Controlling Gibraltar After Brexit Vote. *The Telegraph*, 24 June. Available from: https://www.telegraph.co.uk/news/2016/06/24/spain-proposes-shared-sovereignty-over-gibraltar-after-brexit-vo/. Last accessed 28 March 2018.

Bárd, P. 2018. *The Effect of Brexit on European Arrest Warrants*. Centre for European Policy Studies Paper in Liberty and Security in Europe, No. 2018-02, April.

Barnier, M. 2017a. *Speech by Michel Barnier at the Berlin Security Conference*, 29 November, Berlin. Available from: http://europa.eu/rapid/press-release_SPEECH-17-5021_en.htm. Last accessed 24 March 2018.

Barnier, M. 2017b. *Speech by Michel Barnier, Chief Negotiator for the Preparation and Conduct of the Negotiations with the United Kingdom, at the Plenary Session of the European Committee of the Regions*, SPEECH/17/723, 22 March, Brussels. Available from: https://www.ifa.ie/wp-content/uploads/2017/03/Speech-by-Michel-Barnier.pdf. Last accessed 30 March 2018.

Barnier, M. 2018. *Speech by Michel Barnier at BusinessEurope Day 2018*, 1 March, Brussels. Available from: http://europa.eu/rapid/press-release_SPEECH-18-1462_en.htm. Last accessed 29 March 2018.

BBC. 2011. *George Wright Wins US Extradition Case in Portugal*, 17 November. Available from: http://www.bbc.co.uk/news/world-us-canada-15778384. Last accessed 29 March 2018.

BBC. 2016a. *EU Data Retention Ruling Goes Against UK Government*, 21 December. Available from: http://www.bbc.com/news/uk-politics-38390150. Last accessed 16 June 2017.

BBC. 2016b. *Staying in EU 'Exposes UK to Terror Risk', Says Iain Duncan Smith*, 21 February. Available from: http://www.bbc.co.uk/news/uk-politics-eu-referendum-35624409. Last accessed 30 April 2018.

BBC. 2017a. *Privacy Concerns as China Expands DNA Database*, 17 May. Available from: https://www.bbc.co.uk/news/world-asia-china-39945220. Last accessed 18 June 2018.

BBC. 2017b. *Brexit: Jean-Claude Juncker Criticises UK's Position Papers*, 30 August. Available from: http://www.bbc.co.uk/news/uk-politics-41089257. Last accessed 26 March 2018.

Benwell, M., and A. Pinkerton. 2016. Brexit and the British Overseas Territories. *The RUSI Journal* 161 (4): 8–14.

Bernard, P. 2018. Celebree par Theresa May et Emmanuel Macron, la Cooperation Franco-britannique a l'epreuve du Brexit. *Le Monde*, 18 January. Available from: http://www.lemonde.fr/europe/article/2018/01/18/celebree-par-theresa-may-et-emmanuel-macron-la-cooperation-franco-britannique-vit-a-l-epreuve-du-brexit_5243239_3214.html?xtmc=touquet&xtcr=7. Last accessed 18 May 2018.

Black, J., A. Hall, K. Cox, M. Kepe, and E. Silversten. 2017. *Defence and Security After Brexit. RAND Corporation Europe*. Available from: https://www.rand.org/content/dam/rand/pubs/research_reports/RR1700/RR1786/RAND_RR1786.pdf. Last accessed 27 May 2018.

Blitz, J. 2017. Why Dover Is Braced for Customs Gridlock After Brexit. *Financial Times*, 18 October. Available from: https://www.ft.com/content/7ff7c97c-b33c-11e7-a398-73d59db9e399. Last accessed 19 May 2018.

Boin, A., M. Ekengren, and M. Rhinard. 2006. Protecting the Union: Analysing an Emerging Policy Space. *Journal of European Security* 28 (5): 405–421.

Bond, I., S. Besch, A. Gostyńska-Jakubowska, R. Korteweg, C. Mortera-Martinez, and S. Tilford. 2016. *Europe After Brexit. Unleashed or Undone?* Centre for European Reform, April. Available from: https://www.cer.org.uk/sites/default/files/pb_euafterBrexit_15april16.pdf. Last accessed 24 June 2017.

Carling, J. 2007. Migration Control and Migrant Fatalities at the Spanish-African Borders. *International Migration Review* 41 (2): 316–343.

Carr, S., A. Gallop, E. Piasecki, G. Tully, and T.J. Wilson. (forthcoming). Clarifying the "Reliability" Continuum and Testing Its Limits: Biometric (Fingerprint and DNA) Expert Evidence. In *Forensic Science Evidence and Expert Witness Testimony: Reliability Through Reform?*, ed. R. Roberts and M. Stockdale. Cheltenham: Edward Elgar.

Carrapico, H., and F. Trauner. 2013. Europol and Its Impact on EU Policy-Making on Organised Crime. *Perspectives on European Politics and Society* 14 (3): 357–371.

Carrapico, H., C. Berthélemy, and A. Niehuss. 2017. *Better Safe Than Sorry? Brexit and Internal Security*. Report for the UK in a Changing Europe Funding Initative. Aston University, Birmingham.

Carrera, S., E. Guild, and N. Chun Luk. 2016. What Does Brexit Mean for the EU's Area of Freedom, Security and Justice? *CEPS Commentary*. Available from: https://www.ceps.eu/system/files/What%20does%20BREXIT%20mean%20for%20the%20EU.pdf. Last accessed 28 March 2018.

Cellan-Jones, R. 2017. Frictionless Borders: Learning from Norway. *BBC News*, 29 September. Available from: http://www.bbc.co.uk/news/technology-41412561. Last accessed 5 April 2018.

Christou, G. 2016. *Cybersecurity in the European Union. Resilience and Adaptability in Governance Policy*. Basingstoke: Palgrave Macmillan.

Commons Justice Committee. 2017. *Implications of Brexit for the Justice System*, (HC 2016–17, 750).

Connor, P., and J.M. Krogstad. 2016. *5 Facts About Migration and the United Kingdom*, Factank, Pew Research Centre, 21 June. Available from: http://www.pewresearch.org/fact-tank/2016/06/21/5-facts-about-migration-and-the-united-kingdom/. Last accessed 18 May 2018.

Cornelius, W.A., and T. Tsuda. 2004. Controlling Immigration: The Limits of Government Intervention. In *Controlling Immigration. A Global Perspective*, ed. W.A. Cornelius, T. Tsuda, P.L. Martin, and J.F. Hollifield, 3–48. Stanford: Stanford University Press.

Council of Europe Treaty Series. 2013. *No. 214. Protocol No. 16 to the Convention on the Protection of Human Rights and Fundamental Freedoms*, Strasbourg, 2.X.2013.

Council of the European Union. 2002a. Council Framework Decision of 13 June 2002 on Joint Investigation Teams. *OJ* L162: 1–3.

Council of the European Union. 2002b. Council Framework Decision of 13 June 2002 on the European Arrest Warrant and the Surrender Procedures Between Member States. *OJ* L190: 1–18.

Council of the European Union. 2005. Council Framework Decision 2005/222/JHA on Attacks Against Information Systems. *OJ* L69: 67–71.

Council of the European Union. 2006. *Press Release 21st February*. Available from: http://www.eu2006.at/en/News/Council_Conclusions/JAISchlussfolgerungen.pdf. Last accessed 14 June 2017.

Council of the European Union. 2008a. Council Decision 2008/615/JHA of 23 June 2008 on the Stepping Up of Cross-Border Cooperation, Particularly in Combating Terrorism and Cross-Border Crime. *OJ* L210: 1–11.

Council of the European Union. 2008b. Council Decision 2008/616/JHA of 23 June 2008 on the Implementation of Decision 2008/615/JHA on the Stepping Up of Cross-Border Cooperation, Particularly in Combating Terrorism and Cross-Border Crime. *OJ* L210: 12–72.

Council of the European Union. 2009. Council Decision 2009/316/JHA of 6 April 2009 on the Establishment of the European Criminal Records Information System (ECRIS) in Application of Article 11 of Framework Decision 2009/315/JHA. *OJ* L93: 33–48.

Council of the European Union. 2014. *Council Conclusions on a Homogeneous Extended Single Market and EU Relations with Non-EU Western European Countries*, General Affairs Council Meeting, 16 December.

Council of the European Union. 2017. *European Public Prosecutor's Office: 16 Member States Together to Fight Fraud Against the EU Budget.* Press Release, 3 April. Available from: http://www.consilium.europa.eu/en/press/press-releases/2017/04/03-eppo/. Last accessed 15 June 2017.

Council of the European Union. 2018. *Statement by President Donald Tusk on the Draft Guidelines on the Framework for the Future Relationship with the UK*, 7 March, Statements and Remarks 109/18.

Court of Justice. 2014. Opinion 2/13 Opinion of the Court (Full Court) of 18 December 2014, EU:C:2014:2454.

Court of Justice. 2015. Case C-362/14 Schrems v Data Commissioner, EU:C:2015:650.

Court of Justice. 2017. Opinion 1/15 of the Grand Chamber ECLI:EU:C:2017:592 (EU-Canada PNR Agreement).

Court of Justice. 2018. C-284/16, Judgment ECLI:EU:C:2018:158, 6 March 2018.

Couzens, G. 2017. Gibraltar Border Delays: Spanish MP Demands Answers Over Long Queues. *Express*, 6 April. Available from: https://www.express.co.uk/news/world/788585/gibraltar-border-delays-spanish-mp-answers-long-queues. Last accessed 4 April 2018.

Cremona, M. 2016. A Triple Braid: Interactions Between International Law, EU Law and Private Law. In *Private Law in the External Relation of the EU*, ed. M. Cremona and H.-W. Micklitz, 33–55. Oxford: Oxford University Press.

Cvajner, M., and G. Sciortino. 2010. Migration Careers and Their Development Paths. *Population, Space and Place* 16: 213–225.

Daily Mail. 2017. Prime Minister Theresa May: How I Will Make Brexit a Success for Everyone, 6 September. Available from: http://www.dailymail.co.uk/news/article-4856216/How-ll-make-Brexit-success-EVERYONE.html. Last accessed 28 March 2018.

Davies, R., and J. Burke. 2017. Labout Demands Review into City of London Role in Money Laundering. *The Guardian*, 19 October. Available from: https://www.theguardian.com/business/2017/oct/19/labour-demands-review-uk-banking-role-money-laundering-gupta-south-africa. Last accessed 15 May 2018.

Dawson, J., S. Lipscombe, and S. Godec. (2017). The European Arrest Warrant. *House of Commons Briefing Paper* 1: 14.

DCLG and Home office. (2018). *Controlling Migration Fund: Prospectus.* Available from: https://assets.publishing.service.gov.uk/government/uploads/system/uploads/attachment_data/file/733160/CMF_Prospectus_2018_-_2020.pdf. Last acessed 20 March 2018.

Dearden, L. 2017. London Terror Attack Suspect Was British-Born and Previously Investigated by MI5 Over Extremism, May Confirms. *Independent*, 23 March. Available from: https://www.independent.co.uk/news/uk/home-news/london-terror-attack-suspect-identity-british-born-citizen-mi5-investigate-extremism-islamist-a7645331.html. Last accessed 15 May 2018.

Department for Exiting the Union. 2018. *The Future Relationship Between the United Kingdom and the European Union*. Available from: https://www.gov.uk/government/publications/the-future-relationship-between-the-united-kingdom-and-the-european-union Last accessed on 12 July 2018.

EFTA. 2016. *Agreement on the European Economic Area*, 3 January 1994. Updated 1 August 2016. Available from: http://www.efta.int/Legal-Text/EEA-Agreement-1327. Last accessed 28 March 2018.

El Pais. 2015. Diez puntos calientes en el conflicto entre Gibraltar y España desde 2005, 11 August. Available from: https://politica.elpais.com/politica/2015/08/11/actualidad/1439288228_477478.html. Last accessed 28 March 2018.

El Pais. 2016. Spanish Flag will Fly in Gibraltar "Sooner Than Chief Minister Thinks", 6 October. Available from: https://elpais.com/elpais/2016/10/06/inenglish/1475762366_981489.html. Last accessed 28 March 2018.

Engbersen G., and D. Broeders. 2011. Fortress Europe and the Dutch Donjon: Securitization, Internal Migration Policy and Irregular Migrants' Counter Moves. In *Transnational Migration and Human Security*, ed. T.D. Truong, and D. Gasper, vol. 6. Hexagon Series on Human and Environmental Security and Peace. Berlin and Heidelberg: Springer.

Eurojust. 2017. *Annual Report 2016*. Available from: http://eurojust.europa.eu/doclibrary/corporate/Pages/annual-reports.aspx. Last accessed 25 May 2017: 1–69.

European Commission. 2009. *Awareness of Key Policies in the Area of Freedom, Security and Justice-Analytical Report*. Eurobarometer Survey, January.

European Commission. 2011. *Internal Security—Report*. Special Eurobarometer 371, November.

European Commission. 2012. *Communication from the Commission to the European Parliament, the Council, the European Economic and Social Committee and the Committee of the Regions on EU Relations with the Principality of Andorra, the Principality of Monaco and the Republic of San Marino*, COM (2012) 680 final.

European Commission. 2014. *Security in 2020: Meeting the Challenge*. Available from: https://ec.europa.eu/home-affairs/sites/homeaffairs/files/financing/fundings/research-forsecurity/docs/security_research_brochure_2014_en.pdf. Last accessed 20 June 2017: 1–32.

European Commission. 2015. *A Digital Single Market Strategy for Europe*, COM (2015) 192 final. Brussels.

European Commission. 2016a. *Proposal for a Directive Establishing the European Electronic Communications Code*, (Communication) COM (2016) 590 final, 2016/0288 (COD).

European Commission. 2016b. *Commission Staff Working Document. Horizon 2020 Annual Monitoring Report 2015*, SWD (2016) 376 final: 1–260.

European Commission. 2016c. *Proposal for a Directive of the European Parliament and of the Council Amending Council Framework Decision 2009/315/JHA, as Regards the Exchange of Information on Third Country Nationals and as Regards the European Criminal Records Information System (ECRIS), and Replacing Council Decision 2009/316/JHA*, COM (2016) 7 final, 2016/0002 (COD): 1–38.

European Commission. 2016d. *Proposal for a regulation of the European parliament and of the Council on the establishment of 'Eurodac' for the comparison of fingerprints for the effective application of [Regulation (EU) No. 604/2013 establishing the criteria and mechanisms for determining the Member State responsible for examining an application for international protection lodged in one of the Member States by a third-country national or a stateless person], for identifying an illegally staying third-country national or stateless person and on requests for the comparison with Eurodac data by Member States' law enforcement authorities and Europol for law enforcement purposes (recast)*, 2016/0132 (COD): 1–107.

European Commission. 2017a. *Joint Statement by President Jean-Claude Juncker and Prime Minister Theresa May*, 16 October, Brussels. Available from: http://europa.eu/rapid/press-release_STATEMENT-17-3969_en.htm. Last accessed 26 March 2018.

European Commission. 2017b. *Position Paper Transmitted to EU27 on the Use of Data and Protection of Information Obtained or Processed Before the Withdrawal Date*, TF50 (2017) 14. Available from: https://ec.europa.eu/commission/sites/beta-political/files/use-data-protection-information_en.pdf. Last accessed 18 December 2017.

European Commission. 2017c. *Joint Report from the Negotiators of the European Union and the United Kingdom Government on Progress During Phase 1 of Negotiations Under Article 50 TFEU on the United Kingdom's Orderly Withdrawal from the European Union*, 8 December, Brussels.

European Commission. 2017d. *Proposal for a Regulation of the European Parliament and of the Council Concerning the Respect for Private Life and the Protection of Personal Data in Electronic Communications and Repealing Directive 2002/58/EC (Regulation on Privacy and Electronic Communications)*, (Communication) COM (2017) 10 final, 2017/0003 (COD).

European Commission. 2017e. *Communication from the Commission to the European Parliament, the European Council and the Council. Seventh Progress Report Towards an Effective and Genuine Security Union*, COM (2017) 261 final.

European Commission. 2017f. *Evidence*. Available from: http://ec.europa.eu/justice/criminal/recognition-decision/evidence/index_en.htm. Last accessed 4 July 2017.

European Commission. 2017g. *European Attitudes Towards Security—Special Eurobarometer 464b Report.* Directorate-General for Migration and Home Affairs and Directorate-General for Communication, December.

European Commission. 2017h. *Proposal for a Regulation of the European Parliament and of the Council on ENISA, the "EU Cybersecurity Agency", and Repealing Regulation (EU) 526/2013, and on Information and Communication Technology Cybersecurity Certification ("Cybersecurity Act"),* COM (2017) 495 final.

European Commission. 2018a. *Proposal for a Regulation on European Production and Preservation Orders for Electronic Evidence in Criminal Matters,* COM (2018) 225 final 2018/0108 (COD).

European Commission. 2018b. *Migration and Home Affairs: Cybercrime.* Available from: https://ec.europa.eu/home-affairs/what-we-do/policies/organized-crime-and-human-trafficking/cybercrime_en. Last accessed 29 March 2018.

European Commission. 2018c. *Police and Judicial Cooperation in Criminal Matters,* 23 January. Available from: https://ec.europa.eu/commission/sites/beta-political/files/police_judicial_cooperation_in_criminal_matters.pdf. Last accessed 4 April 2018.

European Commission. 2018d. *Brexit Next Steps.* Powerpoint Slide. Available from: https://www.parliament.uk/documents/lords-committees/eu-select/scrutiny-brexit-negotiations/Slide-1-brexit-next-steps.pdf. Last accessed 8 April 2018.

European Commission. 2018e. *Report on the Protection and Enforcement of Intellectual Property Rights in Third Countries,* SWD (2018) 47 final.

European Commission. 2018f. *Proposal for a Directive Laying Down Harmonised Rules on the Appointment of Legal Representatives for the Purpose of Gathering Evidence in Criminal Proceedings,* COM (2018) 226 final 2018/0107 (COD).

European Commission. 2018g. *Press Statement by Michel Barnier Following This Week's Round of Article 50 Negotiations,* 9 February. Available from: http://europa.eu/rapid/press-release_SPEECH-18-725_en.htm. Last accessed 25 May 2018.

European Commission. 2018h. *Draft Agreement on the Withdrawal of the United Kingdom of Great Britain and Northern Ireland from the European Union and the European Atomic Energy Community, as Agreed at Negotiators' Level on 14 November 2018,* TF50 (2018) 55. Available from: https://ec.europa.eu/commission/sites/beta-political/files/draft_withdrawal_agreement_0.pdf. 14 November 2018.

European Commission and High Representative of the European Union for Foreign Affairs and Security Policy. 2017. *Resilience, Deterrence and Defence: Building Strong Cybersecurity for the EU,* (Joint Communication) JOIN (2017) 450 final.

European Commission and HM Government. 2018. *Draft Agreement on the Withdrawal of the United Kingdom of Great Britain and Northern Ireland from the European Union and the European Atomic Energy Community.* Available from: https://www.gov.uk/government/uploads/system/uploads/attachment_data/

file/691366/20180319_DRAFT_WITHDRAWAL_AGREEMENT.pdf.   Last accessed 26 March 2018.

European Council. 2017. *Special Meeting of the European Council (Art. 50)— Guidelines*, EUCO XT 20004/17, 29 April, Brussels.

European Court of Justice. 2013. *EU law does not preclude Spanish legislation which requires credit institutions, operating in Spain without being established there, to forward directly to the Spanish authorities information necessary for combatting money laundering and terrorist financing*. Press Release N°54/13, 25 April, Luxembourg.

European Court of Justice. 2015. *The Court of Justice declares that the Commission's US Safe Harbour decision is invalid*. Press Release N°117/15, 6 October, Luxembourg.

European Court of Justice. 2017. *The Court declares the agreement envisaged between the European Union and Canada on the transfer of passenger name record data may not be concluded in its current form*. Press Release N°84/17, 26 July, Luxembourg.

European Parliament. 2016. Parliament Backs EU Directive on Use of Passenger Name Records. *European Parliament News*, 14 April. Available from: http://www.europarl.europa.eu/news/en/press-room/20160407IPR21775/parliament-backs-eu-directive-on-use-of-passenger-name-records-pnr. Last accessed 8 April 2018.

European Parliament. 2017a. The European Union's Policies on Counter-Terrorism Relevance, Coherence and Effectiveness. *LIBE Committee*. Available from: http://www.europarl.europa.eu/RegData/etudes/STUD/2017/583124/IPOL_STU(2017)583124_EN.pdf. Last accessed 18 December 2017.

European Parliament. 2017b. *EU Passenger Name Record (European PNR)*, Legislative Train Schedule. Available from: http://www.europarl.europa.eu/legislative-train/theme-area-of-justice-andfundamental-rights/file-eu-passenger-name-record-(european-pnr). Last accessed 18 May 2017.

European Parliament. 2018. *European Parliament Resolution of 14 March 2018 on the Framework of the Future EU-UK Relationship*, 2018/2573.

European Parliament and the Council. 1995. Directive 95/46/EC of the European Parliament and of the Council of 24 October 1995 on the Protection of Individuals with Regard to the Processing of Personal Data and on the Free Movement of such Data (Data Protection Directive). *OJ* L281: 31–50.

European Parliament and the Council. 2002a. Directive 2002/58/EC of the European Parliament and of the Council of 12 July 2002 Concerning the Processing of Personal Data and the Protection of Privacy in the Electronic Communications Sector (e-Privacy Directive). *OJ* L201: 37–207.

European Parliament and the Council. 2002b. Directive 2002/21/EC of the European Parliament and of the Council of 7 March 2002 on a Common

Regulatory Framework for Electronic Communications Networks and Services (Framework Directive). *OJ* L108: 33–50.

European Parliament and the Council. 2013a. Regulation 526/2013/EU of the European Parliament and the Council of 21 May 2013 Concerning the European Union Agency for Network and Information Security (ENISA). *OJ* L165: 41–58.

European Parliament and the Council. 2013b. Regulation (EU) No. 603/2013 of the European Parliament and of the Council of 26 June 2013 on the Establishment of 'Eurodac'. *OJ* L180: 1–30.

European Parliament and the Council. 2013c. Directive 2013/40/EU of the European Parliament and the Council of 12 August 2013 on Attacks against Information Systems and Replacing Council Framework Decision 2005/222/JHA. *OJ* L218: 8–14.

European Parliament and the Council. 2014a. Regulation (EU) No. 516/2014 of the European Parliament and of the Council of 16 April 2014 Establishing the Asylum, Migration and Integration Fund, amending Council Decision 2008/381/EC. *OJ* L150: 168–194.

European Parliament and the Council. 2014b. Regulation 910/2014/EU of the European Parliament and Council of 23 July 2014 on Electronic Identification and Trust Services for Electronic Transactions in the Internal Market and Repealing Directive 1999/93/EC. *OJ* L257: 73–114.

European Parliament and the Council. 2014c. Directive 2014/42/EU of the European Parliament and the Council of 3 April 2014 on the Freezing and Confiscation of Instrumentalities and Proceeds of Crime in the European Union. *OJ* L127: 39–50.

European Parliament and the Council. 2014d. Directive 2014/41/EU of the European Parliament and of the Council of 3 April 2014 regarding the European Investigation Order in Criminal Matters. *OJ* L130: 1–36.

European Parliament and the Council. 2015. Directive 2015/2366/EU of the European Parliament and of the Council of 25 November 2015 on Payment Services in the Internal Market. *OJ* L337.

European Parliament and the Council. 2016a. Regulation 2016/679/EU of the European Parliament and of the Council of 27 April 2016 on the Protection of Natural Persons with Regard to the Processing of Personal Data and on the Free Movement of Such Data. *OJ* L119: 1–88.

European Parliament and the Council. 2016b. Directive 2016/1148/EU of the European Parliament and of the Council of 6 July 2016 Concerning Measures for a High Common Level of Security of Network and Information Systems Across the Union. *OJ* L194: 1–30.

European Parliament and the Council. 2016c. Regulation 2016/794/EU of the European Parliament and of the Council of 11 May 2016 on the European Union Agency for Law Enforcement Cooperation (Europol). *OJ* L135: 53–114.

European Scrutiny Committee. 2013. *The UK's Block-Opt Out of Pre-Lisbon Criminal Law and Policing Measures.* House of Commons, Twenty-First Report of Session 2013–2014: 1–159.

European Scrutiny Committee. 2016. *European Union Agency for Asylum Debate,* 15 November 2015. Available from: https://hansard.parliament.uk/Commons/2016-11-15/debates/0bb691c4-3ce1-4d19-abcd-7bba69a853a9/EuropeanUnionAgencyForAsylum?highlight=eurodac#contribution-DD14A42BAFDF-4241-AD81-54D36F5AB275. Last accessed 24 June 2017.

European Scrutiny Committee. 2017a. *Documents Considered by the Committee on 19 April 2017. Europol: Agreement with Denmark.* Available from: https://www.publications.parliament.uk/pa/cm201617/cmselect/cmeuleg/71-xxxvi/7111.htm#_idTextAnchor016. Last accessed 2 June 2017.

European Scrutiny Committee. 2017b. *Fingerprinting of Asylum Applicants and Irregular Migrants: The Eurodac System.* Available from: https://www.publications.parliament.uk/pa/cm201617/cmselect/cmeuleg/71-xxxii/7109.htm. Last accessed 5 July 2017.

European Scrutiny Committee. 2017c. *EU Asylum Reform: Revision of the Dublin Rules and the Establishment of an EU Agency for Asylum.* Available from: https://www.publications.parliament.uk/pa/cm201617/cmselect/cmeuleg/71-xxiii/7110.htm. Last accessed 2 June 2017.

European Union. 2010. *Internal Security Strategy for the European Union—Towards a European Security Model.* Brussels.

European Union and United Kingdom. 2018. *Joint Report from the Negotiators of the European Union and the United Kingdom Government on the State of Play of the Negotiations Under Article 50 TEU on the Withdrawal of the United Kingdom of Great Britain and Northern Ireland from the European Union and the European Atomic Energy Community,* TF50 (2018) 54, 14 November 2018.

Europol and European Union Intellectual Property Office. 2017. *2017 Situation Report on Counterfeiting in the European Union.*

Eurostat. 2017. *First Time Asylum Applicants, Q4 2015–Q4 2016.* Available from: http://ec.europa.eu/eurostat/statisticsexplained/index.php/File:First_time_asylum_applicants_Q4_2015_%E2%80%93_Q4_2016.png. Last accessed 10 June 2017.

Fahey, E. 2016. Joining the Dots: External Norms, AFSJ Directives & the EU's Role in the Global Legal Order. *European Law Review* 41: 105.

Fahey, E. 2017. The Evolution of Transatlantic Legal Integration: Truly, Madly, Deeply? EU-US Justice and Home Affairs. In *Routledge Handbook on Justice and Home Affairs,* ed. F. Trauner and A. Rippoll-Servent. Abingdon: Routledge.

Fahey, E. (ed.). 2018. *Institutionalisation Beyond the Nation State: Transatlantic Data Privacy and Trade Law.* Cham, Switzerland: Springer.

Falvey, D. 2017. 'Borders at Risk' After 'Inadequate' Home Office Planning Could Leave 'Brexit in Jeopardy'. *Express*, 16 November. Available from: https://www.express.co.uk/news/uk/880172/Brexit-news-eu-illegal-immigration-home-office-borders-uk-parliament-select-committee.   Last accessed 15 May 2018.

Farrand, B. 2018. Combatting Physical Threats Posed via Digital Means: The European Commission's Developing Approach to the Sale of Counterfeit Goods on the Internet. *European Politics and Society* 19 (3): 338–354.

FBI. 2018. *CODIS-NDIS Statistics*. Available from: https://www.fbi.gov/services/laboratory/biometric-analysis/codis/ndis-statistics. Last accessed 18 June 2018.

Finotelli, C. 2007. *Illegale Einwanderung, Flüchtlingsmigration und das Ende des Nord-Süd-Mythos: Zur funkionalen Äquivalenz des deutschen und des italienischen Einwanderungsregimes*. Münster: LIT Verlag.

Friedrichs, J. (2008). *Fighting Terrorism and Drugs: Europe and International Police Cooperation*. London and New York: Routledge.

Galaz, M. 2011. Zapatero reitera ante Carlos de Inglaterra que hay que buscar solución al conflicto de Gibraltar. *El País*, 31 March. Available from: https://elpais.com/elpais/2011/03/31/actualidad/1301554130_850215.html. Last accessed 28 March 2018.

Geddes, A. 2013. *Britain and the European Union*. Basingstoke and Hampshire: Palgrave Macmillan.

Gelder, S. 2017. Tommy Adams Jailed: Brother from Notorious Islington Crime Family Gets Seven Years for Money Laundering. *Islington Gazette*, 2 November. Available from: http://www.islingtongazette.co.uk/news/crime-court/tommy-adams-jailed-brother-from-notorious-islington-crime-family-gets-seven-years-for-money-laundering-1-5263470. Last accessed 15 May 2018.

George, S. 1998. *An Awkward Partner. Britain in the European Community*. Oxford: Oxford University Press.

Gibraltar Police Authority. 2014. *Annual Report of the Gibraltar Police Authority*. Available from: http://gpasurvey.com/images/publications/Annual_Reports/GPA_Annual_Report_2013-2014.pdf. Last accessed 27 November 2017.

Giuffrida, F. 2017. *The European Public Prosecutor's Office: King Without Kingdom?* Centre for European Policies Studies, Research Report No. 2017/03, February 2017.

Gonzalez, M., and P. Guimon. 2016. El Reino Unido pide disculpas a España por el accidente de un submarino nuclear en Gibraltar. *El País*, 21 July. Available from: https://elpais.com/internacional/2016/07/21/actualidad/1469083210_393273.html. Last accessed 28 March 2018.

Gruszczak, A. 2017. The EU Criminal Intelligence Model: Problems and Issues. In *EU Criminal Law and Policy: Values, Principles and Methods*, ed. J. Banach-Gutierrez and C. Harding. London and New York: Routledge.

Guild, E. 2016. The UK Referendum on the EU and the Common European Asylum System. *freemovement.org*, 29 April. Available from: https://www.freemovement.org.uk/brexit-and-thecommon-european-asylum-system/. Last accessed 10 June 2017.

Harding, L., P. Oltermann, and N. Watt. 2015. Refugee Welcome? How UK and Germany Compare on Migration. *The Guardian*, 2 September. Available from: https://www.theguardian.com/world/2015/sep/02/refugees-welcome-uk-germany-compare-migration. Last accessed 18 May 2018.

Hayward, K., and D. Phinnemore. 2018. The Northern Ireland/Ireland Border, Regulatory Alignment and Brexit: Principles and Options in Light of the UK-EU Joint Report of 8 December 2017. Briefing Paper 3, Queen's University Belfast, February.

Henley, J. 2016. The Calais Border Treaty and Brexit: What Is France Saying? *The Guardian*. Available from: https://www.theguardian.com/uk-news/2016/mar/03/calais-border-treaty-brexit-what-is-france-saying. Last accessed 3 April 2018.

Hervey, G. 2018. Boris Johnson Compares Irish Border Post-Brexit to London Congestion Charge. *Politico*, 27 February. Available from: https://www.politico.eu/article/boris-johnson-compares-irish-border-post-brexit-to-london-congestion-charge/. Last accessed 5 April 2018.

Hillebrand, C. 2017. With or Without You: The UK and Information and Intelligence Sharing in the EU. *Journal of Intelligence History* 16 (2): 91–94.

HM Government. 2016a. *The UK's Cooperation with the EU on Justice and Home Affairs, and on Foreign Policy and Security Issues*. Background Note. Available from: https://www.gov.uk/government/uploads/system/uploads/attachment_data/file/521926/The_UK_s_cooperation_with_the_EU_on_justice_and_home_affairs__and_on_foreign_policy_and_security_issues.pdf. Last accessed 1 June 2017: 1–11.

HM Government. 2016b. *National Cyber Security Strategy 2016–2021*. Available at: https://assets.publishing.service.gov.uk/government/uploads/system/uploads/attachment_data/file/567242/national_cyber_security_strategy_2016.pdf.

HM Government. 2017a. *Security, Law Enforcement and Criminal Justice: A Future Partnership*. Available from: https://www.gov.uk/government/uploads/system/uploads/attachment_data/file/645416/Security__law_enforcement_and_criminal_justice_-_a_future_partnership_paper.PDF. Last accessed 22 March 2018.

HM Government. 2017b. *The United Kingdom's Exit from and New Partnership with the European Union*. Available from: https://www.gov.uk/government/uploads/system/uploads/attachment_data/file/589189/The_United_Kingdoms_exit_from_and_partnership_with_the_EU_Print.pdf. Last accessed 18 December 2017.

HM Government. 2017c. *Policy Paper. The United Kingdom's Exit from the European Union: Safeguarding the Position of EU Citizens Living in the UK and UK Nationals Living in the EU*, 26 June. Available from: https://www.gov.uk/government/publications/safeguarding-the-position-of-eu-citizens-in-the-uk-and-uk-nationals-in-the-eu/the-united-kingdoms-exit-from-the-european-union-safeguarding-the-position-of-eu-citizens-living-in-the-uk-and-uk-nationals-living-in-the-eu. Last accessed 14 December 2017.

HM Government. 2017d. *Enforcement and Dispute Resolution: A Future Partnership Paper*. Available from: https://assets.publishing.service.gov.uk/government/uploads/system/uploads/attachment_data/file/639609/Enforcement_and_dispute_resolution.pdf. Last accessed 5 April 2018.

HM Government. 2018a. *Treaty Between the Government of the United Kingdom of Great Britain and Northern Ireland and the Government of the French Republic Concerning the Reinforcement of Cooperation for the Coordinated Management of Their Shared Border*. Available from: https://www.gov.uk/government/uploads/system/uploads/attachment_data/file/674885/Treaty_Concerning_the_Reinforcement_Of_Cooperation_For_The_Coordinated_Management_Of_Their_Shared_Border.pdf. Last accessed 3 April 2018.

HM Government. 2018b. *The Future Relationship Between the United Kingdom and the European Union*. Available from: https://assets.publishing.service.gov.uk/government/uploads/system/uploads/attachment_data/file/725288/The_future_relationship_between_the_United_Kingdom_and_the_European_Union.pdf. Last accessed 21 July 2018.

Home Office. 2013a. *Information About the JHA Opt-In and Schengen Opt-Out Protocols*. Ministry of Justice, February 2013. Available from: https://www.gov.uk/government/publications/jha-opt-in-and-schengen-opt-out-protocols. Last accessed 26 April 2017.

Home Office. 2013b. *List of JHA (Title V) Opt-In and Schengen Opt-Out Decisions Taken Between 1 December 2009 to Date*. Home Office and Minister of Justice, February 2013. Available from: https://www.gov.uk/government/publications/jha-opt-in-and-schengen-opt-out-protocols. Last accessed 26 April 2017.

Home Office. 2018a. *Fact Sheet: The UK's Juxtaposed Border Controls*. Available from: https://homeofficemedia.blog.gov.uk/2017/07/11/fact-sheet-the-uks-juxtaposed-border-controls/. Last accessed 3 April 2018.

Home Office. 2018b. *Over 10,500 Refugees Resettled in the UK Under Flagship Scheme*, 22 February. Available from: https://www.gov.uk/government/news/over-10000-refugees-resettled-in-the-uk-under-flagship-scheme. Last accessed 18 May 2018.

Home Office and Ministry of Justice. 2015. *Background Information: JHA Opt-In Protocol and Schengen Opt-Out Protocol*. Available from: https://www.

gov.uk/government/publications/jha-opt-in-and-schengen-opt-out-proto-cols--3. Last accessed 7 July 2017.

House of Commons. 2011. The Forensic Science Service. *Science and Technology Committee*, 2nd Report of Session 2010–12, HC 855.

House of Commons. 2013. Forensic Science. *Science and Technology Committee*, 2nd Report of Session 2013–14, HC 610.

House of Commons. 2014. *10 Nov 2014 Daily Hansard—Debate*. Available from: https://www.publications.parliament.uk/pa/cm201415/cmhansrd/cm141110/debtext/141110-0002.htm. Last accessed 28 May 2017.

House of Commons. 2017a. EU-Canada Agreement on Passenger Name Record Data. *European Scrutiny Committee*. Available from: https://publications.parliament.uk/pa/cm201719/cmselect/cmeuleg/301-i/30131.htm. Last accessed 30 April 2018.

House of Commons. 2017b. Implications of Brexit for the Justice System. *Justice Committee*, 9th Report of Session 2016/2017, 22 March, HC 750.

House of Commons. 2018a. Oral Evidence: Home Office Delivery of Brexit: Policing and Security Cooperation. *Home Affairs Committee*, 635. Available from: http://data.parliament.uk/writtenevidence/committeeevidence.svc/evidencedocument/home-affairs-committee/home-office-delivery-of-brex-it-policing-and-security-cooperation/oral/77427.pdf. Last accessed 29 March 2018.

House of Commons. 2018b. UK-EU Security Cooperation After Brexit. *Home Affairs Committee*. Available from: https://publications.parliament.uk/pa/cm201719/cmselect/cmhaff/635/635.pdf. Last accessed 29 March 2018.

House of Commons. 2018c. The Land Border Between Northern Ireland and Ireland. *Northern Ireland Affairs Committee*. Available from: https://publications.parliament.uk/pa/cm201719/cmselect/cmniaf/329/329.pdf. Last accessed 14 May 2018.

House of Lords. 2013. *Follow-Up Report on EU Police and Criminal Justice Measures: The UK's 2014 Opt-Out Decision*, 31 October. Available from: https://publications.parliament.uk/pa/ld201314/ldselect/ldeucom/69/69.pdf. Last accessed 22 March 2018.

House of Lords. 2014a. The United Kingdom Opt-In to the Draft CEPOL Regulation. *European Union Committee*, 3rd Report of Session 2014–2015: 1–15.

House of Lords. 2014b. The European Public Prosecutor's Office (EPPO): The Impact on Non-participating Member States. *European Union Committee*, Oral and Written Evidence, 29 April. Available from: https://www.parliament.uk/documents/lords-committees/eu-sub-com-e/europeanpublic-pros-ecutor-office/EPPOVolofEvidence280414.pdf. Last accessed 15 June 2017.

House of Lords. 2016. Brexit: Future UK-EU Security and Police Cooperation. *European Union Committee*, 7th Report of Session 2016–2017.

House of Lords. 2017a. Brexit: The EU Data Protection Package. *European Union Committee.* Available from: https://publications.parliament.uk/pa/ld201719/ldselect/ldeucom/7/7.pdf. Last accessed 18 December 2017.

House of Lords. 2017b. Brexit: Gibraltar. *European Union Committee,* 13th Report of Session 2016–2017, HL Paper 116, 1 March.

House of Lords. 2017c. Exiting the EU and Security, Law Enforcement and Criminal Justice. *European Union Committee,* Number CDP-2017-0015, 13 January.

House of Lords. 2017d. Brexit: Judicial Oversight of the European Arrest Warrant. *European Union Committee,* 27 July.

House of Lords. 2018a. Brexit: Common Security and Defence Policy. *European Union Committee,* 16th Report of Session 2017–2019. Available from: https://publications.parliament.uk/pa/ld201719/ldselect/ldeucom/132/132.pdf. Last accessed 27 May 2018.

House of Lords. 2018b. Brexit: The Proposed UK-EU Security Treaty. *European Union Committee,* 18th Report of Session 2017–2019. HL Paper 164, July. Available from: https://publications.parliament.uk/pa/ld201719/ldselect/ldeucom/164/164.pdf. Last accessed 25 August 2018.

Hulme, B. 2017. Could Brexit Be a Boom to Human Smuggling? *Open Democracy.* Available from: https://www.opendemocracy.net/benjamin-hulme/could-brexit-be-boon-to-human-smuggling. Last accessed 18 May 2018.

Huysmans, J. 2006. *The Politics of Insecurity: Fear, Migration and Asylum in the EU.* London and New York: Routledge.

Inkster, N. 2016. Brexit, Intelligence, and Terrorism. *Survival* 58 (3): 23–30.

Integration Office FDFA/FDEA. 2009. *Bilateral Agreements Switzerland-EU.* Bern: SFBL.

International Centre for Counter-Terrorism. 2016. *The Foreign Fighters Phenomenon in the European Union Profiles, Threats & Policies.* Available from: https://www.icct.nl/wp-content/uploads/2016/03/ICCT-Report_Foreign-Fighters-Phenomenon-in-the-EU_1-April-2016_including-AnnexesLinks.pdf. Last accessed 18 December 2017.

International Centre for Counter-Terrorism. 2018. *The Homecoming of Foreign Fighters in the Netherlands, Germany and Belgium: Policies and Challenges.* Available from: https://icct.nl/publication/the-homecoming-of-foreign-fighters-in-the-netherlands-germany-and-belgium-policies-and-challenges/. Last accessed 30 April 2018.

Jain, K. 2017. Brexit Causes Anguish on Gibraltar. *The Conversation,* 14 March. Available from: https://theconversation.com/brexit-causes-anguish-on-gibraltar-74426. Last accessed 28 March 2018.

Jeney, P. 2016. The European Union's Area of Freedom, Security and Justice without the United Kingdom: Legal and Practical Consequences of Brexit. *ELTE Law Journal* 1: 117–139.

Jones, S. 2018. Inside La Linea, the Spanish Town in the Frontline Against Drug Trafficking. *The Guardian*, 4 April. Available from: https://www.theguardian.com/world/2018/apr/04/spain-la-linea-drug-trafficking-gibraltar-hashish. Last accessed 4 April 2018.

Juncker, J.-C. 2018. *Speech at the Munich Security Conference*, 17 February 2018, Munich. Available from https://www.securityconference.de/mediathek/munich-security-conference-2018/video/statement-by-jean-claude-juncker/. Last accessed 29 March 2018.

Karlsson, L. 2017. Smart Border 2.0: Avoiding a Hard Border on the Island of Ireland for Customs Control and the Free Movement of Persons. *European Parliament, Directorate General for Internal Policies, Policy Department for Citizens' Rights and Constitutional Affairs*, November, PE 596.828.

Kaunert, C., S. Léonard, H. Carrapico, and S. Rozée. 2014. The Governance of Justice and Internal Security in Scotland: Between the Scottish Independence Referendum and British Decisions on the EU. *European Security*, 23 (3): 344–363.

Kjeldsen, T., and W. Nueteboom. 2015. *20 Years of Forensic Cooperation in Europe: The History of ENSFI 1995–2015*. The Hague: ENSFI.

Larik, J. 2017. Brexit and the Transatlantic Trouble of Counting Treaties. *EJIL Talk!* 6 December.

Lavorgna, A., and A. Sergi. 2016. Serious, Therefore Organised? A Critique of the Emerging "Cyber-Organised Crime" Rhetoric in the United Kingdom. *International Journal of Cyber Criminology* 10 (2): 170–187.

Léonard, S., and C. Kaunert. 2016. *The Extra-Territorial Processing of Asylum Claims*. Available from: Fmreview.org/destination-europe. Last accessed 17 May 2018.

London Loves Business (LLB). 2017. *Money Launderers Paid £1.8m into London Banks in Two Weeks*. Available from:http://www.londonlovesbusiness.com/business-news/money-launderers-paid-18m-into-london-banks-in-two-weeks/18879.article. Last accessed 15 May 2018.

MacAskill, E., and D. Boffey. 2018. Brexit Row: GCHQ Chief Stresses UK's Role in Foiling European Terror Plots. *The Guardian*. Available from: https://www.theguardian.com/politics/2018/jun/19/barnier-uk-will-lose-access-to-eu-security-databases-after-brexit. Last accessed 19 June 2018.

Macdonald, A., and J. Aguado. 2017. EU Offers Spain Veto Right Over Gibraltar in Brexit Talks. *Reuters*, 31 March. Available from: https://www.reuters.com/article/us-britain-eu-gibraltar/eu-offers-spain-veto-right-over-gibraltar-in-brexit-talks-idUSKBN1722AS. Last accessed 28 March 2018.

Martín y Pérez de Nanclares, J. 2017. Brexit Y Gibraltar: la soberanía compartida como posible solución de la controversia. In *El Brexit y Gibraltar: Un reto con oportunidades conjuntas*, ed. M.M. Martín Martínez and J. Martín y Pérez de Nanclares. Colección escuela diplomática ministerio de asunto exteriores y de cooperación, September. Available from: http://www.exteriores.gob. es/Portal/es/Ministerio/EscuelaDiplomatica/Documents/coleccion%20 ED%2023_para%20web.pdf. Last accessed 18 May 2018.

Massey, D.S., J. Durand, and K.A. Pren. 2016. Why Border Enforcement Backfired. *American Journal of Sociology* 121 (5): 1557–1600.

May, T. 2013. Home Secretary Oral Statement to Parliament on 2014 Decision. *Gov.uk*, 9 July. Available from: https://www.gov.uk/government/speeches/ home-secretary-oral-statement. Last accessed 22 March 2018.

May, T. 2016. *Speech on Brexit*. Available from: http://www.conservativehome. com/parliament/2016/04/theresa-mays-speech-on-brexit-full-text.html. Last accessed 3 June 2017.

May, T. 2017. *Andrew Neil's Interview with Theresa May*, 29 March. Available from: https://blogs.spectator.co.uk/2017/03/transcript-andrew-neils-brex-it-interview-theresa-may/. Last accessed 20 June 2017.

May, T. 2018a. *PM Speech at Munich Security Conference: 17 February 2018*. Available from: https://www.gov.uk/government/speeches/pm-speech-at-mu-nich-security-conference-17-february-2018. Last accessed 24 March 2018.

May, T. 2018b. *PM Speech on Our Future Economic Partnership with the European Union*, 2 March. Available from: https://www.gov.uk/govern-ment/speeches/pm-speech-on-our-future-economic-partnership-with-the-eu-ropean-union. Last accessed 7 April 2018.

McDonald, M. 2008. Securitization and the Construction of Security. *European Journal of International Relations* 14 (4): 563–587.

Menon, A., M. Chalmers, C. Macdonald, L. Scazzieri, and R. Whitman. 2018. A Successful Brexit: Three Foreign and Security Policy Tests. *The UK in a Changing Europe*. Available from: http://ukandeu.ac.uk/wp-content/ uploads/2018/02/77181-UKIN-A-Successful-Brexit-security-tests-.pdf. Last accessed 2 May 2018.

Migration Observatory. 2015. *Election 2015 Briefing: Why Do International Migrants Come to the UK?* 6 May. Available from: http://www.migrationob-servatory.ox.ac.uk/resources/briefings/election-2015-briefing-why-do-inter-national-migrants-come-to-the-uk/. Last accessed 18 May 2018.

Migration Observatory. 2017. *Migrants in the UK: An Overview*, 21 February. Available from: http://www.migrationobservatory.ox.ac.uk/resources/brief-ings/migrants-in-the-uk-an-overview/. Last accessed 18 May 2018.

Mitsilegas, V. 2017. The United Kingdom in Europe's Area of Criminal Justice. The Triple Paradox of Brexit. *Criminology in Europe* 16 (2): 9–10.

Mitsilegas, V., and B. Ryan. 2010. *Extraterritorial Immigration Control. Legal Challenges*. Leiden: Brill.

Monar, J. 1999. Justice and Home Affairs in a Wider Europe: The Dynamics of Inclusion and Exclusion. ESRC One Europe or Several? Working Paper No. 07/00. ESCRC, Swindon.

Monar, J. 2006. Cooperation in the Justice and Home Affairs Domain: Characteristics, Constraints and Progress. *Journal of European Integration* 28 (5): 495–509.

Monar, J. 2014. EU Internal Security Governance: The Case of Counter-Terrorism. *European Security* 23 (2): 195–209.

MOPAC. 2018. *Request for DMPC Decision: PCD 346*. Mayor of London, Office for Policing and Crime. Available from: https://www.london.gov.uk/sites/default/files/pcd_346_part_1_exchange_of_biometric_data_across_europe_-_the_prum_arrangements.pdf. Last accessed 23 May 2018.

Morehouse, C., and M. Blomfield. 2011. *Irregular Migration in Europe*. Washington: Migration Policy Institute.

Moreno-Lax, V. 2017. *Accessing Asylum in Europe: Extraterritorial Border Controls and Refugee Rights Under EU Law*. Oxford: Oxford University Press.

Mortera-Martinez, C. 2017. *Good Cop, Bad Cop. How to Keep Britain Inside Europol*. Center for European Reform Insight, 1–4. Available from: https://www.cer.org.uk/insights/good-cop-bad-cop-howkeep-britain-inside-europol. Last accessed 5 June 2017.

Mortera-Martinez, C. 2018. Plugging in the British: EU Justice and Home Affairs. *Policy Brief*. Centre for European Reform, May.

National Crime Agency. 2016. *Wanted from the UK: European Arrest Warrant Statistics 2009–May 2016 (Calendar Year)*. Available from: http://www.nationalcrimeagency.gov.uk/publications/european-arrest-warrant-statistics/wanted-fromthe-uk-european-arrest-warrant-statistics. Last accessed 1 June 2017.

National Crime Agency. 2017. *National Strategic Assessment of Serious and Organised Crime*. Available from: http://www.nationalcrimeagency.gov.uk/publications/807-national-strategic-assessment-of-serious-and-organised-crime-2017/file. Last accessed 15 May 2018.

Nazca, J. 2016. Spain Seeks to Jointly Govern Gibraltar After Brexit. *Reuters*, 24 June. Available from: https://www.reuters.com/article/us-britain-eu-gibraltar/spain-seeks-to-jointly-govern-gibraltar-after-brexit-idUSKCN0ZA184. Last accessed 28 March 2018.

Negotiators of the EU and the UK Government. 2017. *Joint Report from the Negotiators of the European Union and the United Kingdom Government on Progress During Phase 1 of Negotiations*, 8 December. Available from: https://ec.europa.eu/commission/sites/beta-political/files/joint_report.pdf. Last accessed 5 April 2018.

Neil, R. 2017. HC Deb, 18 January 2017, vol. 619, cols. 956–7.

Niehuss, A., B. Farrand, H. Carrapico, and J. Obradovic-Wochnik. 2018. *European Union Member States' Judicial Cooperation Frameworks: A Focus on Extradition, Mutual Legal Assistance, and Joint Investigation Teams*. Report for the Home Office.

Nielsen, N. 2013. EU Prosecutor Likely to Expand Powers. *EUobserver*, 28 November. Available from: https://euobserver.com/justice/122285. Last accessed 25 June 2017.

Occhipinti, J.D. 2015. Still Moving Toward a European FBI? Re-examining the Politics of EU Police Cooperation. *Intelligence and National Security* 30 (2–3): 234–258.

OLAF. 2017. *The OLAF Report 2016*. Available from: https://ec.europa.eu/anti-fraud/sites/antifraud/files/olaf_report_2016_en.pdf. Last accessed 15 May 2018.

Organization for Economic Cooperation and Development. 2006. *The Economic Impact of Counterfeiting and Piracy*.

Organization for Economic Cooperation and Development. 2008. *The Economic Impact of Counterfeiting and Piracy*. Available from: http://apps.who.int/medicinedocs/documents/s19845en/s19845en.pdf. Last accessed on 24 April 2018.

Orsini, G. 2016. Securitization as a Source of Insecurity: A Ground-Level Look at the Functioning of Europe's External Border in Lampedusa. *Studies in Ethnicity and Nationalism* 16 (1): 135–147.

Paul, R. 2015. *The Political Economy of Border-Drawing. Arranging Legality in European Labour Migration Policies*. New York: Berghahn Books.

Payne, A. 2017. Theresa May's 'Blackmail' Security Threat to the EU Had to Be 'Toned Down'. *Business Insider*, 20 April. Available from: http://nordic.businessinsider.com/mays-article-50-brexit-letter-to-eu-had-to-be-toned-down-2017-4/. Last accessed 27 May 2018.

Peck, T. 2017. Brexit Won't Stop the UK Won't Sharing Intelligence, Says (British) Europol Chief. *The Independent*, 7 March. Available from: http://www.independent.co.uk/news/uk/politics/brexitwont-stop-the-uk-wont-sharing-intelligence-says-british-europol-chief-a7616886.html. Last accessed 14 June 2017.

Peers, S. 2004. Mutual Recognition and Criminal Law in the European Union: Has the Council Got It Wrong? *Common Market Law Review* 41 (1): 5–36.

Peers, S. 2016. Migration, Internal Security and the UK's EU Membership. *The Political Quarterly* 87 (2): 247–253.

Peers, S. 2017. The Beginning of the End? Citizens' Rights in the Brexit 'Sufficient Progress' Deal. *EU Law Analysis*, 9 December. Available from: http://eulawanalysis.blogspot.it. Last accessed 14 December 2017.

Peers, S. 2018. Differentiated Integration and the Brexit Process in EU Justice and Home Affairs. In *The Routledge Handbook of Justice and Home Affairs Research*, ed. A. Ripoll Servent and F. Trauner, 253–263. London: Routledge.

Pellicer, L. 2015. Montoro dice que Gibraltar debe estar en la lista de paraísos fiscales de la UE. *El País*, 19 June. Available from: https://elpais.com/economia/2015/06/19/actualidad/1434739565_185828.html. Last accessed 27 March 2018.

Picardo, F. 2015. Brexit Would Destroy Gibraltar. *Politico*, 5 March. Available from: https://www.politico.eu/article/brexit-would-destroy-gilbraltar/. Last accessed 4 April 2018.

Politico. 2017. Macron Is Bad News for Britain's Borders. Available from https://www.politico.eu/article/emmanuel-macron-bad-news-for-britain-border-dover-calais/. Last accessed 10 December 2017.

Politico. 2018. Europe's Terror Defenses Pass to Belgian Hands, 2 May. Available from: https://www.politico.eu/article/europol-europes-terror-defenses-pass-to-belgian-hands-eu-law-enforcement-agency-catherine-de-bolle/. Last accessed 22 May 2018.

Porcedda, M.G. 2018. Patching the Patchwork: Appraising the EU Regulatory Framework on Cyber Security Breaches. *Computer Law and Security Review* 34 (5): 1077–1098.

Porcedda, M.G., and D.S. Wall. 2018. Data Science, Data Crime and the Law. In *Research Handbook on Data Science & Law*, ed. V. Mak, E. Tjong Tjin Tai, and A. Berlee. London: Edward Elgar.

Port of Dover. 2018. *Port of Dover Announces Fifth Consecutive Record Year for Freight*. Press Release, 9 January. Available from: https://www.dover-port.co.uk/about/news/port-of-dover-announces-fifth-consecutive-record-y/13341/. Last accessed 3 April 2018.

Prime Minister's Office. 2017a. *The Government's Negotiating Objectives for Exiting the EU: PM Speech*. Available from: https://www.gov.uk/government/speeches/the-governments-negotiating-objectives-for-exiting-the-eu-pm-speech. Last accessed 31 May 2018.

Prime Minister's Office. 2017b. *Prime Minister's Letter to Donal Tusk Triggering Article 50*. Available from: https://www.gov.uk/government/publications/prime-ministers-letter-to-donald-tusk-triggering-article-50. Last accessed 31 May 2018.

Pusterla, E., and F. Piccin. 2012. The Loss of Sovereignty Control and the Illusion of Building Walls. *Journal of Borderlands Studies* 27 (2): 121–138.

Rankin, J. 2016. Belgium Politicians Drop Opposition to EU-Canada Trade Deal. *The Guardian*, 27 October. Available from: https://www.theguardian.com/world/2016/oct/27/belgium-reaches-deal-with-wallonia-over-eu-canada-trade-agreement. Last accessed 28 March 2018.

Reinish, J. 2015. 'Forever Temporary'. Migrants in Calais, Then and Now. *The Political Quarterly* 86 (4): 515–522.

Remiro Brotons, A. 2004. Regreso a Gibraltar: acuerdos y desacuerdos hispano-británicos. Universidad Autónoma de Madrid, ISSN: 1575-720X. Available from: https://repositorio.uam.es/bitstream/handle/10486/3063/14295_10RJ132.pdf?sequence=1&isAllowed=y. Last accessed 18 May 2018. *Revista Jurídica* 10: 133–182.

Reuters. 2016. EU Exit Could Make Britain Safer: Former MI6 Spy Chief, 24 March. Available from: https://uk.reuters.com/article/uk-britain-eu-security/

eu-exit-could-make-britain-safer-former-mi6-spy-chief-idUKKCN0WQ0NE. Last accessed 31 May 2018.

Reuters. 2017. Whole of the UK Needs to Take Back Control of Borders and Cash from EU, Johnson Says. Available from: https://www.reuters.com/article/uk-britain-eu-johnson/whole-of-the-uk-needs-to-take-back-control-of-borders-and-cash-from-eu-johnson-says-idUSKBN1E11M8. Last accessed 13 December, 2017.

Ripoll Servent, A. 2015. *Institutional and Policy Change in the European Parliament: Deciding on Freedom, Security and Justice.* Houndmills: Palgrave Macmillan.

Ripoll Servent, A., and A. MacKenzie. 2012. The European Parliament as a 'Norm Taker'? EU-US Relations After the SWIFT Agreement. *European Foreign Affairs Review* 17 (2/1): 71–86.

Ripoll Servent, A., and A. MacKenzie. 2017. Eroding Germany's Commitment to Data Protection: Policy Entrepreneurs and Coalition Politics in EU Passenger Name Records. *German Politics* 26 (3): 398–413.

Robert, A. 2016. Big Data Revolutionises Europe's Fight Against Terrorism. *EurActiv.com,* 23 June. Available from: https://www.euractiv.com/section/digital/news/big-data-revolutionises-europes-fight-against-terrorism/. Last accessed 28 March 2018.

Romaguera, C. 2013. La verja de Gibraltar registra retenciones de más de siete horas. *El País,* 28 July. Available from: https://elpais.com/ccaa/2013/07/28/andalucia/1375033236_246363.html. Last accessed 28 March 2018.

Roos, C. 2018. The (De-)politicization of EU Freedom of Movement: Political Parties, Opportunities, and Policy Framing in Germany and the UK. *Comparative European Politics,* 1–20. https://doi.org/10.1057/s41295-018-0118-1.

Rudd. 2017. *Justice and Home Affairs Post-Council Statement,* 2 February 2017, vol. 620. Available from: https://hansard.parliament.uk/Commons/2017-02-02/debates/17020250000014/JusticeAndHomeAffairsPostCouncilStatementhighlight=Criminal%20Records#contribution-F8DE59D8-34F0-4076-B773-5E201B4041D5. Last accessed 26 June 2017.

Ruhs, M., and B. Anderson. 2006. Semi-Compliance in the Migrant Labour Market, Centre on Migration, Policy and Society. Working Paper No. 30, Oxford: University of Oxford.

Ryan, B. 2016. Brexit and Borders: Schengen, Frontex and the UK. *freemovement.org,* 19 May. Available from: https://www.freemovement.org.uk/brexit-and-borders-schengen-frontex-and-the-uk/. Last accessed 10 June 2017.

Sandler, T. 2006. Recognizing the Limits to Cooperation Behind National Borders: Financing the Control of Transnational Terrorism. In *The New*

Public Finance: Responding to Global Challenges, ed. I. Kaul and P. Conceiçao. New York: Oxford University Press.

Santos, F. (2016). Overview of the Implementation of the Prum Decisions. Exchange-Forensic Geneticists and the Transnational Exchange of DNA Data in the European Union: Engaging Science with Social Control, Citizenship and Democracy. *European Commission*. Available from: https://estudogeral. sib.uc.pt/bitstream/10316/41091/1/Overview%20of%20the%20implementation%20of%20the%20Pr%C3%BCm%20Decisions.pdf. Last accessed on 25 April 2018.

Sergi, A. 2016. *Brexit Could Make Life Easier for Organized Crime Gangs.* Available from: https://theconversation.com/brexit-could-make-life-easier-for-organised-crime-gangs-60515. Last accessed 3 June 2017.

Sergi, A. 2017. *From Mafia to Organised Crime: A Comparative Analysis of Policing Models.* Cham, Switzerland: Palgrave Macmillan.

Sergi, A. 2018. What's Really Going on in London's Organised Crime Scene: According to a Criminologist. *Independent*, 24 January. Available from: https://www.independent.co.uk/news/uk/crime/mcmafia-london-gangs-crime-accuracy-what-is-it-like-real-life-kray-twins-a8173726.html. Last accessed 15 May 2018.

Sharf, E. 2016. Information Exchanges. Regulatory Changes to the Cyber-Security Industry After Brexit: Making Security Awareness Training Work. *Computer Fraud & Security* 7: 9–12.

Sidharth, K. 2011. Supply and Demand: Human Trafficking in the Global Economy. *Harvard International Review* 33 (2): 66–71.

Slack, J., and T. Cohen. 2016. Quitting EU Would Make Britain Safer, Says Former MI6 Chief: Sir Richard Dearlove Suggests Brexit Would Make It Easier to Deport Terrorists and Control Our Borders. *The Daily Mail*, 23 March. Available from: http://www.dailymail.co.uk/news/article-3506991/UK-safer-Europe-says-former-MI6-chief-Sir-Richard-Dearlove-suggests-Brexit-make-easier-deport-terrorists.html. Last accessed 27 May 2018.

Smith, M. 2017. *Nine in Ten Brits Think Further Terror Attacks Are Likely.* YouGov Survey, 24 March. Available from: https://yougov.co.uk/news/2017/03/24/nine-ten-brits-think-further-terror-attacks-are-li/. Last accessed 31 May 2018.

Soleto Muñoz, H., and A. Fiodorova. 2014. DNA and Law Enforcement in the European Union: Tools and Human Rights Protection. *Utrecht Law Review* 10 (1): 149–162.

Spijkerboer, T. 2007. The Human Cost of Border Control. *European Journal of Migration and Law* 9: 127–139.

Stewart, H. 2017. Brexit MPs Angry as Theresa May Accepts Continuing Rule of EU Court. *The Guardian*, 9 October. Available from: https://www.theguardian.com/politics/2017/oct/09/brexit-mps-angry-as-theresa-may-accepts-continuing-rule-of-eu-court. Last accessed 7 April 2018.

Stone, J. 2017. Brexit: David Davis Rushes to Repair Damage After Undermining Trust in Negotiations. *The Independent*, 12 December. Available from: https://www.independent.co.uk/news/uk/politics/brexit-david-davis-phoned-guy-verhofstadt-legally-binding-brexit-deal-a8105876.html. Last accessed 29 March 2018.

Stone, J. 2018. EU Officials Tear into UK's Fantasy Brexit Negotiating Strategy as Talks Turn Bitter. *The Independent*, 24 May. Available from: https://www.independent.co.uk/news/uk/politics/brexit-latest-uk-eu-customs-plan-northern-ireland-theresa-may-a8368101.html. Last accessed 25 May 2018.

Suárez de Vivero, J.L. 2009. *Aguas Jurisdiccionales en el Mediterráneo y el Mar Negro*. Brussels: European Parliament.

Talani, L.S. 2013. London: The Laundry of Choice? Money Laundering in the City of London. In *Dirty Cities: Towards a Political Economy of the Underground in Global Cities*, ed. L.S. Talani, A. Clarkson, and R.P. Pardo. Basingstoke, Hampshire and New York: Palgrave Macmillan.

Tannam, E. 2017. Brexit's Implications for Northern Ireland May Be Destabilising, but Not Fatal. *LSE Blog Post*. Available from: http://blogs.lse.ac.uk/brexit/2017/04/06/brexit-and-peace-in-northernireland/. Last accessed 15 June 2017.

Taverne, M.D., and A.P.A. Broeders. 2015. *The Light's at the End of the Funnel!: Evaluating the Effectiveness of the Transnational Exchange of DNA Profiles Between the Netherlands and Other Prüm Countries*. Zutphen: Paris Legal Publishers.

Taylor, B. 2017. *Leaving the European Union: Frontex and UK Border Security Cooperation Within Europe*. House of Lords, LIF 2017/0039.

The Economist. 2018. Gangster's Paradise: Brexit Presents New Opportunities for Organised Crime, 24 January. Available from: https://www.economist.com/news/britain/21735569-crooks-stand-benefit-new-lines-business-smuggling-goods-and-people-brexit. Last accessed 15 May 2018.

The Guardian. 2016. Nigel Farage Defends Linking Brussels Attacks and EU Migration Rules. Available from: http://www.bbc.com/news/uk-politics-35879670. Last accessed 31 May 2018.

The Law Society of Scotland. 2016. *Written Evidence: FSP0001*. Available from: http://data.parliament.uk/writtenevidence/committeeevidence.svc/evidencedocument/eu-home-affairssubcommittee/brexit-future-ukeu-security-and-policing-cooperation/written/43327.html. Last accessed 2 June 2017.

The Telegraph. 2017. Exclusive: Brexit Should Have No Impact 'Whatsoever' on Links with Europol, Says Anti-slavery Commissioner. *www.telegraph.co.uk*, 28 August. Available from: https://www.telegraph.co.uk/news/2017/08/28/brexit-should-have-no-impact-whatsoever-links-europol-says-anti/. Last accessed 28 March 2018.

Tonge, J. 2017. *The Impact and Consequences of Brexit for Northern Ireland*. European Parliament Policy Department C: Citizens' Rights and Constitutional Affairs PE 583, 116: 1–12.

Trauner, F. 2014. Migration Policy: An Ambiguous EU Role in Specifying and Spreading International Refugee Protection Norms. In *EU Policies in a Global Perspective: Shaping or Taking International Regimes?*, ed. Gerda Falkner and Patrick Müller, 149–166. London: Routledge.

Treadwell, J. 2012. From the Car Boot to Booting It Up? eBay, Online Counterfeit Crime and the Transformation of the Criminal Marketplace. *Criminology and Criminal Justice* 12 (2): 175–191.

Treadwell, J., and T. Ayres. 2014. Talking Prada and Powder: Cocaine Use and Supply Among the Football Hooligan Firm. In *Football Hooliganism, Fan Behaviour and Crime*, ed. M. Hopkins and J. Treadwell. Basingstoke, Hampshire and New York: Palgrave Macmillan.

Uçarer, E. 2016. The Area of Freedom, Security and Justice. In *European Union Politics*, ed. M. Cini and N. Perez-Solorzano Borragan, 5th ed., 281–294. Oxford: Oxford University Press.

UK Government Statistics. 2018. *National DNA Database Statistics*. Available from: https://www.gov.uk/government/statistics/national-dna-database-statistics Last accessed 18 June 2018.

United Nations. 2018. *Special Political and Decolonization (Fourth Committee)*. Available from: http://www.un.org/en/ga/fourth/. Last accessed 18 May 2018.

Usher, J. 1997. Variable Geometry or Concentric Circles: Patterns for the European Union. *International and Comparative Law Quarterly* 46 (2): 243–273.

Valle Galvez, A. 2017. Gibraltar, the Brexit, the Symbolic Sovereignty, and the Dispute. A Principality in the Straits? *Gibraltar Reports. Academic Journal About the Gibraltar Dispute* 2 (2): 67–96.

Van Tiem, B. 2016. What Brexit Could Mean for Refugee Protection in Britain. *Open Democracy*, 8 August. Available from: https://www.opendemocracy.net/britte-van-tiem/what-brexit-could-mean-for-refugee-protection-in-britain. Last accessed 18 May 2018.

Vollmer, B. 2011. *Irregular Migration in the UK: Definitions, Pathways and Scale*. Available from: http://www.migrationobservatory.ox.ac.uk/wp-content/uploads/2016/04/Briefing-Irregular_Migration.pdf. Last accessed 9 December 2017.

Wainwright, R. 2016. *Foreword, in Maajid Nawaz and Julia Ebner the EU and Terrorism: Is Britain Safer In or Out?* Quilliam, May. Available from: http://www.quilliaminternational.com/wpcontent/uploads/2016/05/The-EU-and-Terrorism_Maajid-Nawaz-and-Julia-Ebner.pdf. Last accessed 15 June 2017.

Wall, D.S. 2016. Policing Cybercrime in the EU: Shall I Stay or Shall I Go? *British Society of Criminology Newsletter* 78 (Summer).

Warrell, H. 2017. Terror Attacks Shaped UK Election but Failed to Lift May. *Financial Times*, 8 June. Available from: https://www.voanews.com/a/terror-attacks-may-drive-security-issues-upcoming-brexit-talks/3889359.html. Last accessed 15 May 2018.

Weyembergh, A. 2017. Consequences of Brexit for European Union Criminal Law. *New Journal of European Criminal Law* 8 (3): 284–299.

Wilson, T. 2015. The Global Perspective. In *Annual Report of the Government Chief Scientific Adviser 2015: Forensic Science and Beyond: Authenticity, Provenance and Assurance—Evidence and Case Studies*, ed. M. Peplow. London: Government Office for Science.

Wilson, T.J. 2016. Criminal Justice and Global Public Goods: The Prüm Forensic Biometric Cooperation Model. *The Journal of Criminal Law* 80 (5): 303–326.

Wilson, T.J. 2018. The Implementation and Practical Application of the European Investigation Order in the United Kingdom: An Academic Perspective. In *Los avances del espacio de Libertad, Seguridad y Justicia de la UE en 2017: II Anuario de la Red Española de Derecho Penal Europeo (ReDPE)*, ed. Á. Gutiérrez Zarza. Madrid: Wolters Kluwer edit.

Winstock, A.R. 2015. *What Did We Learn from GDS2015? An Overview of Our Key Findings*. Global Drug Survey 2015. Available from: http://www.globaldrugsurvey.com/the-global-drug-survey-2015-findings/. Last accessed 15 May 2018.

Witte, G. 2017. As Brexit Tremors Ripple, the Rock of Gibraltar Shudders. *Washington Post*, 14 January. Available from: https://www.washingtonpost.com/world/europe/as-brexit-tremors-ripple-the-rock-of-gibraltar-shudders/2017/01/14/f86c0b70-d764-11e6-a0e6-d502d6751bc8_story.html?utm_term=.b540d29cd10f. Last accessed 28 March 2018.

Woods, L. 2017. Transfering Personal Data Outside the EU: Clarification from the ECJ? *EU Law Analysis*, 4 August. Available from: http://eulawanalysis.blogspot.co.uk/2017/08/transferring-personal-data-outside-eu.html. Last accessed 6 April 2018.

Wright, R. 2018. Europol Head Warns of Security Impediments After Brexit. *Financial Times*, 7 March. Available from: https://www.ft.com/content/b74ec3d0-2213-11e8-9a70-08f715791301. Last accessed 31 May 2018.

INDEX

© The Editor(s) (if applicable) and The Author(s),
under exclusive license to Springer Nature Switzerland AG,
part of Springer Nature 2019
H. Carrapico et al., *Brexit and Internal Security*,
Palgrave Studies in European Union Politics,
https://doi.org/10.1007/978-3-030-04194-6

Printed by Printforce, the Netherlands